OUTSIDE the MARGINS

For Bryce Milligan

a muse poet with wings

Introduction:
Imaginary Borders

I

Translation is a significant border crossing, since it brings a text from its first language into a new one, spreading beyond the limits of its original expression. While this is obvious, establishment publishers view American English honorifically (less than 3% of *all* U.S. books are translations, and only a fraction are books of poems). These commentaries map translated books from university presses and independent imprints, which also publish most of the new poetry.

Poetry is greatly underappreciated by our reading public, and it has an infinitely smaller readership than prose. Poetry in translation faces another level of neglect, since publishers must compensate translators (although they are grossly underpaid). Yet when it falls upon university presses or low budget independents to publish books of poems, few readers buy them. Now with electronic books and self-publishing, many more poets are seeing print, but it also means that a surfeit of mediocrity drowns out superior work. This happened to a lesser degree during the 1960s-1970s when little magazines and small presses published with passionate involvement.

Always I believed the Spanish language poems of the last century to be the most astonishing in the world: from Machado to Jiménez to García Lorca, and down the decades to Ángel González. This also included the Latin Americans—from Peruvian César Vallejo to the Chileans Pablo Neruda, Vincente Huidobro, Nicanor Parra, Enrique Lihn, Oscar Hahn, and to the Mexicans Octavio Paz and Jaime Sabines. During a long stay in Mexico, I met the authors Juan Rulfo, José Emilio Pacheco, Salvador Elizondo, Augusto Monterroso, Paz, and younger poets who became friends, (Francisco Hernández and the late Carlos Isla). The greatest collection of Spanish poems—*Roots and Wings: Poetry from Spain 1900-1975* (a bilingual anthology edited by Hardie St. Martin, at 528 pages, published by Harper & Row in 1976)—was a gift from the late poet Len Randolph, who then directed the literature program for the National Endowment for the Arts. I have referred back to that volume more than any other during the past 40 years, and that poetry remains alive.

Authors have been forced from their homelands by wars, political upheavals, and human rights violations—including "ethnic cleansing" and "genocide" (horrific realities that mean the slaughter of innocent civilians, which cannot be softened by words). It is true that some artists remained in their homelands (often under the occupation of military regimes), which does *not* ignore those who migrated willingly and settled elsewhere. Yet all have crossed real and stylistic borders.

The idea of "regional" writing once meant that writers who lived away from the East Coast were regional authors automatically, even if their work *never* reflected those regions. When I lived in New York City (my birthplace), the tired cliché about works written and published west of the Hudson River were considered "regional" still seems to hold validity for parochial elites. But one must live somewhere, and with the great migration of writers around the nation, any validity in that cliché has disappeared. Good artists live everywhere, travel the country, and nationally recognized émigré authors have settled beyond New York.

II

The world of books has been central since I began to read. Reading was followed by attempts to write, and eventually becoming involved in every aspect of independent publishing—as editor/publisher, typesetter/book designer (during the era of hands-on cutting and pasting), along with the necessary tasks to bring out 112 titles in 35 years under the independent Latitudes Press imprint (1966-2000).

The first book reviews appeared in *San Francisco Review, New Orleans Review, December, Motive*, and *Southwest Review*, when I was a graduate teaching fellow in English at the University of Houston during the mid-1960s. I was a regular unpaid reviewer for *Library Journal*, while living in Brooklyn from 1968 to the mid-1970s. Returning to Austin, Texas, I wrote essays for *Texas Observer* and reviews for *Small Press Review*. I moved to Fort Worth in 1983 and wrote on human rights in *National Catholic Reporter*, and reviews for the *Fort Worth Star-Telegram*. After settling in San Antonio in 2003, I began the *Poetic Diversity* column for the *San Antonio Express-News*.

Most texts were written in the third person. That viewpoint—an obvious ruse of "objectivity"—responds from roots buried in subjectivity, since I write about personal enthusiasms. Taking a hatchet to any book, even one glorified by popularity, may stimulate a primal sense of revenge, but that demands a younger role. I remain biased toward poetry and the translations of poems, toward independent imprints and the authors they publish. The reasons—aside from the belief that these artists have created challenging works—reflect the reality of standing outside the margins of popular consciousness, and that their works have been overlooked by establishment publishers and mainstream media.

Yet these commentaries are merely readings, responding as a second voice in a fraternal dialogue. I was never employed by a commercial institution, but have worked independently only. The Latitudes Press motto was *Independently Poor*, yet we published works that will endure, including internationals Octavio Paz, Macedonio Fernández, Paul Celan, Rafael Alberti, Carlos Drummond de Andrade, Jorge Luis Borges, Stanislaw Lem, Carlos Fuentes, Jaime Sabines, Denise Levertov, Enrique Lihn, Ernesto Cardenal, Rosario Castellanos, Juan José Arreola, José Emilio Pacheco, Severo Sarduy, Ingeborg Bachman, Brian Swann, Salvádor Elizondo, John Reeves, Julio Ortega, and Cecilia Bustamante. North American authors: Thomas Merton, Mark Van Doren, Arthur Miller, John Barth, John Howard Griffin, W.S. Merwin, Gary Snyder, Robert Bly, Herbert Gold, Marge Piercy, Marvin Cohen, Donald Hall, Vassar Miller, Paul Christensen, George Garrett, Russell Hardin, Naomi Shihab Nye, William Mathews, Charles Simic, Russell Banks, Charles Baxter, C.W. Truesdale, Ronnie Dugger, Angela de Hoyos, and many others.

III

The truest poetry puts intelligence to work and allows intuition to play. While intellect offers ideas and concepts, intuition appreciates shapes, forms, proportions. Bodily awareness is how the poem moves in space. Other awareness must be alive, like self-criticism and sensitivity to the feelings and behaviors of others. Insight must be aligned with empathy, and a commitment to understanding.

Just as some are born with a gift for words or numbers, others hear music in the silence, perceive beautiful shapes where most see confusion, or move gracefully rather than clumsily. Some know who they are without consulting a mirror, always at ease with fellow humans. We all have the potential to develop such abilities. In poetry all these gifts are significant. It is just as important to hear the music as to read the words, to recognize shapes as to ponder meaning. Poetry heightens awareness, and the poem leaps suddenly from a poet's experience—entering ours.

Poetry (with a capital P) can be found in verse or in prose. It can also be aural lyricism in music, poetic tableaus in the visual arts, elastic bodies in dance, theater pieces, and films that may include all these genres.

"Well, that means *anything* could be Poetry," you may argue.

"Yes, but it does *not* mean that everything *is* Poetry."

Verses that are merely broken lines of prose—what most contemporary creative writing programs produce—constitute typing, which usually begins at the left margin, spilling words down an invisible staircase or sprinkling them across the page. In these days of computers we can even read "poems" that are centered, but this simply makes clichés of visual form. Without true Poetry at the core, such texts will *not* lift the spirit beyond the page.

First and last, I remain a perpetual reader who desires textual challenges and pleasures, approaching writing as a lover of literature and language, fascinated by knowledge and experiment. Not posing as an established poet or critic, I remain an amateur. My professionalism amounts to being truthful, but without pretending to know the truth. While I have read my poetry in the lively, marginal spaces left within our withering civilization, most attention lives in solitude, searching for the scribbling cure that will heal obscure wounds into a meaningful scar.

Outside

the Margins

Walking Meditations

This hefty bilingual edition of *Campos de Castilla* (2005), by the venerable Spanish poet Antonio Machado, is the first complete English translation of his famous 1917 book, translated by Dennis Maloney and Mary G. Berg. It would be a major publishing event if the independent White Pine Press had the promotional clout of an establishment house. As it stands we have a literary event of the first magnitude, since *Campos de Castilla* has been translated into 40 languages, continues to be heralded as one of the classics of 20th century, and dearly loved by millions.

Machado's walking meditations through the Spanish countryside are open to anyone with eyes to see and a love of natural beauty—from mountains and rivers to an "old elm, split by lightning/ and half rotted" that "has sprouted a few green leaves." He evokes wheat fields, olive groves, sheepherders, and a blind donkey trudging around a water wheel. Yet these are not merely nature poems or odes to a passing agricultural way of life. Machado was attentive to a once supreme Spain, unprepared to enter the modern era, and to the loss of his love, Leonor, who haunted his steps with a deep grief untainted by misty romanticism.

In a cogent Introduction, Berg writes: "He is a poet of solitude and landscape, of precise immediate images and larger national (and human) concerns. Preoccupied with time and the relationship between interior and exterior realities, Machado writes with simultaneous simplicity and depth that resonate on many levels."

Machado says, "Our hours are minutes/when we anticipate knowledge,/and centuries when we know/what it's possible to learn." While these proverbs recall the Greek philosophers, they are as fresh as his varied narratives of village life and lore under a rural sun. A teacher of high school French, Machado was married at 34 to the young daughter of his pensión proprietors. But Leonor died of tuberculosis at 18, and the poet never remarried. After alluding to her death in "Caminos" ("Lord, you've already torn from me what I loved most"), Machado writes, "Hope says: some day/you will see her, if you will only wait./Despair says: all you have left of her is your bitterness./Beat, heart. . . The earth/has not swallowed everything."

Machado knew the seminal writers of his time, dedicating elegies and praises to Spanish philosophers Miguel de Unamuno and José Ortega y Gassett, to his near-contemporary, poet Juan Ramón Jiménez, as well as to Henri Bergson of France and the Nicaraguan modernist poet Rubén Dario.

Undoubtedly the humblest of this illustrious generation, the first of Machado's "Proverbs and Folksongs" declares,

> I never chased fame,
> nor longed to leave my song
> behind in the memory of men.

Instead he adored the innocent Leonor, solitary walks, and

> subtle words
> almost weightless, delicate
> as soap bubbles.
> I like to see them paint themselves
> in the colors of sunlight and float,
> scarlet, into the blue sky, then
> suddenly tremble and break.

"In January of 1939, as the Spanish Civil War was ending with the defeat of the Republican forces, Machado and his family fled across the Pyrenees into France, where the poet died in the town of Collioure on February 22, 1939," writes Berg. "Found in his coat pocket after he died were scribbled words recalling his childhood in Seville: 'These blue days and this sun of childhood,' his last evocation of the landscape of memory." It was the last imaginary border Machado would cross.

This 319-page bilingual edition contains several long, vivid narratives of Spain's heroic and quixotic history, its landscape and inhabitants. The translators have crafted an intelligent, dependable English version of the complete *Campos de Castilla*.

Antonio Machado's subtle wit and lucid wisdom are not lost in translation. From his great sequence, *Proverbs and Folksongs*, he has the last word.

> Man has four things
> that are no good at sea:
> anchor, rudder, oars,
> and the fear of going down.

Light and Shadows

Roots and Wings. But let the wing grow roots and the roots fly.
—Juan Ramón Jiménez

The poetic light of being was embodied by Juan Ramón Jiménez (1881-1958), and its shadows were inhabited by Federico García Lorca (1898-1936). Jiménez was not a sun, but he always charted our star by day and that borrowed light passed directly to the moon. Lorca stared at the moon in new ways.

Jiménez, the 1956 Nobel Laureate, became a voluntary exile during the Spanish Civil War, settling in Puerto Rico. Like Lorca's *Poet in New York*, he had visited the Manhattan colossus, writing critically about it. Robert Bly translated from Jiménez's *Diary of a Poet Recently Married* (1916) in a bilingual selection of poems by Jiménez and Lorca (Beacon Press, 1983). Bly writes in the introduction.

> Jiménez said that he lived his life in such a way as to get the most poetry possible out of it. His poems ask the question: what sort of life shall we live so as to feel poetry, ecstasy? We can understand the subject matter of Jiménez' poems if we understand that it is in solitude a man's emotions become very clear to him. Jiménez does not write of politics or religious doctrines, of the mistakes of others, not of his own troubles or even his own opinions, but only of solitude, and the strange experiences and the strange joy that come to a man in solitude. His books usually consist of emotion after emotion called out with great force and delicacy, and it must be said that his short, precise poems make our tradition of the long egotistic ode look rather absurd. . . . This is what he calls "naked poetry." It is poetry near the emotion.

Bly's version of "Vino, Primero, Pura" reveals the story of naked poetry.

> At first she came to me pure,
> dressed only in her innocence,

and I loved her as we love a child.

Then she began putting on
clothes she picked up somewhere;
and I hated her, without knowing it.

She gradually became a queen,
the jewelry was blinding . . .
What bitterness and rage!

Soon she was back to the single shift
of her old innocence.
I believed in her a second time.

Then she took off the cloth
and was entirely naked . . .
Naked poetry, always mine,
That I have loved my whole life!

Bly's translation of "Oceans" (*Light and Shadows*, White Pine, 1987) suggests a solitary pause, as imagination's boat strikes the depths of consciousness.

I have a feeling that my boat
has struck, down there in the depths,
against a great thing.
                              And nothing
happens! Nothing . . . Silence . . . Waves . . .

—Nothing happens? Or has everything happened,
and are we standing now, quietly, in the new life?

The last lines of Dennis Maloney's version of "New Leaves" in the White Pine collection strike a spiritual postscript to the tranquil "Oceans": "Don't run, go slow/it is only into yourself/that you must go!//Go slow, don't run/for the child of yourself, just born/eternal/cannot follow!" The determination to look inward, of diving deeply into the solitary self, becomes an ecstatic awakening into a new life.

Jiménez influenced Lorca early on, taking him under his wing—that wing which grew roots, soaring beyond the younger poet's first love of music. Lorca was a piano student under his mother's tutelage (Vincenta Lorca Romero was a gifted pianist), writing music compositions before he wrote poems. The early poetry is full of music and light, including "Juan Ramón Jiménez" for his mentor. Over time elegiac shadows spread across his passionate lines of desire. "Malguena" evokes Spanish folk music and awareness of the *duende*. "Death/is coming in and leaving/the tavern.//Black horses and sinister/people are riding/over the deep roads/of the guitar."

In the bilingual edition of Lorca's *Selected Verse* (Farrar, Straus, Giroux, 2004), editor Christopher Maurer quotes from Lorca's lecture on the *duende*:

> The *duende* must know beforehand that he can serenade death's house . . . With idea, sound, or gesture, the *duende* enjoys fighting the creator on the very rim of the well. Angel and muse escape with violin, meter, and compass; the *duende* wounds. In the healing of that wound, which never closes, lie the strange, invented qualities of a man's work.

Poet W.S. Merwin's translation of Lorca's "Song of the Barren Orange Tree" begins and ends with the dark song's refrain: "Woodcutter./Cut my shadow from me./Free me from the torment/of seeing myself without fruit."

> Why was I born among mirrors?
> The day walks in circles around me,
> and the night copies me
> in all its stars.
>
> I want to live without seeing myself.
> And I will dream that ants
> and thistle burrs are my
> leaves and my birds.

Woodcutter.
Cut my shadow from me.
Free me from the torment
of seeing myself without fruit.

—*Roots and Wings: Poetry From Spain 1900-1975*

That Lorca was unable to bear fruit was perhaps the "shadow" that he wanted cut away; but this also evokes the shadow of *duende*, as the "night copies me/in all its stars." Lorca and Jiménez remained in touch with childlike wonder in their poetry, but from different perspectives. The older man was involved in publishing books and a magazine, always pushing the evolution of Spanish literature. The younger Lorca, who seemed never to let go of the "little boys" who "eat/brown bread and delicious moon" or to escape "the stone in the fruit" (in poet James Wright's translation of "August"), remained encased "In a drop of water/the little boy was looking for his voice." (in Merwin's version of "The Little Mute Boy").

Federico García Lorca became famous for *The Gypsy Ballads* (1928), for the powerful "Lament for Ignacio Sánchez Mejías" (1935), for later plays, *Blood Wedding* (1932) and *The House of Bernarda Alba* (1936). Because he was brutally assassinated by Franco's regime in 1936, at age 38, Lorca will remain beloved worldwide. But Jiménez is the greater poet, probably known more for his charming novel, *Platero y yo* (1917) than for his magnificent poetry. One of his lines was the epigraph for Ray Bradbury's novel *Fahrenheit 451*: "If they give you ruled paper, write the other way."

Juan Ramón Jiménez wrote the *other* way.

Almost Music

Spanish poet Ángel González (1925-2008) sings to the theme of music in his last book, *Almost All the Music and Other Poems*, translated by the late poet E.A. Mares (Wings, 2007), observing that "music's power of suggestion is much more intense and richer than that of poetry."

González clarifies this statement in his *Prologue*.

> Music is produced with pure sounds, uncontaminated, without reference to any concrete reality not their own: there is nothing to interfere with its limitless capacity to produce dreams. Poetry, on the other hand, is made of words, and words inevitably carry ideas or notions that orient and limit its possibilities of suggestion, although they don't entirely nullify them. Poetry seduces us not only by what it says but also, and in a very important way, by what its memorable euphony expresses irrationally, placing the word on the verge of music. Those effects of poetry derived from rhythm that we can think of as "musical," speaking in figurative language, can also occasionally be achieved through the accumulation of certain rhetorical artifices: rhymes, harmony of vowels, alliterations. However, we should not forget that everything in poems, including what takes us furthest away from normal language, has the same substance as words and the phonemes that compose them. And their signifying functions have nothing to do with the functions of musical notes. Poetry is a purely verbal deed.
>
> As a result of my efforts, I almost experienced music with my fingers in the form of a guitar. Then I lashed at it in the shape of a violin, and later I insisted on flutes, marimbas, and keyboards. There were some moments, a few happy ones for me—I don't say the same for my neighbors and friends—when I came to believe I had experienced it, but such was not the case. It was all an illusion, the result of confusing desire with reality. With the passage of time, and already close to old age, I had no choice but to

admit the disillusioning truth: music had been an illusive presence in my life, intangible, like one of Tantalus's apples provoking me with its nearness and hiding its body, its transparent immaterial body, at the very moment my hands were about to touch it.

Briefly related, that was the history of my relations with music. It is, above all, a story of frustration. Perhaps in an unconscious way, my dedication to poetry obeyed, possibly, the intention of doing with words what was forbidden me with pure sounds.

The majority of poems in this collection were not selected for their possible sound or "musical" qualities, rather because music appears in them as a theme, or a motive for dealing with other themes. Some of them, in which music is not the theme or even a motive, are here because they try to approximate the form of a "song."

Listen to the nostalgic "Dawn Tango" calling silent instruments. "The concertina/sends a shiver traveling/low necklines and spinal columns./Imprisoned by amplified guitars, by deep and agonizing guitars,/the concertina stretches out/its indolence and its hoarse, transplanted sound of the sea." Alas, "There is a light moment/when people dance./There is a murky moment/during which I faint./There is a broken moment/when everything is weeping." Yet "Hope takes aim from behind the violin:/an all but impossible tenuous hope./I know you won't return./The woman sings." Finally, the "song flees,/ drunk and sobbing,/towards the street . . ."

"A Song for Singing a Song" then "Insists, damages/your soul./ It comes perhaps from a time/remote, from an impossible epoch/lost forever./It goes beyond the limits/of music. It has substance,/aroma, like the dust of something/indefinite, a memory/that never really happened,/a vague hope never realized./It is called simply:/song.//But it isn't only that.//It's also sadness." Emotions stir music into poetry. All the arts are born of emotion. Analysis follows, pretending to be precise in its impurity.

González scripts playful references to poetry in the second section, bordering at times on his unique brand of anti-poetry. The entire text of the opening poem ("There, Where Words Fail") cuts both ways. It could be about Lorca's execution, or merely a string of cryptic overstatements that toy with melodrama. "Poet of the ineffable.//He was finally able to say/What no one had ever said.//They sentenced him to death."

"Countermand (Poetics I'm in favor of some days.)," begins: "This is a poem.//Here it's permitted/to put up posters,/throw trash, take a piss . . .//The endless afternoon,/the tediousness of this day,/the sheer stupidity of time,/will be held responsible." Not as outlandish as Nicanor Parra, this Ángel's dry wit whips against a history of writing "serious" poems. "To Poetry" becomes a love poem.

> They have said the most obscure things about you.
> Also the most brilliant.
> The words entwined as
> strands of hair, silk and gold in a single tress
> —an adornment for your beautiful shoulders—
> Now,
> as beautiful as you are,
> recently combed,
> I want to take you by what I most love.
> I want to take you
> —although I am old and poor—
> not by the gold and silk tress,
> but to take you (passionately) by your simple, fresh,
> pure, perfumed, angrily buoyant
> and smooth hair, and have fun with you.
> I want to take you out into the street,
> disheveled,
> your dark hair
> undulating in the breeze
> —free, loose, and bouncy—
> long and black as cackling laughter.

"Penultimate Nostalgia" forms a bridge from earlier "serious" poems to some light-hearted ones, but it also slices into deeper realms.

> That sweet violin,
> the one that played tangos,
> hounded by the labored murmur of accordions

and the happy mob . . .

Gasoline was beginning its reign
on the astonished streets,
but the jasmines had not yet begun their retreat

The violin,
bard of this drama
and impossibly sweet,
brilliant vagabond of space,
pursued those solitary hearts . . .

More music images follow that "Imprecise, murky time," as "the blues returned, and their syncopations/filled the risky morning/with restlessness and outbursts of laughter." And "Now/that everything has passed,/we feel nostalgic," but "On the other hand, we forget/the cadavers,/the battlefields,/the hunger in the countryside,/the reasons for the hunger." He admits in the last lines, "I am also nostalgic with age./I was also very happy. Also, I remember./I was also a witness of other times."

Those "other times" are *not* forgotten. González's five books published in Spain during the cataclysmic years of Franco dictatorship and the lingering wounds of civil war got negative attention from the government, so he exiled to America. Earlier political poems appear in *Roots and Wings*, the anthology edited by Hardie St. Martin, who introduced us to the history of modern Spanish poetry.

Poet E.A. Mares is an excellent translator of this subtle poetry. Ángel González settled in his translator's hometown, Albuquerque, where eventually they met. "The honors he has received do little to reveal the man," declares Mares' *Preface*.

> Ángel is a quiet, reflective person, absolutely unpre-
> tentious. He has a sharp and penetrating sense of humor
> yet he is the gentlest of persons . . . . Ángel deeply empa-
> thizes with the insulted and the injured of this earth. Wary
> of empty abstractions and political ideologies, his concern
> for the *other*, for the concrete, personal and social experi-
> ence of ordinary people, is matched by a fine complemen-

tary lyricism that endows his most engaged poems with literary excellence.

Reading this poetry is an enchanting start for soaring with one of the angels "to the *largo* cadence of the afternoon."

Exiting the Wound

Peruvian poet César Vallejo was born in 1892 in a small Andean town and died at the age of 46 in Paris in 1938. His body was buried in a pauper's grave.

Vallejo's poetry first arrived into English in 1943, included in the pioneering anthology, *Twelve Spanish American Poets*, translated and introduced by American poet H.R. Hays. Another translator, Thomas Merton, called Vallejo "the greatest catholic poet since Dante—by catholic I mean universal."

I read Vallejo's poetry first in Spanish and then in the translations by Hays, before exploring the imagery of the originals with Julio Ortega, a Peruvian critic and expert on Vallejo, when he was lecturing at the University of Texas in Austin. Vallejo's most ardent supporters—American poets James Wright, Robert Bly, John Knoepfle, and Hardie St. Martin—reintroduced his poetry to English-language readers during the 1960s and 1970s. Bly wrote that "Vallejo's art shows us what it's like not to go about recapturing ideas but to actually think. We feel the flow of thought, its power like an underground river finding its way for the first time through some shifted ground—even he doesn't know where it will come out."

At the time English-language poetry was still controlled by the New Criticism, casting poets out beyond the margins of their texts, so academic explicators could lecture about "meaning" in poetry. The poet was expected to be impersonal and to exhibit neoclassical restraint. Thus the most subjective linguistic venture had to aspire to an aesthetic of objectivity, as if poets were without bodies or emotions. Vallejo's poetry breaks down the textual object, pierces the vulnerable skin of ego, and reveals the poet's gaping wound. Next to the elegant masters of metaphor, Vallejo writes like a wild, tortured being. The New Critics were unaware of his work, and likely would have dismissed it, since there was no way to discern T.S. Eliot's objective correlative in Vallejo's fractured code.

Vallejo knew the intellectuals of Paris, traveled to Marxist Russia where he experienced brief fame, and then on to war-torn Spain, where Federico García Lorca supported his work. He was sketched by Picasso, but would never be a candidate for The French Academy. In a startlingly fresh idiom, he criticized the "pseudo-new" of André Breton's surrealism. His originality—never stylized and always evolving—resists imitation. "A Man Walks By" opens currents of intense anger and compassion, crying out to be free. This 1937 poem, written as the Spanish Civil War raged, lances the glories of Modernity. Glimpses of the grim poverty he experienced among ordinary people alternate with terse, sardonic questions concerning "high culture" in the face of Fascism, bloodshed, and the massive destruction by military barbarism. His mocking critique of Modernist Art—ego's royal reign and existential metaphysics—finds direct expression in conversational speech and interrogatives, scalding the pretensions of "high" culture with savage wit. In one stroke he destroys the polite formality of genres, creating a new poetics at the heart of actual experience. Unconcerned with the precious elements of poetry, Vallejo teaches us not to lose awareness of our painful humanity roiling in the caldron of modern existence.

A Man Walks By

A man walks by with a loaf of bread on his shoulder.
Am I going to write about my double after that?
Another scratches, plucks a louse from his armpit, kills it.
Of what value to discourse on psychoanalysis?
Another has entered my chest with a stick.
Then to dialogue about Socrates with the doctor?
A cripple passes by, holding the hand of a child.
After that am I going to read André Breton?

Another trembles from cold, coughs, spits blood.
Will it be possible then to allude to the profound self?
Another searches in the mud for bones and peels.
How dare to write about the infinite after that?
A bricklayer falls from a roof and dies.
Now to innovate the trope and the metaphor?

A merchant cheats a customer out of a peso.
To speculate, then, on the fourth dimension?
A banker falsifies the balance sheets.
With whose face to cry in the theatre?
An outcast sleeps with a foot on his back.
Next to speak to anyone about Picasso?

Someone goes to a funeral weeping.
How then to join the Academy?
Someone cleans a carbine in his kitchen.
Of what value to speak of the beyond?
Someone passes by counting with his fingers.
How to chat of the ego without screaming?

In the seventh canto of *Trilce* (1922) appears what Vallejo phrased as that "heroic exit through the wound." *Trilce* leaps beyond surrealism, with the command that we must "refuse symmetry firmly."

> The book was born from the greatest emptiness. I'm responsible for it. I assume complete responsibility for its aesthetics. Today, and more than ever perhaps, I sense an until now unknown most sacred obligation gravitating over me, as a man and an artist: Being free! If I don't have to be free, I won't ever be. I feel the arch of my forehead gaining its most imperative force of heroism. I offer myself in the freest form I can and this is my greatest artistic harvest. God knows how far my freedom is true and real! God knows how much I suffered so the rhythm didn't overrun this freedom and slide into license! God knows what hair-raising ledges I've looked down from, full of fear, afraid everything was gong to die in my poor living soul!

Vallejo seems to be in dialogue with an impossible reader—himself.

"How hard it is to be oneself and see only what is there!" These wild strophes of Being are the tortured music of grief. "What matter that I cry from not being able to cry, and laugh at the little I've laughed." It took heroic courage to live openly and to face the wound. "Whether I pretend I'm alive/or pretend I was not born,/I won't be able to get free." He glares at the wound, knowing he will die of it never healing. Instead he stacks his bones at the edge of the abyss. "And what if after so many words,/the word itself doesn't survive!//To have been born to live off our own death!/It would be better, frankly,/ if we were all swallowed up, and to hell with it!"

French poet Pierre Reverdy, the most authentic voice among Europeans of that time, ends his cubist poem "X" with these lines (Kenneth Rexroth translation):

> Winged hands advanced to open everything
> Then in the tight livid warp is revealed
> the unheard of wound I want to cure

Perhaps Reverdy's "unheard of wound" and Vallejo's "heroic exit through the wound" refer not only to the wound of mortality, but to the rupture between male and female. Vallejo reveals this idea in the lines: "And female is the soul of the absent./And female is my soul." The female is his complement, though she is the "soul of the absent." Yet even in her absence and in his attending grief, she is part of his psyche in the "still burning repose of being."

In discussing Vallejo's poetry, Robert Bly wrote of 20th century Europe: "The European psyche knows it is wounded. It's a profound wound, and it will not heal, and it's only in our time that the wound is beginning to live and be lived again—also in words. I don't believe it's possible to write post-Lawrentian poetry, or 'wound poetry,' without solitude." Without solitude a blunted consciousness becomes the curse of civilization. It has always been the poet's role to awaken society. "We, whose task is wakefulness itself," wrote Nietzsche from his dream of philosopher-poets discovering a new world. Carl Jung characterized a similar modernity.

> The man whom we can with justice call "modern" is solitary. He is so of necessity and at all times, for every step towards a fuller consciousness of the present removes him further from his original "participation mystique" with the mass of men—from submersion in a common unconsciousness.

The 20th century's landscape is littered with such lucid, despairing quotes. The Portuguese poet of multiple identities, Fernando Pessoa, writes, "I am myself the loss I suffered." Eliot lost that intense fire in later work, but Vallejo never gave up the flame. Instead he fanned it, writing, "Absurd, only you are pure./Absurd, this excess sweats/only before you/golden pleasure." The specter of death was always in Vallejo's vision. The black riders who herald death are the archetypical beasts of lower consciousness. He wrote the title poem for his first book, *Los heraldos negros*, which he self-published in 1918, during his mid-twenties in Lima.

The Black Riders

There are blows in life so powerful—I can't tell you!
Blows like the hatred of God;
as if the undertow of all who suffered
gets dammed up in the soul.
I can't tell you!

They open dark gulches
in the fiercest face and the strongest back.
Perhaps they're the horses of barbaric Attilas
or the black messengers sent by death.

There are the backslidings of Christs of the soul,
an adoration blasphemed by destiny.
These bloody blows are the cracklings
of bread that burn against the oven door.

And man, poor man! He turns his eyes
to the clap of hands behind his back.
Mad eyes shift and all that's been lived
dams up a pool of blame in his stare.

There are blows in life so powerful—I can't tell you!

In *Trilce* (1922), he tells his friends they are dead. "So I say life/is in the mirror,/and you are the original, death." When Vallejo was literally starving in Paris, he broke all tradition by entering his own poem to die. The poem was a time capsule waiting for a rainy Thursday in autumn, and it became a self-fulfilling prophecy. He actually died in Paris on a rainy Thursday in autumn.

Black Stone on a White Stone

> I will die in Paris, in a sudden downpour,
> on a day I can already remember.
> I will die in Paris—and I don't run from it—
> perhaps on a Thursday, like today, in autumn.
>
> It will be a Thursday, because today,
> Thursday, as I set down these lines,
> my arms have been forced on wrong,
> and never have I turned onto my road
> to see the whole way alone.
>
> César Vallejo is dead.
> They beat him, without his doing anything to them.
> They hit him hard with a stick and also with a rope.
>
> The witnesses are the Thursdays and the bones,
> the solitude, the rain and the roads . . .

In 1937, the year before he died, Vallejo wrote "A Brief Funeral Liturgy for a Hero of the Republic"—a series of images that narrate the event. It begins with "A book was lying at the edge of his waist/A book was sprouting from his corpse/They carried the hero away." But the book continues to grow even though the hero's blood becomes "vaporous, infinite." And "I saw it—a book,/a book behind, a book above,/sprouted from the corpse violently." This is a small ritual for a man who is now doubly dead. But he has left us the book of his remains (*Poemas Humanos*, published posthumously by his French widow in 1939).

The corpse is Vallejo, this time unnamed, identified by the book he has created from his mortal wound. César Vallejo becomes "the dead hero" who transcends his own death by discovering the "heroic exit through the wound."

Sublime Blue

The *Elemental Odes* by Noble Laureate Pablo Neruda (1904-1973) are mature poems from the Chilean's astonishing career. The "Early" designation means that the Spanish poems are from the first of three volumes. A few political poems have *never* been translated, until William Pitt Root began wrestling with these deceptively simple lines during the 1980s. Composed to fit newspaper columns, their slender "deception" resides in a dynamic whipping from one realm to another.

Sublime Blue, a bilingual edition (Wings Press, 2013), opens with "The Invisible Man," critiquing unnamed predecessors, while also being self-critical. Midway the poem shifts, since he "cannot/live without life,/be a man without mankind," unlike "my brother/the poet" who "suffers/because of his passion/for the sea,/he loves exotic ports/for their names,/he writes of oceans/he doesn't know,/he passes right alongside of life." The unknown Romantic poet "falls and rises/without ever touching earth," declaring "himself cursed,/with great difficulty carries the cross/of shadows,/he believes himself unique/in all the world."

In a brilliant Introduction, Root assesses this poem as "the antidote to the 'I' as all-devourer and to the private ego as self-reflexive"—artistic poses Neruda "regarded as defunct Romantic responses inadequate to contemporary existence." Neruda confesses that he "fought against my own self-absorption and so was able to settle the debate between the real and the subjective deep within myself." Genuine humility shines forth, as he "accepts the investiture earned in the street, among the masses. Today's social poet is still a member of the earliest order of priests. In the old days he made his pact with darkness, and now must interpret the light." But the light of a truthful poet "is dangerous to a capitalism on its last legs."

Neruda was dangerous to the Chilean elite, giving the poor real hope. In "Ode to Poverty," he knows "the bankrupt wit, the torn suit,/the shoes split wide open," yet not romanticizing it, as "stalking me/through the streets/ever since I was born." Poverty followed "through barracks and hospitals, through peace and war." Then Neruda leaps into defiant confrontation. "Now,/Poverty,/I follow you./As you were relentless/I am relentless./Alongside/every poor person/you will find me singing."

In Root's masterful characterization, Neruda's "phrases fall like thin wrists of water cascading from great heights, exploding at intervals against ledges and obstacles protruding from a sheer cliff-face. Fluent, sinuous, riddled with delightful surprise, the offhand form is also suited to the tone of seemingly casual surmise that can so suddenly pool in a conclusion of great clarity and depth." Water imagery is apt, because Neruda loved the sea, living decades near the Pacific in a house built like a ship, where he died and was buried. In "Ode to Hope," the sea brings redemption at "Marine twilight,/in the middle of/my life,/the waves like clustered grapes,/the solitude of the sky," as "Waves whisper to the solid coast: 'All will be made whole.'"

Sea, sky, and an anonymous blue flower "that has invaded my whole house," Neruda recollects in his *Memoirs*. "I don't know if all human beings have the gift of seeing the sublimest blue. Is it revealed to select few? Has some blue god denied them its contemplation?" Neruda could not name that sublime blue flower. "Ode to the Blue Flower" evolves similarly "from what depth/do you extract your blue radiance?/Does your silk trembling/below the earth/commune with the depths of the sea?" Humble questions, but with no self-assured answers, raising "a small banner/of blue flame, of irresistible peace,/of indomitable purity."

While there are trenchant odes to numbers, to atoms, and to gloom, "Ode to Restlessness" never demands others "to be ruled by my words,/I don't wish/for a sea without tides, poetry/without people/vacant/paintings or music/without the wind!"

"A complete poet is a complete human being—not a specialist, a technician comprehensible chiefly to fellow technicians—who works as the universe itself works," writes Root in his introduction, "building out of elemental materials those increasingly profound structures in which may live and breathe the astonishing and mysterious varieties of the human spirit."

Pablo Neruda is that poet and these translations complete a human song. This great poet of the world has been speaking truth to power for generations unto this very day, because translators like William Pitt Root have understood, bringing lucidity to these humane poems of fraternal love into countless languages.

Parra-Phrasing

Nicanor Parra's *After Dinner Declarations* might be the most savagely witty book ever written, translated by Dave Oliphant in a bilingual edition (Host Publications, 2009). The Chilean antipoet (b. 1914) is still alive and well, threatening to outlive us all, while having the last laugh. His *Deprecations* (pun intended) makes fun of himself (*Parranoid* is one self-deprecating moniker), as well as the names attached to literary prizes he received—Mexican author Juan Rulfo (1917-1986), poet Vicente Huidobro (1893-1948), plus later awards not satirized (Cervantes Prize in 2011, Neruda Prize in 2012), although their namesakes appear in playful utterances.

Parra's inside jokes about *literati* mix praise with ridicule in unequal measure, but he greatly admires Shakespeare, Cervantes, and Juan Rulfo, reserving the sharpest barbs for dictators, while tossing prickly pears at Chilean poetic rivals—Huidobro, Neruda, Gabriela Mistral (1889-1957), and Pablo de Rokha (1894-1968). Mistral and Neruda won the Nobel Prize, and Parra has been nominated several times.

One strophe concerns dreaming of the prize, but he answers with a question: "If they didn't give it to Rulfo/Why would they give it to me?" He declares himself "A full-time Rulfologue," but warns us "Not to confuse Rulfologue with Rulfist" or "Rulfian" or "Rulfophile" or "Rulfomaniac" or "Rulfopath" or "Rulfophobe" or "Rulfophage" in an absurd academic list, even as he declares that "I'm a compulsive illiterate."

Yet "Parra has been a serious student of Shakespeare," writes Oliphant, "partly because he considers the Bard the first antipoet. . . . Hamlet exemplifies the antipoetic position par excellence." Parra calls him the "Champion of Methodical Doubt."

> Although Parra's five poem-speeches concern his concept of antipoetry, mainly as it contrasts the work of other literary figures, they also touch on such perennial motifs as ecology, human rights and responsibilities,

philosophy . . . and math and science, the latter owing to his work as a professor of physics trained at Brown and Oxford. Parra even manages to satirize, by way of his honorary doctorate, both professors and the medical profession, aiming his barbed witticism at pedantic doctors of philosophy and the "Health Business." . . . Parra has conceived a new, or revived a traditional, genre for his anti-poetry: the address given on receiving an honor or award, which, in the antipoet's case, he finds so undeserved, and for which he remains ironically speechless, with no words to express his gratitude and disbelief. The Chilean often turns his satire on himself, as when he speaks of working on the last "bad" speech of the twentieth century and the first "good" speech of the twenty-first, unable to decide which page goes with which speech.

In 1966 Parra and James Laughlin (publisher of New Directions) traveled to the Abbey of Gethsemani in Kentucky to visit with Trappist monk Thomas Merton, who had translated some of Parra's antipoems. The two poets corresponded before and after, but their conversation was brief.

Merton's final books—*Cables to the Ace* (1968) and *The Geography of Lograire* (1969), both from New Directions—contain Mertonian versions of antipoems. Before meeting Parra, he had welcomed Nicaraguan poet-priest of liberation theology, Ernesto Cardenal, to the novitiate at Gethsemani. Cardenal (b. 1925) introduced him to the significant Latin American poets, Parra among them.

In a 1965 letter to Parra, Merton writes:

> I like your irony very much and I cannot tell you how much in agreement I am with you about contemporary society. We are in a time of the worst barbarity. It is sufficient to look at what is happening in Vietnam and everywhere, most of all here. Sermons are worth nothing in this situation. It is necessary to state, without judgment, the truth. And that apocalyptic truth cannot be expressed in apocalyptic symbols, but only in its clichés.

Merton felt that with the rise of our totalitarian state, public language was rendered meaningless (especially in advertising), since the products of narcissism were endowed with the "transcendental properties of being." He described *Cables to the Ace* as "a series of poems, which are largely experimental . . . full of ironies and ambiguities appropriate to the moment when we are saturated with the wrong kind of communication." He went further in *The Geography of Lograire,* observing the decadence of the western myth and "its unmitigated arrogance towards the rest of the human race." The text includes a "warning": "IF YOU HAVE HEART FAILURE WHILE READING THIS THE POET IS NOT RESPONSIBLE."

Parra had issued a similar "warning" in *Poems and Antipoems* (New Directions, 1967): "The author will not answer for any problems his writings may raise."

Figures of Speech

Figures of Speech is the only book by Enrique Lihn (1929-1988) to appear in the United States since 1978, when the Chilean's first book, *The Dark Room and Other Poems*, was published by New Directions. This bilingual volume, translated by Dave Oliphant (Host, 1999), contains 62 poems, mainly from later books, including signature texts on the poetic process that are among his most powerful.

Lihn was obsessed—in a self-critical way—with the paradoxical nature of art and the limits of communication. From perception to naming emerges poetic evocation; from text to reader, intense listening and dialogue; and from the original idiom to the translated language, comes cross-cultural interpretation.

"There is no lucidity like that of Enrique Lihn," says Nicanor Parra, referring *not* to meaning, but to the poet's self-awareness and linguistic clarity in creating it. "Those who insist on calling things by their names/as if they were clear and simple/cover them simply with new ornaments," proclaims Lihn in "If Poetry Is To Be Written Right": "They do not express things, they dig around in the dictionary,/they render language more and more useless,/they call things by their names and those answer to their names/but they undress themselves before us only in the dark."

In his thoughtful Introduction, Oliphant clarifies this as "Lihn's preoccupation with the function of language, how it should be utilized, how it can stand in the way of true understanding, and yet how the poet would be nothing without his words. The idea that poetry is 'nothing' is, from beginning to end of Lihn's writing career, the cause of his sense of futility as a creative artist, and yet remains for him the subject that he must forever confront and the object that he must continue to make."

Poems about poetry are generally reflexive rather than reflective, but the effect of these texts prevents the reader from slipping into a cozy romanticism about *Ars poetica*, challenging one's assumption of what a poem means. "By An Uncontrollable Force" begins with the following lines.

I hope these poems have been written
     by an uncontrollable force, with the inadequacies
     of such a case.
I may have botched them, but will not forgive
myself if I have done so beyond the bounds
of a certain sincerity that even the words
     are permitted;
and seldom did I believe I could write in such a
     dated manner
as this, naturally.

The voice pretends to speak beyond the margin, as if the poet remains in the wings while his poem performs on stage. This is grounded by a comic self-deprecation, leaving open to debate this "uncontrollable force." Is it neurotic and uncontrollable, or is the poetry actually under artistic control?

I see a summer fade where it finally existed
and its knot is now in my throat
that never aspired to song yet neither to cold
     speculation.
Overstatements strike me as justified, in truth
     we live by them, each in his way
just as one can die of an excess of common
     sense.
Sea and sun, for instance, are naturally
     exaggerated
or if one wishes: rhetorical
while of the logical mad we already have
     the most perilous supply.

Lihn characterized his own poetry accurately. He was neither lyrical nor coldly philosophical. His discursive sermons are littered with oxymorons, wordplay, and wit, illuminating his own truth, somewhat like Parra's leaner antipoems, which broke the mold of *Modernismo*. Lihn begins to play with absurdity in the final passage.

> Soon all the tricks of language
> —and language itself is the original artifice—
> wanted to place themselves here at the service
> of a poetry that's neither artificial nor natural;
> a no-man's land it may be but a familiar spot
> where those poles have come to touch
> and in the best of cases by an uncontrollable force.

Since "language itself is the original artifice," what would this "poetry that's neither artificial nor natural" be? Lihn does not say directly, but his poems map this "no-man's land." His "familiar spot" cannot be found by logic, psychoanalysis, or automatic writing. The texts cut against these methodologies, yet contain a rigorous logic, a humane insight, and a painfully ironic spontaneity.

These aspects are strikingly evident in the naked *Death Diary*. Chilean poets have written memorably about death—Gabriela Mistral's *Sonnets of Death*, Pablo Neruda's "Nothing but Death," Nicanor Parra's gallows humor, Oscar Hahn's *The Art of Dying*—but *only* Lihn (among Chileans) wrote about his own dying. "Pain Has Nothing To Do With Pain"—an 80-line discourse—offers this warning: "The words we use to mean those things, like pain and death, are contaminated/There are no words in the mute zone." Yet a voice from the "mute zone" takes up the discourse!

"A dead man who has a few months of life would have to learn/a clean language for hurting, despairing, and dying/which beyond mathematics would be accessible only to specialists/of an impossible and equally valid knowledge/a language like a body with all its organs operated on/that would live for a fraction of a second in a brilliant fashion."

If Lihn was frustrated by the veils of language obscuring reality, how futile was his attempt to evoke the final unknown? His evocation of death emerges as the image of a dying body. By "operating" on the body of language, he transforms prosaic function into poetic creation. In the eternal instant rises the poem.

Lihn insists that "this is already stating/the merely obvious with help/of a figure of speech/my words obviously cannot cross the barrier of that unknown tongue/before which I am a baboon called upon by extra terrestrial beings/to interpret/the human language . . ." In death-bed poems he tries to transcend the melodramatic rhetoric of death by facing the silent reality of dying.

"Limitations of Language" offers another perspective on the inexplicable. "Language awaits the miracle of a third person,/(but not the one that's absent from Arabic grammars)/neither a character nor someone dead/A real subject who may speak for himself, in an inhuman voice/of what neither I nor you is able to say/blocked by our *personal* pronouns . . ."

Of course there can be no such person, but the second stanza teases us with a fresh variation. "We have here a man, pressing the trigger close to his temple/He sees something between that gesture and his death/Sees it during an elemental bit of time/so short that it will form no part of that/If something could prolong his death without placing it in time/a drug (discover it!)/The first pallid echoes would be heard/of an unpublished description of what it is not" (this published version of "what it is not" ends without a period, leaving open the search).

"The Artificial Hand" is Lihn's closure "that brought/paper and pencil in the bag of the terminally ill," but it will not "sign a decree/making an exception that will return him to life." Instead he rejects the false hope it represents.

> His orthopedic hand moves like an idiot who would play
> with a rock or a piece of wood
> and the paper fills itself with signs like ants on a bone.

These last poems take discourse into a silent nothingness.

Oliphant has divided *Figures of Speech* into six sections, revealing a range of styles and themes. The first opens with "Portrait" (dated 1952, printed posthumously in 1998), which rants against Catholicism. "As 'Portrait' indicates," writes Oliphant, "Lihn could be psychologically incisive in his clinical analysis of himself, yet always with an ironic touch that lends his observations a somewhat comic objectivity. This is true as well of his treatment in 'Belle Epoque' and 'News From Babylon' of the oppressive religious atmosphere of his childhood, which yet inspired his writing and was the basis for much of its vital 'neurotic' imagery."

The second section contains 14 poems about writing, including sonnets, which illuminate aspects of the translating craft, demonstrating Lihn's technical control and Oliphant's linguistic ingenuity, although they are among the weakest poems. When English feels forced into a rhyme scheme, results are pedestrian.

Concerning one poem ("The Wailing Wall"), Oliphant relates a back-story. "The English translation was first published in 1978, but without the Spanish, which Lihn and I both somehow lost along the way." In 1987 Oliphant asked him to reconstruct it in Spanish. In 1988 Lihn had 'reconstituted approximately' the original poem, while declaring, 'The reconstruction was improbable.'" Lihn was not fluent in English, but the "improbable" Spanish reconstruction holds up and the exchange reveals the poet's confidence in his translator.

A set of nine poems on art constitutes the second section, displaying fresh perspectives of Degas, Kandinsky, and "Monet's Years at Giverny." While Lihn was discursive, conversational, and often noisy, his contemplation of a painting closes with a calm vision of "the moment that consumes the substance/and leaves only the embers of Being/that conflagration that comes from clouds and wind/and burns—spread out on the waters —its image" [from "J.M.W. Turner (1775-1851)"].

The fourth part features poems of travels beyond Chile ("this horrendous/trivial country"), and on to Madrid, Rome, New York, and Toronto, plus two poems written during a 1985 stay as a visiting professor at the University of Texas in Austin. One of the love poems in section five, "Echo of Another Sonata," recalls Lihn's themes and subjects in memory of Eros.

> In your opinion one love erases another
> and it's so, dear, but in love not everything
> belongs to the arrow and the quiver
> —the first versions—nor to the wound that bewilders
> all pleasure all pain
> twin of death, metaphor of birth

The victims of Eros survive the crime
of which, gladly, they are its passive agents
its authors in a mysterious moment and do not forget
I at least: my memory of you
independently of love retains it
as in that painting by Magritte the morning sky
    has not dissipated in the street at night
nor its precious moon: clotted light
in the lamp that darkly illumines that street
    It's true, the oxymoron
is no more than a figure of speech and can commit
            a premeditated sin
But not I, so I hope, if I tell you:
one love doesn't erase another
Memory, also, in its way, loves
and, as someone said: "there's nothing forgotten."

This edition excludes what Oliphant calls "Lihn's more overtly political poems," but without explanation, although the personal poems bare a political edge. Never a political revolutionary, Lihn nonetheless wrote indictments of Latin American tyranny and U.S. imperialism (see "The Defeat" and "Age of Sarcasm" in *The Dark Room*), exploring in an ironic voice the limits of language and self. Since Lihn doubted the little gods of poetry, he held no illusions about the smaller Latin American dictators. Critiquing the politics of death and the poetics of life with equal intensity and clarity, he became a force in the last century's revolution of the word.

Lihn's *Death Diary* entries close the book, returning us to the opening discourse. *Figures of Speech* invites readers into a dialogue, begun by a poet and his translator, in which we can participate. Reading the original texts leaves no doubt about their significance. For those who read Spanish but have not read Lihn, this representative selection stands as a useful beginning. For those without Spanish these accurate versions are always evocative.

Dave Oliphant worked at translating Lihn's poetry for three decades, discovering it while editing a magazine at the Catholic University of Chile in Santiago. Oliphant's activities as poet and critic, while editing and publishing poets under his independent Prickly Pear imprint, tend to identify him with Texas—almost to the exclusion of the important contributions he has made in the poetic exchange of this hemisphere. His dedicated work on Enrique Lihn's poetry and the antipoems of Nicanor Parra should change that perception.

Ashes and Light

The poems in Oscar Hahn's *Ashes in Love* (Host, 2009) suggest droll meditations on love and death, create surreal thresholds, animated nightmares, and contradictory mirrors. Born in Chile in 1938, Hahn taught Latin American literature for decades at the University of Iowa, but because he was a supporter of Chile's President Salvador Allende, he was imprisoned after the 1973 military coup by dictator Augusto Pinochet. Yet these later poems are not overtly political, although there remains a critique inherent in "The bone is a hero of the resistance."

The "Self-Portrait by Van Gogh" ends with "A drop of blood slides down the mirror/I dip my brush and paint wounds on my face/My head's a sunflower in flames." There are fabulous encounters with St. John of the Cross and Miles Davis, a poem on Duke Ellington at the Cotton Club, odes to dead parents and unknown phantoms, and the wildly witty "Autobiography of the Unconscious."

"I ruined this poem," laments "The Perfectionist," "I cut words/and twisted the neck of its syntax/till I left it speechless.//After so much punishment/it ended up nothing//I don't know what it said/I don't know how it ends."

Yet he knows how life ends. In "The Senses of the Dead," Hahn writes, "The dead are mute/They don't want to tell us what they know//The dead are deaf/They don't want to listen to our outcries.//They don't have mouths but speak among themselves/about the great secret they can't tell us."

There are stunning poems in *Ashes in Love* and in the two earlier Hahn books translated by James Hoggard—the classic *Arte de morir* of 1977 (*The Art of Dying*, 1988) and the banned *Mal de amor* of 1981 (*Love Breaks*, 1991), both published by the independent Latin American Literary Review Press. While these poets are dissimilar except for elegant craftsmanship, James Hoggard lucidly translates the Spanish-language master into English in this bilingual edition.

The prolific Hoggard—Texas Poet Laureate, novelist, essayist, translator—offers his eighth book of poems, *Triangles of Light*

(Wings, 2009), a remarkable evocation that assumes the voice of American painter Edward Hopper.

As with the deceptive simplicity of Hahn's lines, Hoggard also "translates" the seemingly bare surfaces of Edward Hopper's haunting art. Immersed in the persona of the artist, *Triangles of Light* provides readings that reflect ever-changing light. Here is Hoggard's poem about the book's magnificent cover painting by Hopper.

Sun in an Empty Room

No, hell no, I was not
meditating on death
or notions of emptiness.
I meant what I presented:
unadorned slabs of light
on two unaddled walls,

but when you asked
what I was looking for
in peopleless planes,
I said, *Myself—what else?*
for light is where self is
if self itself ever is.

Neither misery nor peace
finds voice or home here,
though a window does
and with it a blur of leaves,
salves for a claustrophobe.
There's nothing abstract here,
and nothing metaphorical,
and except for several ghosts
of gridmarks I've left
all planes are walls or floor,
and chiaroscuro is flesh,
and shadows, stains to mark
where light finds speech.

There are not illustrations for every poem, but viewing Hopper's art we discover that Hoggard's meditations are clear-eyed homages in "language as sparse and telling as the painter's gestures," opines William Pitt Root. Every artwork pauses along an endless journey. As artists create shadows of their imaginings, viewers experience them with our own lights. If a text is a translation or a poem about a painting, other pauses emerge, which can be read differently according to our moods, which change as surely and as often as the effects of light. Hopper's paintings are supreme studies in light, although obviously his medium was paint.

"Sunlight in a Cafeteria" reveals the light in Hopper's voice:

> Painting them, I paint
> us all—I paint us
> into symmetry,
> the speech I know:
>
> light a transient thing
> entering this room,
> overwhelming this room

"I only remember moments now," begins "Moonlight Interior," with "my brush the mnemonic device/through which I discover/and sometimes even invent/events of a fragmentary past. If Hopper's brush remembers, Hoggard's poems project a classic shape for these canvases. "I do see the world triangularly/and there have often been times/that finely tight shape/moved past me to my paint. . ."

"Hopper's implied narratives look simultaneously simple and complex," writes Hoggard, "and so they should, for they imply multilevel conversations with self and the world and those extensions of self, the things one makes that tradition calls art."

James Hoggard's poems are lucid conversations with Edward Hopper, just as his translations of Oscar Hahn create a charming dialogue with the poet. He keeps good company, skillfully transporting these artists into our conversation.

Art of Memory

Marjorie Agosín has been pointing out atrocities for decades—in poems, essays, and anthologies—from the Holocaust that murdered many in her family to the Pinochet dictatorship in Chile that disappeared thousands, sending her immediate family into exile in the States. Now we know without a doubt what happened in Chile, as recent U.S. State Department records have been declassified. The disclosures address the Nixon/Kissinger efforts to destabilize the democratically elected socialist government of Salvador Allende, and the USA-supported coup that assassinated him and brought General Augusto Pinochet to power in 1973.

"One is born with human rights, thus one is sacredly connected to all living things," Agosín writes in *An Absence of Shadows* (White Pine, bilingual edition, translated by Cola Franzen, Mary G. Berg, and Celeste Kostopulos-Cooperman, 1998). Her sense of sacred connections inspires compassion for the victims of political oppression and strengthens a sense of solidarity with peaceful struggles against violence and injustice. The desecration of human dignity ignites her moral outrage: "When human rights are violated, so is the sacredness of the world."

Agosín's passionate concern for the *Other* (and devotion to life as *res sacra*) link her directly to the tradition of Chile's poet-activists, including the Nobel Laureates Gabriela Mistral and Pablo Neruda. Mistral led the first movements for child welfare, women's rights, and new laws to protect the indigenous peoples of Chile during the last century. Her bold, honest poems observe the desolation of poverty, evoke the loving courage of families, and commemorate the spiritual beauties of motherhood and nature. Neruda opposed right-wing regimes in defense of the working poor, and was exiled until the brief flowering of democracy under Salvador Allende.

Agosín's family, friends, and supporters of President Allende escaped to the United States before General Augusto Pinochet's military coup culminated in the assassinations of Allende, members of his government, and thousands of "disappeared" Chileans. "Although

I came of age in a foreign country speaking a foreign language," she writes, "I witnessed from afar the brutality of the Pinochet dictatorship that mutilated an entire generation." Her work in the 1980s and 1990s remembers "those voices muzzled in dark and silent torture chambers, especially the women and children, who were forbidden to sing and denied the opportunity to grow."

Her poetic vision becomes a sanctuary for lost spirits and the art of memory. "The disappeared women slipped in among my dreams," and "more than anything else they would ask me not to forget them." The texts evolve beyond memorials into psychic incarnations. "I am the disappeared woman/in a country grown dark/silenced by the/ wrathful cubbyholes/of those with no memory." She warns: "Don't conspire with oblivion/tear down the walls of silence/I want to be the appeared woman/from among the labyrinths/come back, return/name myself./Call my name." The most tender lyrics embrace surviving women, who "search, inquire and weep," as they attempt to reconnect the dismembered bodies. "Look,/these are photographs/of my children;/this one here has an arm/I don't know if it's my son's/but I think it might be/that this is his sweet little arm." But since "we Chileans/ are good about forgetting," Agosín calls out those who are in denial. "You who vainly/made your tongue/a map of forgetfulness;/you who vainly/keep silent before/the memory of hollow stars."

In "El Salvador," she says, "You don't want to think about a garden of the dead because that would be like returning to Auschwitz. As you can see, history returns in the memory of the living, who are the guardians of the dead." There are only a few references to the perpetrators, since her poetry always remains life affirming and healing, refusing to indulge in obsessions with absolute power or pornographic sadism, speaking the truth about the pathology of evil. "Some of my Chilean countrymen have betrayed not only their dreams of democracy but also their souls. The former dictator is a senator-for-life, an assassin is portrayed as a venerable grandfather, and torturers walk freely the streets of Santiago without fear or remorse."

General Pinochet (1915-2006) was arrested in England and returned to Chile, where he was placed under house arrest and charged with 300 counts of human rights violations, tax evasion, and embezzlement during and after a 17-year reign. There is no doubt where Agosín stands regarding Pinochet, as "The President" makes certain. "Nothing interrupts his movement./He diligently marches among the shadows/of the dead./The general doesn't hear the cries/of widowed mothers./The general doesn't stop before/the dancing ears on the pavement./Nothing stains his white suit."

In several poems about the "eternal ceremony of torture," we experience a depth of feeling that only poetry can invoke for both a real body and for the symbolic body of Chile. "The pain, savage and exact, without guile,/explores over the sands of the body,/glows, speeded over the burning/traces of a thousand bonfires./Someone toys with the misery/of this prostrate body,/of this solitude between/the howling/legs." Most of the dark chamber scenes are projected from the viewpoint of blindfolded victims, who are seers of an inward vision.

Primal imagery flows in "What Lies in the Depths of Your Eyes?"

> In the depths of your eyes,
> half-sleep,
> complicitous and generous sun,
> undulating air,
> wandering seasons,
> yellows sheltering
> in blue facades.
>
> In the depths of your eyes,
> the sea, rivers transformed into
> caresses
> into the roundness of living children.
>
> In the depths of your eyes,
> while darkness courses over their contours,
> and blindfold is a dubious maimed nurse,
> you are there
> because you are made of light
> because you are a butterfly luminous in the mirrors.

This collection includes recent work from the late 1990s and two award-winning titles from White Pine Press—*Circles of Madness: Mothers of the Plaza de Mayo* (1992) and *Zones of Pain* (1998). Agosín has been anthologized widely under various rubrics—Chilean, Latin American, Latina, feminist, human rights—and a dozen books have been published in the States, usually in bilingual editions, reaching a wide readership. Because human rights are abused daily on a global scale, Agosín's tone remains ever vigilant and deadly serious. Her sense of tragedy throbs with pain. She will not debate the niceties of ethical discourse or analyze the politics of diplomatic immunity. No, she simply cries out against injustice. She is too humane to rationalize one moment of horror and too sensitive to look away from the suffering.

Among the Angels of Memory, an expanded 2005 edition of *The Angel of Memory* (Wings, 2001) takes a different form, offering new poems through a fresh translation by Laura Rocha Nakazawa. It concerns Helena Broder—maternal great-grandmother and her "messenger angel"—who allows the poet "to answer questions about the dead and the living." The book won the 2006 Latino Book Award, and was praised by Isabel Allende, Julia Alvarez, and actor-activist Liv Ullmann.

The portrait reveals a fascinating Helena, beginning with a prose poem in her great-grandmother's voice, a transforming text evoking Helena's thoughts on leaving the Old World and crossing the Pacific to the port of Valparaíso, Chile. Her entry into the New World suggests "lights were like dancing fireflies and the savage flowers bent to welcome us into a twilight of unexplored dreams."

At the end of the poem Helena acknowledges Frida, Agosín's mother, as the one who "will remember with precision the date of your arrival in Chile, in 1939." Frida will also "recall the translucent tulle bonnet flowing in the wind, the delicate neckline that insinuated the softness of your neck, still fresh, your delicate breasts, your silver candelabra and the garnet bracelet that has inherited the fate of all our migrations, and now rests peacefully in the hands of your great-granddaughter."

Earlier memoirs—on her mother (*A Cross and A Star*, White Pine, 1997), of her father (*Always From Somewhere Else*, White Pine, 2000), and *The Alphabet in My Hands: A Writer's Life* (Rutgers University

Press, 2000)—were all composed of impressionistic vignettes. These first three memoirs had as their central conflict the rise and ruthless rule of Pinochet's CIA-supported regime in Chile, when her family immigrated to the States shortly before the assassination of President Salvador Allende, a family friend. For her parents, double exiles from Europe and South America, life in the States has been emotionally difficult. They have *not* embraced American culture or English, remaining devoted to the Spanish idiom of Chilean culture, although they have endured virulent anti-Semitism everywhere.

This memoir first returns to the European Holocaust of World War II, where many of Agosín's relatives died in concentration camps. The fortunate ones escaped to Chile. She writes of Helena Broder as one who

> knew how to give destiny the slip,
> how to predict the right moment to fly
> in 1939, dressed as if
> for an evening party . . . .

In the Introduction to *The Angel of Memory*, she recalls her own childhood as "Eight years of being an inquisitive young girl, daring to penetrate the forbidden questions, or the body of blazing memory." This internal landscape of family intimacies and secrets—of brushing Helena's hair, of eyeing the quiet room where she lived in Chile, resonates with the old world's past. "Your room was not like a Chilean's room, my mother used to say. The blankets, the water jars, the inkwell and the luminous candles were not from this America. You brought your Vienna and its lilacs with you. Without a doubt, you were a queen among us, with your magician's gaze and your wise sayings."

The poems in *Among the Angels of Memory* are divided into two sections, before and after Helena's passage to Chile, navigating the memoir from various vantages. Those before departure ("The Old World") concern the human side of the Holocaust, including deft portraits of Nazi functionaries rather than descriptions of Hitler's war. Agosín's tone of ironic understatement carries deep grief. The utter predictability of "Unpredictable Northern Train" clearly echoes her tone.

Like a darkened traveler,
the train conductor
confident, precise,
checks that all passengers,
including the shorn women,
those dressed like brides and death,
and the gasping elders,
board this train
that will deliver them
to the place from which
there is no return,
to the place of nameless horrors
to the most inexplicable secret
the secret we all know.

The train conductor
is well respected for his work,
deserves a medal
for his punctuality.
He knows that the fate of those trains:
stations of blue gas,
the home of that fog,
that silence beyond all silences,
where bodies burn like dead flowers.

The conductor "considers himself noble in this obedience," because "After all,/it is only Jews who travel/on these trains/and it is his duty,/his passionate vocation,/to make Jews disappear." Those who disappeared on trains reverberate in memory with those who were disappeared during Pinochet's reign.

Disappearance seems to be the paranoid pattern of all dictatorships. If there are no victims, then apparently there is no enemy. In all the post-World War II slaughters, most victims are *not* imprinted with a number, or not even counted, like our denials about "collateral damage." Most do not have first-hand knowledge of unspeakable atrocities, but the Agosín family does. "Cousins" addresses the aftermath of just such an event, about her first cousins gassed in Auschwitz.

On holy days
their seats were vacant
and my father, with his sacred cup,
invoked their names:
Julia, Sonia, Silvia.

Their names become a litany filled with scant remnants that were discarded by history—but not lost to memory.

I too came to love them,
was comforted to see
their handwriting
on frayed postcards
from Vienna, then
Prague, and later still
the cities with austere names.

Those "cities with austere names" began with the dreaded Auschwitz, "where there were no calendars,/where there is no memory,/where there is no voice,/where women keep silent,/are shorn." Agosín does not "know how to remember them" and feels that she does "not deserve life/without them." Halfway through, she gives way to the anguish of direct statement and breaks the skin of the poem.

Telling you this story
distresses me,
and I can only say it in a poem
as I am unable to tell it to anyone.
I don't want to hear things like:
"Again, the Jews and their memories."
"That happened years ago."
"I don't know anything about that."
That is how they talked when
the neighbor, the grandfather,
and his small grandchildren were abducted.

One wonders if anyone is listening? Why such calloused remarks blaming the victims of prejudice? Because the patterns are universal, and must be consciously overcome individually. Every group has been victimized at some time in history, and all nations have a history of blood on their hands. But that does not change Agosín's view of human rights. "One is born with human rights," she asserts in *An Absence of Shadows*, thus one is sacredly connected to all living things." She never rationalizes the Israeli or U.S. occupations, but stands in solidarity with Palestinian and Iraqi civilians, because "when human rights are violated, so is the sacredness of the world." No matter the locale or time frame—from *Dear Anne Frank*, to books about Latin American atrocities—she remembers and writes. In the first part of *Among the Angels of Memory*, she declares in "The Golem of Prague":

> Know that we live in memory,
> or in the metaphor of memory,
> or in a memory that allows neither oblivion
> nor promises,
> or in the imagination of a memory
> that plays with distance,
> a small somber bell sounding
> upon the kingdom of the dead.

In "Memory and Exile" Agosín writes that "The exile of our ancestors managed to stir my imagination to the rhythms of solitude and it was possible for me to build lives, alternating melodies and words. Exile became fundamental to a form of writing that had begun in a closely guarded fashion but which was filled with a powerful desire to create life." Her own exile as a teenager from Chile became inhabited by memory and expressed through the medium of her Spanish language. "Exile from a world to which I never had access became the essence of my writing. That is to say, it facilitated the possibility of invention, of doubt, of daydreaming. Literature and its aesthetic expression of language were the most powerful ways to recover what had been lost."

Agosín means a dynamic, evolving memory, not merely a static recounting of facts. "I invented the family I never had and those whose lives I assumed had ended in a forest of barbed wires, dead or feigning death. I made them come to life, gave them hair and voices." The last poem of this section ("Traces") begins—

> More than a memory,
> or the place where memory lives,
> like a texture,
> more than a presence,
> among the phantoms and flickering spirits,
> in the wandering heart of night,
> among the flames
> in that unsettled place,
> I found traces,
> only traces,
> cast-off, shipwrecked syllables,
> shattered alphabets.

From traces of those who lit a flame, she creates "lucid testaments of history," as one who "walks among the rubble/and listens to a lament,/a cadence,/traces,/a name,/a people who lament,/people who pray and are resplendent."

"The New World" contains intimate texts about Helena, including poems in her voice and from the poet's double viewpoints. Some are based on childlike experiences and others are mature reflections derived from Frida's stories. The opening transitional texts are the brief "1939" and "Chile, 1939," which closes with "the angels of memory /arrive at your feet." A suite of variations follows on the émigré's life in Chile, evoking Helena's thoughts and focusing on the tangible (photographs, maps, an address book). "I Thought You Were an Angel, Helena" observes "a strange/guest among/your own belongings," leading to a child's question and response.

> Who were you looking for, so light and small,
> in your white nightgown,
> with your tiny lantern?
>
> I thought you were an angel

and I played at discovering
each one of your messages,
messenger of intense life,
of the frail memory,
a gardener of nocturnal flowers.

Most question the unknown and "Helena Broder Contemplates
the Sky" suggests an answer. "It was an imaginary city,/the sky,/where
nested the names/of the dead and the living." "Helena's Maps" is a
startling reversal, identifying entirely with Helena's dislocation while
speaking of the poet's lost homeland.

Stunned, tied to the amazing
circling of my hand,
I look for my country.
The map lies
on a decrepit, distant table
in the lost dominions of exile.

I search for my rivers
disfigured and yellow
in this fragile geography of exile.
I cannot find my beloved Andes,
scattered and blue.

Stanzas later Agosín's bewilderment returns, ending the poem
with a symbol that identifies her as a schoolgirl in Santiago.

Stunned, I find myself
in a borrowed, fugitive geography
that does not belong to me.

I am searching with maddened faith
for what became of that house
with doors full of happiness
and I seek out my blue school uniform,
dead on some flimsy chair.

The rhetoric of exile, its "lost dominions," are upheld by real yet wounded objects—the map "on a decrepit, distant table" and the school uniform on "some flimsy chair." Even while exile implies vulnerability and diminution, living grief creates the persistence of memory. Only forgetfulness signifies ultimate loss. "Writing from exile must be a permanence, constantly articulating the present, the past, the memories, and lack of memories," Agosín clarifies in "Memory and Exile," "as a way of being and living in a world where the possibility of remembering and being a witness is not outside of history but a part of history."

"Conversations with God and Helena Broder" faces just such madness.

> I am a Jew
> wrestling with you; a Jew
> who does not understand
> why in my eyes burn
> the villages of Lithuania,
> the cells of Terezin,
> the piled up bodies
> of Rwanda.

Since Helena did *not* live long enough to know about Rwanda, the poet takes on her voice. God is silent, and "His presence/had no answers,/but questions." Agosín still believes in "the strongest proof/ of survival,/the miracle of being. . . ." Helena survived eight years in Chile, but in "The Ritual of Goodbye" the very young poet cannot attend the funeral. "You are going,/and the doves will not return to the balcony,/only the absence of your steps,/shall invoke your presence."

Yet that real "absence" remains a "presence" in memory that is transcribed in "The House of Memory":

> At dawn,
> the space of poetry comes
> in the clear hours.
> My hand feels this divine
> presence,

humble, fertile glory.
My fingers glide over the words,
as if each one of them
were a love story,
a fragrance among syllables.
I knit words,
luminous waves over the page,
calmly, I take dictation.
And you, on the other side of the words,
in the resonant clarity of light,
smile.

Poetry is the story of love,
eternal flame
to mitigate the solitude of those who
love each other in the dark.

From memory to poetry to translation, her bridges are for love but never hatred, crossing time, place, and language. Agosín "translates" Helena's Viennese spirit presence into Spanish. "I translate without oblivion,/only presences of a voice over another,/like a hand that resembles/a garden in the shadows/to be born translated in a different light." The poem evokes love and living in every image, "in this cluster of human/voices,/in the constellations of beings without borders."

In a *MultiCultural Review* interview, Agosín speaks of a covenant with Spanish and with those who have translated her work into English:

> I felt that without language I had no voice; I had no identity; I was nothing. It took many years until I learned—I don't want to say mastered but was able to communicate in—the English language, and became a person in English. Then I acquired a sense of self in a new language. That to me was very important for without translations we are speechless. But what I also learned about translation was that even though I became someone once I learned English, I did not want to lose my Spanish

self, which was really my Spanish language, because you are what you speak. But memory is also very complicated because it consists of what one chooses to remember. So perhaps a translator has to choose the right words, and that again makes translation an act of choices. The translation of poetry is the translation of the spirit. So a translator does not simply translate; the translator also becomes that voice. To become someone else you have to be in love with someone else. And in that sense I strongly believe that translations are acts of love. If it were not for that act of love of the translator, great literature would not exist in other languages. To write in Spanish is a gesture of survival, and because of translation my memory has now become a part of the memory of others.

Gathered together, such intimate sources provide textured remembrances of free associations, exquisite impressions, and startling images. These deeply personal poems take on narrative forms in most cases, as she is a faithful storyteller, exploring every branch of her luminous family tree in memoirs, essays, stories, and poems. Yet her narratives are more concerned with "the story of love" than with family chronicles, and they are imbued with a subtle sense of the "presence" of loved ones rather than with a catalogue of the dead. Agosín is essentially a lyric poet. Even when she reclaims family history or critiques human rights abuses, the poems are acts of love.

Raised in Santiago, Agosín continues to remember and to write in Spanish, even though she speaks excellent English and teaches at Wellesley College. However, she teaches what she lives—the literature and human rights struggle, a cultural lineage of which her work has become an organic part. She has been recognized by the United Nations and Jewish organizations for her activism. She has written tirelessly about the victims of 20th century violence, always with emphasis on women and children, including her editions of significant anthologies of writing by women.

Marjorie Agosín's intuitive vision of poetic transformation discovers value in truths instead of mere facts, creating an ecstatic expression for a spiritual life.

Writing in Mexico

I

Despite the deplorable consequences of NAFTA and globalism, we might expect one shift to be a new wave of translations from diverse cultural voices. This is *not* the case, since the publishing establishment fixates on entertainment and its bottom line. Fortunately literary independents and university presses are translating some of those voices, including the significant Trinity University Press series ("The Writers World"), which includes *Mexican Writers on Writing* (2007), edited by Margaret Sayers Peden, who also translates several texts in this anthology.

The collection covers the Spanish invasion of Mexico and represents such early writers as Sor Juana Inéz de la Cruz and others. This essential history gives context to our understanding of the modern era, first represented by Octavio Paz (1914-1998), Mexico's greatest poet and first Nobel Prize Laureate, in 1990. His 1971 essay ("Translation: The Literary and the Literal") provides profound reflections. "The universality of the spirit was the answer to the confusion of Babel: there are many languages, but meaning is one," asserting that we also encounter the irony that "The sun in an Aztec poem is different from the sun in an Egyptian hymn—no matter that they speak of the same star." Paz offers a detailed, clarifying discourse on the translation of art, which has been our most difficult cultural dialogue.

Mexico's first feminist, Rosario Castellanos (1925-1974), reflects on her creative process, and Emilio Carballido (b. 1925), an influential playwright and theater director, illuminates dramatic compositions. Both bring wit and charm to their fresh insights of genuine humility.

Carlos Fuentes (1928-2012), Mexico's greatest novelist, contributes "Decalogue for a Young Writer"—ten trenchant commandments for any writer or serious reader. Among many brilliant lessons, he touches on our moment with these remarks. "The twentieth century left us with a stricken, deeply wounded sense of progress. Today we are aware that scientific and technical achievements do not assure the absence of moral and political barbarism." Yet he sees that "the artistic response to the political and economic crisis of the modern has been a practically unlimited freedom of style. But on one condition: that freedom never forget what it owes to tradition, and that tradition never forget what it owes to creation."

Elena Poniatowska (b. 1932), author of classic "testimonial literature" and works in other genres, begins her essay with "I write to belong." Later she points out that "I live to the rhythm of my country and I cannot remain on the sidelines. I want to be here. I want to be part of it. I want to be a witness. Testimonial literature provides evidence of events that some would like to hide, denounces and therefore is political and part of a country in which everything remains to be done and documented." No one is more engaged than Poniatowska with the struggles of the poor.

José Emilio Pacheco (b. 1939), perhaps Mexico's reigning poet after the deaths of Paz and Jaime Sabines (1926-1998), reveals his defiantly humble poetics, insisting that "We are all poets of transition:/poetry never stands still."

The next generation of critics proves his point, heeding Fuentes' advice. Alberto Ruy Sanchez, Angeles Mastretta, Carmen Bullosa, and Juan Villoro honor literary traditions while breaking new ground. Their essays (in English for the first time) turn on marvelous personal anecdotes at the root of imaginative storytelling. The youngest contributors are equally daring. The 2000 "Crack Manifesto" features five novelists—Pedro Angel Palou, Eloy Urroz, Ignacio Padilla, Jorge Volpi, and Ricardo Chávez Castañeda—discussing this movement and their approaches. The final essay by Volpi, on the art of the novel, stands out as this group's most compelling.

Margaret Sayers Peden, who has won major awards for translations of more than 50 books by Spanish-language masters, has edited this brilliant book to relish and ponder the neglected literature of Mexico. During the 20th century Mexican poetry was treated as the stepchild of literature in the hemisphere. There are several reasons why, but foremost it was the provincial insularity of American culture that resisted most "foreign" poetry until the 1960s. Second, famous Latin American poets—Neruda, Vallejo, Borges, and Parra—flew into our view while Mexican poets, except for Paz, were checked at the border. Then their crossing was overwhelmed by the Chicano Movement and the emergence of Latino-Latina writing. In this millennium Mexico's contemporary voices have an opportunity to be heard.

II

The River Is Wide: *Twenty Mexican Poets*, a bilingual anthology, translated and edited by Marlon L. Fick (University of New Mexico Press, 2005) should stand for decades as the most significant collection of Mexican poetry. Indispensable to this refreshing literary event are 20 talented poets and one intrepid editor.

It was Fick who opened a passageway to discovering a nearly unknown country of poetry. "After an invitation to read my poems at Palacio de Bellas Artes, I fell in love with Mexico, found a job, got married, and stayed." In 1997 he began a four-year search for Mexico's bards and, as he found many in the capital, went to work with their enthusiastic support. Fick has delivered over 100 original poems in Spanish printed on facing pages with accurate, lyrical translations.

Except for Jaime Sabines (1926-1998), Mexico's favorite poet who encouraged this project, all are still writing, including the oldest and best known, Ali Chumacero, born in 1918. Considered among 20th century literary masters in Mexico—along with Sabines, Paz, Rulfo, and Fuentes—Chumacero's work has been in 20 languages but *not* recently in English (since the 1950s versions by William Carlos Williams). His religious critique ("The Wanderer's Response") casts a brooding eye, and a slightly baroque vision upon the "zither of the soul."

Both Rubén Bonifaz Nuño (b. 1923) and Tómas Segovia (b. 1927), authors of acclaimed books, display modern sensibilities—especially Nuño, who states in the untitled text that "I shouldn't talk/ in symbols; but speak plainly/about real things of the spirit." Recipient of the Octavio Paz Prize and winner of the Juan Rulfo Prize, Segovia told the press, "If you see me as a winner, you don't get me. I'm not a winner. You've given an award to a loser." He is also brutally frank in a cascading "Alone," which begins "Now I spread myself open, alone like a miser in his hovel," ending with "I'm the only one thinking of her/because I speak to no one, because I am alone,/I am nothingness, I am alone."

Poets born between 1938-1947 are represented by long poems. Óscar Oliva's cinematic "At the Wheel of a Car" drives wildly over personal history, ending by "braking sharply/so I don't run over everything I've come to write about,/including myself." In "Lost City," Elva Macias envisions Mexico's bloody history in which "All these kingdoms have an end:/their eagerness to conquer eternity/in the minds of men." Elsa Cross' "Poem Under the Willow" finds lyric intensity in nature rather than in cities. "Thoughts come like locusts/to devour your peace./They flower, leading to chaos,/like the wind committing a crime in the leaves." Gloria Gervitz's discrete utterances (in the voice of "Pythia") evoke the mystery of identity—"touch me/in this darkness of the thought. . ./in my incomprehensible otherness."

The most brilliant section features poet Francisco Hernández. His masterful narrative, "How Robert Schumann was Defeated by Demons" (1988), transcribes musical poetry about the Romantic composer's descent into madness. His shorter poems are also boldly original. The entire text of "Until the Verse Remains" reads: "Strip away all the flesh/until the verse remains/in the sonorous dark of the bone./And the bone is smoothed, polished and sharpened/till it becomes a needle so fine/it passes through the tongue without pain,/ though blood stops up the throat."

The generation born during the 1950s contributes varied styles to this rich diversity. Héctor Carreto's witty anti-poems are deliciously irreverent, and Juan Cú's hilarious "Additions to the Book of Whores" created a scandal in Mexico. Both had the last laugh. National Prizewinners Coral Bracho and Myriam Moscona celebrate female sensuality in subtle lyrics that are lovely and fresh. Vernóica Volkow's poems focus on "subjects" as a discipline of attention, from which she makes memorable artifacts. Lillian Van Den Broeck's brief takes from "The State of Anonymity" are clever variations, ranging from jokes to wise aphorisms.

Sweeping lines in "Flocks" by Jorge Esquinca turn birds into "young Sibyls/hotly debate between passion for the airy prophesy/and the terrestrial night/of the friendly tree." Jorge Ruiz Esparza's existentialist dramas gather energy by exploring sexuality, identity, and fear. Arranged alphabetically, these poets appear before the three youngest poets placed at the back: Francisco Ávila Fuentes and Hernán Bravo

Varela, both born in 1979, and Bernardo Emilio Pérez (b. 1980).

Finally there is the late Jaime Sabines, who died a few months after approving Fick's translations, and to whom the book is dedicated. If Sabines stands below Paz in international recognition, he has no rival in the hearts of Mexican readers.

III

A very welcome addition to the contemporary wing of the pantheon of Mexican writers is Jazmina Barrera Velázquez, yet in her twenties.

Foreign Body, a collection of insightful meditations, won the 2013 Literal Essay Award. Throughout these brilliant, concentrated essays, she creates a dialogue with familiar artistic voices, adeptly characterizing their various views in relation to her fresh perceptions. Barrera's first book strikes pointedly with spare, intense prose, exploring the text of her "foreign" body.

"Migraine" masterfully blends sly wit with a bold idea. "Migraine is an illness of the ego," she proclaims. "Some other illnesses tend to be of the superego, like the cold that you give yourself from not wearing a sweater, or the stomach infection that you caught from eating beef tacos." She locates the Freudian ego in the brain. "There we think, we perceive: we are. A pain in the foot is a pain that comes to one from a distance," as if that extremity were a stranger.

In a perfect characterization of ego, she knows that "When the head hurts you hurt, and when you hurt, the world hurts." Barrera then turns over similes to evoke the pain, developing "my migraine as a kind of pet. As if I had adopted a tarantula that would nest in my head." They hate each other, "but we spend so much time together that it is inevitable that we feel a certain affection," contemplating "the other as a permanent threat and at the same time as a type of familiar company." The migraine and the ego are one. The eventual diagnosis: Not a migraine but merely stress and tension. "How evocative was for me the name of that non-being, now unnameable, like one of Lovecraft's monsters."

"Back (Moles)" postulates the reverse terrain of the back, for "Without our backs we are like broken puppets." With a photograph

Barrera observes it as "surely the flattest part of my body . . . I would have to describe on its surface various elevations, a kind of valley, some mishaps, and at least eight moles." Then flows a lovely evocation of moles [*lunares* in Spanish]: "since it is believed that those spots appeared through the influence of the moon." She has "an enormous scar from the removal of my largest mole. I have always felt that procedure was a betrayal of my body."

With precision and charm Barrera's essays examine the body's tics and tears; encounter tiredness and cold, her laughter at being lost, shape-shifting shadows, and the subtle dynamics of memory.

Each literary adventure is discrete, except for "Death (In Life)," which is painfully funny and acidly sardonic. "The problem with being dead in life is that your bed becomes your coffin . . . is that the diagnosis always comes too late . . . the problem with being dead in life is that the flies know it."

Barrera's "Shadow" is "This 'other' that resembles us, but is faceless, that is like us, but has the capacity to widen, to become thin, or to grow depending on the light . . . The shadow personifies an immaterial presence." Some believe "that when someone dies he can leave his shadow, that is, his spirit, in the place where he died." Barrera concludes with the sense "that fantastic stories have made the shadow into a character who is not necessarily evil for being mysterious and eccentric."

Dave Oliphant, who brought the poetry of Nicanor Parra and Enique Lihn into English, lucidly translates the essays in a bilingual edition that includes Barrera's text in Spanish. Rose Mary Salum publishes *Literal* magazine and books by contemporary Latin American voices.

Barrera studied English literature at UNAM in Mexico City, and was awarded a grant from the Foundation for Mexican Letters. In *Foreign Body*, Jazmina Barrera Velázquez has composed the brightest essays since Octavio Paz's illuminating prose works.

Tangible Remains

During the 1970s and 80s Italian poetry was well represented in translations by North American poets—W.S. Di Piero, Brian Swann, and Ruth Feldman from Princeton University Press, and by Alfredo De Palchi and Sonia Raiziss from Chelsea Editions. Due to economic constraints that heyday has passed, but two contemporary Italian poets have been published by independent imprints.

Barbara Carle's *Tangible Remains* (Ghenomena Editions, 2009) collects 50 texts inspired by common objects that are identified only on the contents page at the back. Her explicit goal is to make readers "avoid reducing the poem to its title," which works if we enter into her playful gambit. This speculative dimension would be a trivial gesture if her poetry were not so evocative and imaginative.

Number 3, perhaps among those difficult to guess, is as lithe and deft as most of these remarkable texts.

> Fitted hollow
> accommodates
> bodies for
> intimate
> epiphany.
>
> Nests with
> sheer curves.
> Imperturbably
> absorbs weight
> creates lightness.
> Frees dreams
> with pleasure.

The Italian translation by Antonella Anedda and the author is even more sensual in alluding to this *vasca de bagno* (a bathtub).

Perhaps Number 22 is easier to identify.

Holds water
without clouds.
Rolls sleekly
over the tongue.
Passes what it keeps
        between lips
yet remains complete.
Inclines to be tipped.
Stands
without a hand.

You are right, if you guessed a glass. In a few texts Carle tells us too much, but usually we must grapple with these charming mysteries. Number 32 begins:

Plane of expectancy.
Cleanly cut
clearly indispensable.

This object "Rustles, tears, crumples, folds. . ." Also it "Assumes all shapes/yet retains a blankness/that eclipses the limits of possibility." Expectancy that eclipses our limits—what is it? Your eyes are looking upon it: a piece of paper.

The final poem (Number 50) consists of only fifteen words.

Frames light.
Filters death.
Closes.
Slams.
Opens.
Damns.
Silences.

Perhaps it suggests a door or a gate, until we read the simple and brilliant closure: "That draws you out of your mind." It turns out to be a window through which Barbara Carle's meditations draw us beyond conventional mindsets toward actually contemplating objects generally taken for granted. *Tangible Remains* highlights lucid perspectives rather than mere descriptions, and Barbara Carle has created a poetic vision of the overlooked things of our world.

Franco Buffoni has been among Italy's most celebrated poets since the 1990s, a professor of comparative literature in Rome who also edits a highly respected journal of literary criticism. *Wings: Selected Poems 2000-2005* (Chelsea Editions, 2008) is a sophisticated bilingual edition that includes three startling sequences—two fleeting tableaus of boyhood from *The Profile of Mount Rosa* and *Theios*, and the graphic strophes of torture from *Guerra*.

Buffoni's impressions under Mount Rosa's shadow recall a sensitive, studious boy, tracing snowmelt in town and valley, observed through evolving perspectives. At age eleven, he decides that "there is no reason to get carried away/in games played with cousins,/to follow them in their hurling of bricks at/the neighbor's dahlias," merely to "truly feel part of the gang." Instead, he instructs himself to "go calmly back to your drawings,/to your homework maps to complete/you will win." However he adds the warning: "You will have to suffer."

In *Theios*, stressful male sexuality turns language from lyric innocence into harsh experience, and "Time, fictitious spaceship/moves us indelicately" along that path. Impressionist becomes expressionist, realizing boys are being "bent pounded/gnawed smoked militarized," because they "must be inhabited." Resisting violence in himself alerts us to the ingrained cultural violence in which we are all soaked.

Guerra faces the "Ghost in the blood and bones of history/ that will pursue me from my infancy," and he spies them "in lodges academies coffee houses/where decorations of gods, goddesses and seasons/personifications of virtues/victories cities states confessions insist/from the stucco, if I describe you it is to consign you/to the silence of my memory."

This limpid poetry of memory thrives in postmodern fragments, but always superbly rendered by poet Emamuel di Pasquale, an award-winning translator. We perceive a larger design viewed from above, emerging in precise, intricate details. It is never a matter of understanding these clear passages in English, but only of connecting one to the next, first to last.

Silky Lyric Threads

Meena Alexander's view registers as emotionally challenging. The opening of *Raw Silk* (TriQuarterly Books, 2004) encircles the experience of 9/11—when the twin towers collapsed and our world flattened. We do *not* hear the prattle of newscasters or the pontifications of politicians. Manhattan island, permanent home to this celebrated exile from India, receives a loving gift of exquisite compassion through echoes of Kabir and Indian ancestors, through dialogues with García-Lorca's "Poet in New York," in composer Oliver Messiaen's *Quartet for the End of Time*, and also by way of her sensual, delicate phrasings on the empathetic edge of grief.

From "Late, There Was an Island" begins, "There is an uncommon light in the sky./Pale petals are scorned into stone.//I want to write of the linden tree/That stoops at the edge of the river//But its leaves are filled with insects/With wings the color of dry blood.//At the far side of the river Hudson/By the southern tip of our island//A mountain soars, a torrent of sentences/Syllables of flame stitch the rubble//An eye, a lip, a cut hand blooms/Sweet and bitter smoke stains the sky."

"Rumors for an Immigrant" moves beyond borders to "There is no homeland anymore,/all nations are abolished, a young man cries." "Petroglyph" expands to "The earth our green and fragrant home," but refracts into "our green imperiled home." Her poems leap through a consciousness that connects us to a global lyric of suffering that we rarely hear. "Blue Lotus" discovers its root in India. "When I dream of my tribe gathering/by the red soil of the Pamba River//I feel my writing hand split at the wrist./Dark tribute or punishment, who can tell?/You kiss the stump and where the wrist//bone was, you set the stalk of a lotus." Later she reveals "the sign of the four-cornered world, *gammadion*, which stands for migration, for the scattering of a people," and begins "learning the language again,//a new speech for a new tribe."

Meena Alexander's poetic process follows a silk thread throughout. Follow the thread from "scraps of torn silk" ("Ancestors") through

"Raw Silk" and "the body, old sari/washed with blue soap" in "Porta Santa," to the final closure of "Triptych in a Time of War" (uttered in the voice of the first poet to write in the first-person, the ancient priestess Enheduanna): "You hear her words unfurl on the screen,/ bare sound, filled with longing,/syllables of raw silk, this poem."

Sofia M. Starnes was born in Manila and educated in Madrid. She entered the States in 1986 to become a citizen in 1989. *Fully Into Ashes* (Wings, 2011) stands as a true book of poetry and not a mere collection. Her lyrics are hushed ceremonies of spiritual awakening, opening slowly as wisdom. "The soul sweet-talks/its way into the throng/of lung, rib cage, hip. The lips/are doorsill, in and out;/I do not know which-way./What kills a rose?" But this climactic instant of beauty is not a death since the rose bush lives on and the classic image resonates in memory.

"Distances" ends with a "wasted whiff" that "strikes/heart, a little beyond." As in her third book, *Corpus Homini: A Poem for Single Flesh*, winner of the Wings chapbook contest in 2008, this book maps an open landscape "where both the spiritual and the physical are intimately wed." These poems evoke the holy spirits in nature toward "the divine elevation of all that is real." Never sanctimonious, their humble saints inhabit a poetic garden, flowering with a second innocence.

Listen to "The House That Spoke": "Here is a task to undertake—/let's build a house out of a sigh,/to be, through memory, a language: brick-work,/brick-word, rumors from swung rattan,//spelling out our tales./And the sigh will be the rust stain on the wall,/a pipe's great story which we failed to hear/in summer patches."

Romantic perhaps, but not sentimental. Starnes' original images create a fresh awareness of human experience "because I consider belief to be experience."

The book's three intricately-integrated sections "fell into three clear stages," she explains, "ah, once more that intriguing and illuminating trinity." These are apt words to characterize her poetry— intriguing, illuminating (and insightful, to make a trinity).

Her Artist's Statement reads: "There is 'Find'; that is, the initial awareness of whatever life proffers. Then, there is 'Ache,' our growing experience of loss and longing that define us. And ultimately, there is 'Gift,' when what becomes clear to us is that we are most often on the receiving end, having paid no price to equal its worth, of all that is Good." Through continuous stages of discovery and suffering, we feel the sweet, bountiful sense of wise mercy.

Other poems roam up to 50 lines, yet *never* wander aimlessly. Her graceful rhythms recall Emily Dickinson. Their music echoes classical Spanish guitar solos and the shapes reflect paintings (Goya, Donatello, Boucher). Yet comparative speculations are relatively meaningless in light of her meaningful words.

Two elegies for her parents recall their earthly things. "The Scarf" ends when her "father tucks/a white luminous robe around himself—/not crowned, not wept—/a small verb: merely dozing." "The Armoire"—"dense as a thicket"—reveals "its overlap of living/ things on things thought lifeless." An earlier poem of a girl now grown with "a liturgy of ghosts," ends with "Loss is an old but ample word for ghost;/prize is the better word for angel." Such lovely strophes thematically connect her vision. "Look!" exclaim the last lines of "The Monument Restorer": "Full are the man and the field,/full are we under the sun."

The praise of Starnes finds balance in a droll wit. "I thought I'd break the secret to you now," begins a later poem, "that in our yard a saint has set aside//his rucksack and a ruby glass of wine." Halfway, she pauses but carries on. "You don't believe me (in sanity,/who would) but there's a lily martyr/at the door. . ."

Her "Saints in the Garden" ends with "I'll try again: they peep in, push and wedge, widen/my glance—as masquerades, a feast; or thoughts,/a life. Or awe, that silver negative that yields//the changeless sky, the changing gist of trees."

Sofia M. Starnes is one of those poets rescued by independent press editors, who are attuned to unique discoveries that commercial presses never know.

Reading Rumi
and Other Ecstatic Poets

"Nafas" means "breath" in many Middle-Eastern languages, and has been used by poets as a metaphor for wind and spirit. This word's genius aptly characterizes *Reading Rumi in an Uncertain World* (Wings, 2005), as performed by American poets Robert Bly and Naomi Shihab Nye.

These two voices embody the breath of poetry on winds of translation. We hear ecstatic poems by Rumi, Hafez, and Kabir in versions by Bly; renderings of Sufis Bahauddin Valad and his son Rumi from the books translated by Coleman Barks and John Moyne; and Nye reading contemporary poems of the Middle East.

They also read their own recent poems in harmony with two subtle musicians who had never performed together (Bly's regular accompanist David Whetstone playing sitar and Oliver Rajamani improvising fluently on the oud and percussion instruments), transforming the poetic duo into a resonant quartet. What may sound like a highbrow recital was as natural as inviting friends over for a visit. The performers arrived without pomp, proceeding to entertain and to enlighten 500 enthusiasts with sublime poetry and music.

Perhaps the most-read poet in the world today, Rumi (1207-1273), was unknown in the West except to scholars until mid-20th century, although he never fell into obscurity in the Persian-speaking world. Rumi's best translator, poet Coleman Barks, writes that he "had never even heard Rumi's name until 1976, when Robert Bly handed me a copy of A.J. Arberry's translations, saying, 'These poems need to be released from their cages.'" Barks says that he "felt drawn immediately to the spaciousness and longing in Rumi's poetry," and he worked closely with John Moyne and other scholars on his translations for *The Essential Rumi* and *The Soul of Rumi*. Their translation of the prose meditations of Rumi's father, Bahuddin Valad, also appeared in *The Drowned Book*. Most of the selections in Part II of this DVD are from these three remarkable books.

In a preface to Rumi's poems in *The Winged Energy of Delight*, Bly suggests the reasons for Rumi's appeal to American readers. "Rumi is astounding, fertile, abundant, almost more an excitable library of poetry than a person. In his poems, Rumi often adopts the transparent 'you,' using it so beautifully that each of us feels as if we too were being spoken to. Coleman Barks has echoed that tender 'you' so brilliantly in his translations that we will never get over our gratitude. When I started reading Rumi, all at once I felt at home. I think many readers of his work have that feeling. It's almost as if his poems resonate in some echo chamber that we retain in memory."

We experience this feeling with the audience in Part I, which opens with Nye reading six contemporary poets of the Middle East, including poems composed in English by Alise Alousi of Iraq and Hanan Mikha'il 'Asrawi of Palestine.

In between we hear Palestinian exile Mahmoud Darwish's fanciful dialogue of a prisoner with a guard, who cannot fathom the impossible changes taking place in "The Prison Cell" (as translated by Ben Bennani).

> —Where did this moon come from?
> —From the nights of Baghdad.
> —And the wine?
> —From the vineyards of Algiers.
> —And this freedom?
> —From the chain you tied me with last night.

Bly's set includes Kabir, one of the first poets he translated. We hear hearty laughter, as he quips that "Kabir was an Indian saint with a great big foot," alluding to his "razor-sharp intellect, an outrageous boldness in speech, inspired scolding of the fuzzy-minded. . . ." The poem that follows is a delicate fortress, a magnificent warning from Kabir's ecstatic vision, anointed by sublime wit.

Think While You Are Alive

The idea that you will join with the ecstatic
just because the body is rotten—that is all fantasy.

What is found now is found then.
If you find nothing now,
you will simply end up with an apartment in the City of Death.
If you make love with the divine now, in the next life
you will have the face of satisfied desire.
So plunge into the truth, find out who the Teacher is,
believe in the Great Sound.
Kabir says this: When the Guest is being searched for, it is the
intensity of the longing for the Guest that does all the work.
Look at me, and you will see a slave to that intensity.

The poets then turn to their own poems to complete the first half of the program. Naomi Shihab Nye reads from *19 Varieties of Gazelle: Poems of the Middle East*, a National Book Award nominee, and her recent book, *You and Yours*. Daughter of Palestinian journalist Aziz Shihab, she has witnessed the tragedies of war, editing several anthologies of poetry from the Middle East.

Her strongest poems are about children victimized by war, but the first stanza of "Red Brocade" reveals a very different tone.

The Arabs used to say,
When a stranger appears at your door,
feed him for three days
before asking who he is,
where he's come from,
where he's headed.
That way, he'll have strength
enough to answer.
Or, by then you'll be
such good friends
you don't care.

Part II opens with brief poems by Rumi (translated by Barks and Moyne), then Nye alternates passages by Bahauddin Valad. The English translation of "Forgiveness and Impulse" reads "To know whether a particular sin has been forgiven, look within to see if you still feel the urge to do it. If you do, it hasn't. Keep praying for the impulse to be removed."

This gets a laugh, so Bly counters with Rumi's "Chickpea to Cook."

> A chickpea leaps almost over the rim of the pot
> where it's being boiled.
> "Why are you doing this to me?"
> The cook knocks him down with the ladle.
> "Don't you try to jump out.
> You think I'm torturing you.
> I'm giving you flavor,
> so you can mix with spices and rice
> and be the lovely vitality of a human being.
> Remember when you drank rain in the garden.
> That was for this."

Then Bly reads another Rumi teaching poem ("On Resurrection Day").

> On Resurrection Day your body testifies against you.
> Your hand says, "I stole money."
> Your lips, "I said meanness."
> Your feet, "I went where I shouldn't."
> Your genitals, "Me too."

The stanza draws laughter, so Bly reads it again—gleefully. Throughout the evening he repeats lines and stanzas, calling upon Nye to do the same, which she never does (unless he requests it.) But these repetitions are actually useful when a poem washes over us too quickly on first hearing. Barks' version of "On Resurrection Day" ends with a stark tonal shift.

> They will make your praying sound hypocritical.
> Let the body's doings speak openly now,
> without your saying a word,
> as a student's walking behind a teacher
> says, "This one knows more clearly
> than I the way."

When Bly reads the ultimate Rumi teaching poem—"Love Dogs" in the Barks translation (no pun intended)—we hear an echo of Kabir in the last line.

> One night a man was crying, "Allah! Allah!"
> His lips grew sweet with the praising,
> until a cynic said, "So! I have heard you
> calling out, but have you ever gotten any response?"
> The man had no answer to that.
> He quit praying and fell into a confused sleep.
> He dreamed he saw Khidr, the guide of souls,
> in a thick, green foliage.
> "Why did you stop praising?"
> "Because I never heard anything back."
> "This longing you express is the return message."

Near the end of "Love Dogs," Bly entreats David Whetstone's sitar to whine like a dog—and it does—as he reads the final message of Rumi's lesson. "Listen to the moan of a dog for its master/ That whining *is* the connection./Give your life/to be one of them." Different centuries, cultures, and gods—yet the same ecstatic vision.

Also the same uncertain world, but when has it *not* been uncertain? Born in what we now call Afghanistan, on the eastern edge of the Persian Empire, uncertainty was the only certainty in Jelaluddin Rumi's life. His family was forced into exile by the Mongol armies of Genghis Khan.

Yet one thing must be certain—the ecstatic poetry of the spirit is what we hear throughout the performances.

Internal Refugees

Two world poets—Mahmoud Darwish (1941-2008) and Samih al-Qasim (1939-2014)—had comparatively few books in English, although their Arabic poetry has been translated into many languages. Both books are bilingual, but if one does not read Arabic, one can marvel at the sight of the original texts.

Darwish's *Why Did You Leave the Horse Alone?* (Archipelago Books, 2006, translated by Jeffrey Sacks) and Al-Quasim's *Sadder Than Water: New and Selected Poems* (1958-2003), his first book in English, from Ibis Editions, 2006, translated by Nazih Kassis)—offer a rare chance to read this extraordinary poetry.

From Adina Hoffman's insightful introduction to *Sadder Than Water*, we learn that Al-Qasim and Darwish were close friends since the late 1950s, when they read early political poems at festivals to thousands, "making them famous throughout the Palestine community and eventually the entire Arab world."

Both reflect the complex, personal grief felt under Israeli occupation, witnessing the destruction of their traditional culture. Darwish departed with his family as a child, returning after 26 years in exile. Al-Qasim never left. Both had books censored and were imprisoned for espousing "radical political views" (like demanding free speech and individual rights!).

Of exile, Darwish sardonically writes that it "establishes for us two languages:/a spoken one . . . so the pigeons will grasp it and preserve the memory,/and a classical one . . . so I can explain to the shadows their shadows!"

Darwish explores powerlessness in "Ishmael's *Oud*," evoking his native village razed by Israel, which then appropriated the land.

> He carries his time disguised
> in the clothes of a singing madman. The war had ended
> and the ashes of our village disappeared
> in a black cloud on which
> the phoenix had not yet been born, as

we expected. The night's blood had not dried on
the shirts of our dead.

Darwish resigned from the executive committee of the Palestine
Liberation Organization (PLO) in 1993, rejecting the Oslo accords
because Israel had not been forced to withdraw from the occupied
territories. He lived as a Palestinian citizen of Israel—or as he termed
it, an "internal refugee." Yet whenever his books were published he was
incarcerated or remained under house arrest.

Darwish explained how he was doubly imprisoned by being
considered a "poet of resistance," feeling caged by being "again the
prisoner of a political reading." He emphasized "this obsession to
always want to serve the cause by the way of poetry, which is useless.
It serves neither poetry nor the cause." Darwish's later work "had
become introspective and mythical, and was stirred by a metaphysical
hunger," writes John Palattella in *The Nation*. "He had tried repeat-
edly to demolish the myth of his poetry's political relevance 'because
to inhabit the myth is like living in a prison, denied of any sudden
flowering, of any intellectual enrichment.'"

Samih al-Qasim was born in Jordan to a Druze family from
Galilee. He grew up in Palestine. He was an integral part of the resistance literature movement against Israeli oppression and was one of
the first members of the Druze community to refuse to serve in the
Israeli military.

He was arrested and imprisoned several times by Israeli security
forces for political activism. He was jailed on the first day of the Six-
Day War. "In prison I discovered—when the Israelis were declaring,
'Jerusalem is in our hands'—that I had to make one of two choices,
either to find a cave in the mountains, isolated from mankind, or to
find a higher stage in the struggle. I lost my belief in nationalistic big
words."

He uses no "big words" in one of the powerful, ironic poems in
this collection ("End of a Talk with a Jailer").

From the narrow window of my small cell,
I see trees that are smiling at me
and rooftops crowded with my family.

And windows weeping and praying for me.
From the narrow window of my small cell—
I can see your big cell!

The title poem from a 2003 collection runs 62 pages—an inventive incantatory sequence on time, death, legends, memory, language, and being steadfast (or *samid*, say the Palestinians, who have remained). "The ancient singers are yours," intones this long spiritual mediation, and "The deserts./The secret of conquests—they're for your name." A few blazing desert strophes of "Sadder Than Water" read:

Sadder than water,
in death's wonder
you've distanced yourself from this land.
Sadder than water
and stronger by far than wind,
longing for a moment to drowse,
alone. And crowded by millions
behind their darkened windows.

*

And you stand in the doorway of the will,
your voice trickling, your silence bleeding,
extracting the bullets from the family portraits,
following the missiles' path
into the heart of your household things
counting the holes from bombs' shrapnel
within the body of the sleeping girl—
kissing the wax of her soft fingers
at the edge of the bier.
How can you mold the elegies' madness?

*

All paths lead home. And home leads to prison.
And prison leads to the grave.
But the gypsy at the door is blind;
what harm could she do with her eye?
The door remained as it was, before she knocked—
a veil concealing the heavens from the earth.

No. Don't believe what the stories say, or the legends.
You were born of sadness, in sadness, for sadness.
You were born to remain in the land,
but to remain in it slain
and sad—sadder than sadness,
sadder than water,
sadder than sand.

This could represent the story of any war-torn region, any defeated people and, while al-Qasim tends toward elementary imagery, he means Palestine, which has always been under occupation and never declared as a nation. It remains merely a "territory" of shrinking proportions on the Israeli map.

Darwish also inhabits the mythic realm in *Why Did You Leave the Horse Alone?* with these lines: "I don't know the desert/But I planted words at its edges . . ./The words said what they said, and I left/like a divorced woman, like her broken husband . . .//But the mirage presses me eastward/to the ancient Bedouin/I lead the beautiful horse to water/I feel the pulse of the alphabet in the echo// In the desert absence said to me: Write!//So I wrote: Whoever writes his story will inherit/the land of words, and possess meaning, entirely!/I don't know the desert/but I bid it farewell: Peace/to the tribe east of my song: Peace to the descendants, in their plurality, upon the sword: Peace//And it is not exile/for the sea and the desert to be/the song of the traveler to the traveler: I won't return as I went,/I won't return . . . even secretly!" ("One Traveler Said to Another: We Won't Return As . . .").

Darwish peeks at his poetics in "Poetic Arrangements":

The poem is what lies between a between.
It is able to illuminate the night
with the breasts of a young woman.
It is able to illuminate, with an apple,
two bodies. It is able to restore,
with the cry of a gardenia,
a homeland!

The poem is in my hands. It is able
to arrange the affairs of myths
with the work of hands. But
when I found the poem,
dispossessed my Self
and I asked it: Who am I?
Who am I?

Identity was learned by drawing upon Arabic myths that the poets heard in childhood. Then, by abstracting daily lamentations impossible to avoid hearing, they created challenging encounters with grief and ecstasy. These sparkling glimpses into a little-known reality portrayed in the western media have been illuminated by these masterful (and as yet) controversial voices. As with the strongest contemporary poetry in English, these fine translations have been published by progressive imprints, believing that poetry must be translated and read, even if it does not sell.

Alas, metaphorical prisons remain just as real as imaginary borders, but readers will perceive in the poetry of Mahmoud Darwish and Samih al-Qasim a vision for our starving blind spots.

Exile's Return

As Edward Said frequently observed, part of being Palestinian
is being denied the right to narrate one's own experience.
—Raja Shedadeh

The exile of Aziz Shihab (1927-2007) validates Edward Said's observation, and *Does the Land Remember Me?* (Syracuse University Press, 2007) recovers a crucial right of humane, truthful expression. (This compelling memoir by the Palestinian journalist and diplomat was reissued by Syracuse as a 2011 paperback).

Aziz Shihab often went to Palestine (as a member of the International Board of Governors of Physicians for Peace), but in 1993 he traveled there to be with his dying mother. There were secondary considerations—making a decision about a plot of land he owned, while feeling a surge of hope after the recent Oslo Accords, which turned out to be disastrous for Palestinians.

Reflecting on a difficult landscape during a time of violent change, Shihab's discourse remains critical of the inhumane humiliation of Israel's occupation, yet not without being self-critical about the complexities of his exiled identity.

Born in the Palestinian quarter of Jerusalem in 1927, Shihab emigrated in 1950, becoming a U.S. citizen in 1956. He had to choose between living under a regime that confiscated his family's home, or making it as an outsider in an adopted country. Early on, when he candidly said that Jerusalem was his birthplace, most Americans assumed he was Jewish rather than Arabic. "I was plagued with that explanation for years, and I always thought it was because of the general American ignorance about the Middle East. I could never even acknowledge the existence of the Jewish state," he confesses, "that took by force my home and other Palestinian homes and properties, with the financial and military help of the United States."

But he silenced anger, keeping a separate peace. Shihab took a job at the *St. Louis Globe-Democrat* that lasted only a few months, when they realized he was Palestinian. All the while he harbored an attitude that would *not* have been tolerated during those years. "My dilemma was to live quietly and obediently in a country that helped make me into a refugee and which I chose to make my home, pretending it is the greatest home for justice in the world." His only serious option was to "go back to Palestine and live miserably under Israeli occupation and possibly die fighting injustice."

In the third chapter Shihab mentions "three experiences of feeling suspended by a thin thread a thousand feet above the ground, as if I did not belong to the world and the world did not belong to me." The first hanging thread was his family's eviction from their home in 1949—literally "with only the clothes on our backs"—at gun point—by Jewish émigrés from Brooklyn, claiming the modest house as a gift from God (crudely translated by Israeli government force). The second hanging thread was leaving Palestine in 1950, since he "could not imagine future suicide bombers who, in their hopelessness, would sacrifice others and themselves."

The third incident—powerfully dramatized—tells of being rudely strip-searched and interrogated by Israeli soldiers at the Jordan River checkpoint. This central scene escalates, due to a scrap of paper on which he had inscribed the name of Yasser Arafat, whom he knew on a first-name basis and intended to interview. The interrogation ends abruptly with an ironic twist when the Israeli captain mercifully releases the journalist, learning that Shihab was there to be with his dying mother. They agree to continue conversing under better circumstances, initiating a personal dialogue, which clarifies the absurdity of deadly monolithic stereotypes.

Several days later when they meet at a restaurant, the captain—out of uniform and on his first trip into occupied territory—accompanies Shihab to his mother's home in Sinjil village. Introduced as Rafi from Iraq—his actual name and homeland—the Iraqi Jew receives a warm welcome. Allowing the gentle subterfuge, the Israeli captain comes under the spell of the Palestinian family's sweet generosity. Later that week the journalist meets the captain at a café, accompanied by his father and sister. Captain Rafi, in full uniform, introduces the journalist as his American friend. They invite Shihab to their Tel Aviv home, treating him with courtesy and affection.

Rafi's father, Mr. Atar, tells an intriguing tale of departing Iraq. "It's a long story and a sad one, but you are like my son and I am going to tell you the truth. Yes, we were forced out, not by the Iraqis, but by the Israelis. Bombs started exploding and we were being harassed. When we got here, Israel treated us first like heroes, then they wanted to give us the menial labor jobs which European Jews refused. To my shock, I found out that it had been Israeli agents who planted the bombs." When Shihab later asks if peace is possible, the captain thinks *not*, explaining that "Both sides are caught in a web of hatred, blame, holier-than-thou attitude and lack of flexibility. I am not optimistic." He learns that Rafi's sister was widowed after a sniper killed her husband. Asking about children, Rafi says: "Two are alive and grown and another one was killed when a suicide bomber attacked a supermarket."

"This is awful," Shihab laments. "Someone has got to find a solution."

These conversations evoke genuine fraternal dialogue, as both listen respectfully, striving to understand. Such communication stands firmly in opposition to the double monologues of governments and mainstream media that rarely achieve understanding, and seem to care only about winning stereotypical arguments.

Along this narrative's path, the signs essential to dialogue are marked LISTEN and OBSERVE. As Shihab walks through the present, personal flashbacks—some sad, many humorous, all poignant—provide deeper context and a layering of attentions. He encounters characters whose lives have been trampled on daily and whose viewpoints have been ignored. He listens with a sharp ear for revealing dialogue that allows us to hear normal Palestinians speaking for themselves. His observing eye sets vivid scenes replete with fascinating characters that one can understand *only* outside their own blind spots. Eliciting cultural insights—often-humorous ones—Shihab also registers the wisdom and blindness among his countrymen.

Serious themes emerge in this literary tapestry, concerning human rights issues at the edge of abject poverty and displacement at the loss of property. Paralleling these hardships, we begin to appreciate the stoic adaptations of peaceful Palestinians to the daily irrationalities of military occupation. Shihab's narrative voice remains truthful throughout, keeping a covenant with readers, who will trust his point of view, since it includes a clear dimension of self-criticism. A natural storyteller from a culture in which oral history remains a central force, old stories unfurl like modern tales. A traditional wedding ends with an unexpected funeral; a single day includes visits—to a Bedouin's tent, to a banquet of American evangelists, and to a hospital. On another day he searches a refugee camp for lost luggage. His attempt to locate the courthouse becomes a nightmare during another trip.

As the memoir evolves, Shihab slowly realizes a social distancing—from being an *insider* to becoming an *outsider*, in particular revolving around what decision he shall make about his property. Will he sell it or will he return to build on it? His mother, who can no longer look after it, pleads with him *not* to sell. He asks a relative: "Why is everyone in the village so interested in the fate of my tiny piece of land?" Khalid responds: "They want to know if you are still with us, if you feel our fears and our pain. Whether you sell it or not, will determine the peace between you and everyone in this village." But this question involves another problem, since a nephew has squatted there and begun to build on the land, but without paying a cent or even asking permission. For several intense chapters these concerns are discussed in conversations, which are by turns emotional, logical, and absurd.

In a passionate dialogue with Abu-Ghazaleh, a former judge who had secured the initial title to his property, Shihab expresses views on the prevailing political situation, confessing disappointment with his countrymen. The judge responds: "I think you have been brainwashed, my friend." Shihab honestly considers the possibility of having been "brainwashed" by his comfortable American lifestyle.

While the basic conditions of exile include duration of separation, disorientation in a new social context, and a complex series of adjustments—an exiled writer learning a second language might be the most challenging condition of all. Shihab's mastery of English to the extent of becoming a career journalist (never losing fluent Arabic), stands as a remarkable achievement. He was an editor of *The Jerusalem Times* (English version), worked for seven years at *The San Antonio Express-News*, and a decade with *The Dallas Morning News*, retiring in 1986. After that he published *The Arab Star* for three years, while continuing as a correspondent on Middle East affairs for Reuters and *The New York Times*. His development as a stylist in *Does the Land*

Remember Me? goes beyond his journalism and advances beyond the charming vignettes in his first book, *A Taste of Palestine*, published by Corona Press (1993).

In refusing to be denied the right to his own narrative, Aziz Shihab engenders a deeply insightful understanding of the Palestinian wounds that remain unhealed under the shadow of a wall.

Inclined to Speak

The eclectic styles by these poets of Arabic descent speak eloquently in this major anthology of poetry, *Inclined to Speak*, from University of Arkansas Press (2008). They do *not* sing as one monolithic chorus but as 39 diverse soloists; and the sophisticated texts do *not* aim to establish a threshold for the latest ethnic literature of the decade or for the next phase of multiculturalism. Rather, these gifted poets are creating some of North America's strongest and most passionate contemporary poetry.

The poets are neither tourists nor terrorists, but esteemed professors, lawyers, translators, and editors; people doing business and community work; parents raising families and corresponding with relatives from their countries of origin. They are not having an identity crisis or mapping an Arab Diaspora. They are peaceful citizens, thoughtful and humane, just like most of us.

There are political poems here from fresh perspectives, but no propaganda or screeds. In fact, they argue convincingly with satirical wit. Where there is anger there is also compassion; where there is social criticism, there is never didacticism. They remind us that stereotypes and prejudice, war and genocide are overcome only by bridges of dialogue and not by walls of separation. Like all poets they write of love and nature, of language and ideas, always with spirit and attitude.

The first line of *Inclined to Speak* (in Elmaz Abinader's "Living with Opposition") brings us to the edge of openings. "Someone has told you, It's an attitude problem./I hear this, say something like, I wonder whose." Yes, since attitudes are formed by culture before experience. This powerful poem about her father, a gentle man who "is tired of being foreign, of trying/so hard just to breathe, to get a little light/of his own," is one of many beautiful odes and elegies for family elders, who either emigrated or remained home. What could be more human than that?

Marian Haddad observes her father in a hospital as "he smacks his lips, rolls/his tongue inside, *Agua,*//He says, though he is/not

Mexican, *Agua*,//a language he has learned/in America, and he, Arabic.//Three languages roll deftly/on this dry tongue."

Assef Al-Jundi mentions his late father (a Syrian poet), taking him to Amman and Beirut in quest of a student visa, when the U.S. Embassy in Damascus was closed after The Six Day War.

Naomi Shihab Nye writes of breaking off the hands of "mother's praying statute/when I was four—/how she tearfully repaired them,/ but the hairline cracks/in the wrists/were all she said/she could see—//the unannounced blur/of something passing/out of a life."

Just as 9/11 was a defining moment for most Americans it was particularly painful for Arab-Americans. As Saladin Ahmad writes, "In a word, brother, it is dangerous," especially after the "war on terror" was concocted. Samuel Hazo writes of it directly. "Nightmares of impact crushed us./We slept like the doomed or drowned,/then woke to oratory, vigils,/valor, journalists declaring war/and, snapping from aerials or poles, the furious clamor of flags."

Yet the lyric impulse emerges even in tragedy. Kazim Ali in a musical turn hears "The violin's empty stomach resonate/Music is a scar unraveling itself in strings." Sinan Antoon writes that "the Tigris and Euphrates/are two strings/in death's lute/and we are songs/or fingers strumming." D.H. Melhem listens to the "Broadway Music" of a homeless trio (who are not Arabic) with her fine-tuned ear of empathy.

Presented in alphabetical order are 160 texts—impressive narratives by Sharif S. Elmusa, Hedy Habra, Sam Hamod, Lawrence Joseph, Mohja Kahf, Pauline Kaldas, Jack Marshall, Khaled Mattawa, Philip Metres, Haas H. Mroue, Adele Ne Jame, Kevin Gerard Rashid, Deema K. Shehabi, Matthew Shenoda; lovely lyrics by Alise Alousi, Nuar Alsadir, Lisa Suhair Majaj, Gregory Orfalea; stunning prose poems by Lara Hamza, Nathalie Handal, Fady Joudah, David Williams, and Eliot Khalil Wison; and ingenious experimental work by Etel Adan, Walid Bitar, Ahimsa Timoteo Bodhrán, Suheir Hammad, Sekeena Shaben, and Zaid Shlah.

Hayan Charara has made shrewd editorial choices, contributing a masterful language excursion in his long poem ("Usage"). His thoughtful introduction discusses the poetic, political, and social dimensions, as well as the thematic and personal issues that Arab-

American poets confront daily. This groundbreaking anthology appears at a time when deeper understanding of our diversity is most crucial.

lands. Even as the ancestral circle was broken on the physical plane, millions internalized their sacred rituals and fused the remembered past with faith in the unknown. "Stripped of all but the ability to express the most complex emotions in a pure sound, enslaved Africans reached across the barriers of language, culture, and circumstance to forge links with one another, in the midnight of the Middle Passage, with comforting sound." From this deep sounding their sacred music was kept alive. The earliest "Negro Spirituals"—rooted in African rhythms and the scriptures of the Bible—became the foundation of African-American theology. The masks have evolved through centuries of discourse—much of it racist—against which Brown stands firmly. But his book is *not* a catalogue of recriminations, rather it is a deep, integrated text of insightful discoveries, aesthetic interpretations, poetic illuminations, and spiritual epiphanies. We are engaged in a penetrating dialogue with historians, sociologists, philosophers, theologians, and artists —all within an encircling purpose of understanding what it means to be "authentically black and truly Catholic."

The overarching theme of identity—African *and* American—draws upon the "ground-breaking analysis" of Robert Farris Thompson and a body of enlightened scholarship that supercedes the shadowy bias of studies about the Middle Passage and centuries of slavery. Brown then carries on a conversation with Frederick Douglass and W.E.B. Du Bois, acknowledging their insights but pointing out misconceptions. For instance, he objects to the labels "slave narratives" and "sorrow songs" adopted by these classic black thinkers and repeated by the white editors of narratives and songs. Brown's view is that "slave narratives" were actually "documents of *liberation*" and that the "sorrow songs" were "too spirited and lively in the composition and execution to be simply considered songs of an 'unhappy people.'"

Father Brown observes African "performance theology" between the lines of Colonel Thomas Wentworth Higginson's depiction of black Union soldiers preparing for battle (*Army Life in a Black Regiment*). The former slaves (nominally-free citizens), who led the white regiments against the South, were more than the dedicated troops and composers of Negro Spirituals. They viewed themselves as "the mighty arm of the heavenly host," he asserts, "waging war on the forces of Satan."

Of all the texts examined, it is the biblical tale of Jacob (and the songs based on it), which holds a central focus in this liberating vision. "Wrestling Jacob" specifically "calls for the divine through the act of self-naming and by the act of restoring a right relationship (balance) in the community." Jacob's cautionary tale goes to the heart of identity. "Those men and women of Africa who were named *slaves*. . . took a twisted version of Christianity and retwisted it into a culture of liberation, transcendence, creativity, and wholeness."

What does it mean now for African Americans to be truly Catholic? The short answer, quoted by Brown as a "prophetic gift" and a challenge to the white hierarchy, comes from the black nun, Sister Thea Bowman. She asserted in a 1989 speech to the Catholic Bishops that "It means that I come to my church fully functioning. That doesn't frighten you, does it?"

The long answer, developed in the final part of this book, provides a bracing sense of what it means to be "fully functioning" congregants of the sacred circle. To be Catholic means being *catholic* in the original sense of the word—universal, all-inclusive, edified, and just. He envisions a church that must be unified and integrative in both membership and leadership, that it must be genuinely multicultural in liturgy, ritual and structure. "One of the greatest tragedies of the failure of leadership in the Black Catholic Church," he writes, "may be the inevitable consequence of raising up leaders and apostolic ministers who felt obligated to 'wear the mask' of perfection and super-womanhood and manhood in the face of those who denied us the right to be anywhere in the building, except as servants/slaves."

Dr. Joseph A. Brown directs the Black American Studies program at Southern Illinois University (Carbondale) and teaches African American Aesthetics, drama, and film. He has directed many theatrical productions and has published *Accidental Grace* (1986), *A Retreat with Thea Bowman and Bede Abram* (1998), *Sweet, Sweet Spirit* (2007), and *The Sun Whispers, Wait* (2009).

To Stand on the Rock suggests that we discard the masks and leap into the dance, singing "Anybody ask you who you are, tell them you a child of God." This does *not* frighten the liberated author of this truly liberating book.

The Call to Emptiness

In "Notes for a Philosophy of Solitude," Thomas Merton writes that "One who is called to solitude is not called merely to imagine himself solitary. . . to cultivate the illusion that he is different, withdrawn, elevated. He is called to emptiness."

John Howard Griffin says that the monk "Made it clear that he did not come there into the silences and solitude of the hermitage to seek Christ, but rather because he believed that is where Christ wanted to find him."

These themes are engraved in this enlightening collaboration—of photographs and paintings by Merton, integrated with Griffin's photographic portraits and commentaries, all emerging harmoniously in *A Hidden Wholeness: The Visual World of Thomas Merton* (Houghton Mifflin, 1970).

Merton (1915-1968) entered the Trappist Abbey of Gethsemani in Kentucky on December 10, 1941. Twenty-seven years later *to the day* (December 10, 1968), he died of accidental electrocution, in Bangkok during his journey to the Far East.

Primarily the book covers the final years of the monk's life, when he became a hermit, and began taking photographs—first with cheap cameras and later with Griffin's camera, a splendid Swiss Alpa, which Merton called a Zen camera (although he took a less expensive Canon with him on that fateful trip).

Griffin mentions that the monk's first negatives were mailed to his young son, Gregory Parker Griffin, to make prints and contact sheets.

> The films poured in, all sizes and all formats, depending on what kind of camera Merton had borrowed. They ranged from superb negatives made with a Rolleiflex to miserable ones made with an Instamatic.
>
> I suggested that he would never have much satisfaction with the results until he got a good camera. He replied that although his pictures were beginning to sell for book

jackets, he did have a vow of poverty and did not want to ask permission to buy one.

That problem was solved when Griffin loaned the Alpa "indefinitely" to Merton. He had the camera for three years, making a provision in his Will that it be returned to Griffin in the event of the monk's death. Griffin (1920-1980) had *not* expected to outlive Merton, never considering that the monk's photographic work would come to such an abrupt end.

Griffin was tense when the Canon arrived in the mail a few weeks after Merton's untimely death. He writes in *A Hidden Wholeness*.

> I tried to open the box, but my hands trembled so uncontrollably my wife had to finish the job. I was overwhelmed to see what care Merton had taken of this equipment. . . I glanced at the frame counter and saw that eighteen shots had been taken of the roll of thirty-six frames.
>
> More carefully than I have ever done anything in my life, I removed that roll of film and held it in my hand, realizing that on eighteen frames were undeveloped images of scenes Tom had been the last to see as he clicked the shutter, and we would be the first to see when they assumed form and detail in the developer.

The final frames were from Merton's Asian trip where he attended an ecumenical council and had dialogues with the Dali Lama in India. Before that final trip, we see the photographic diary of the monk's spiritual solitude and Griffin's images of Merton (including the Official Portrait taken in 1963). Griffin visited with the monk from 1963 until early 1968, both taking photographs. After Merton's death, Griffin lived at the hermitage for 160 days during several visits from 1969 until 1972, researching the first Official Biography (never completed due to serious health issues).

The title of *A Hidden Wholeness* is from Merton's meditation ("Hagia Sophia" of 1963): "There is in all visible things, an invisible fecundity, a dimmed light, a meek namelessness, a hidden wholeness. This mysterious Unity and Integrity is Wisdom, the Mother of all. . . . There is in all things an inexhaustible sweetness and purity, a silence that is a fountain of action and of joy. It rises up in wordless gentleness and flows to me from the unseen roots of all created being. . . ."

A Hidden Wholeness, produced in a large, glossy format, is in eight sections. The first reflects the monk's simple cabin and the environment of surrounding woods in lucid images by both photographers, marvelous shots of penetrating clarity into the visual spirit of the hermitage. The most outstanding image is of Merton's worktable—where light has its own way with the desk, chair, typewriter, and shadows, as if it had arrived to discover the hermit.

The second section includes numerous photographs of the monk, including those that appeared in *Life* magazine. The third—"Serious Photographs and Calligraphs"— includes 28 Merton prints and seven black tempera on white paintings that he called Calligraphs. Here are his purest photographic visions of the unadorned theater of nature— dried roots and tree stumps, weeds declaring among boulders and rocks, peeling paint and leftover snow. One spread illustrates perfectly Merton's sense of musical variation, and we almost hear Mozart's figures in the light. Another image features a crude, handmade broom leaning against the cinder block wall, lifting a peasant skirt to dance in the radiant light.

Griffin explains Merton's distinction of "serious photographs" in his Prologue.

> Merton distinguished between his serious work and the documentary uses he made of photography. In the latter, he captured faces and places and events as any good photographer would, though with his own personal characteristics of wit and composition. In the serious work he was captured by the play of light, the ambience, and the inner life of the things he photographed. For him, the best images were silent but communicative. He aimed for the image that was true to its subject and had the mysterious ability to communicate fresh insights into it.

The tempera paintings recall some of Paul Klee works in that both artists created an original, freely agile, almost childlike effect. (One photograph features a Klee print on the cabin's whitewashed wall.) But the actual look of Merton's abstractions suggest miniature versions of Franz Kline's large black on white canvases.

Section IV contains a series of Griffin photographs of Merton, roaming around the woods with the Alpa camera, and Section V ("Merton Among Friends") features portraits of French philosopher Jacques Maritain and several other visitors to the hermitage, in 1966.

Section VI includes Merton's photographs from Asia, where the subjects change drastically. Instead of stones, we see mountains. Instead of raindrops on a window, we encounter oceans. The massive landscapes and seascapes impressively reveal Merton's graceful ability to adapt to nature's intrinsic forms. He photographed giant Buddhas as intimately as the simple crucifix hanging on the bare cabin wall. He chanted the *Psalms* in the same hour as he recalled Zen Koans. In silence was music. East meets West. Yet these seeming contradictions "connected" in all of Merton's Art, bringing forth the "hidden wholeness" Griffin discusses perceptively.

Merton's photography "began to reveal, in a way nothing else did, certain aspects of his interior vision and his qualities as a man." He photographed "the natural, unarranged, unpossesed objects of his contemplation, seeking not to alter their life but to preserve it in his emulsions," Griffin points out. "This concept" of "going out to the to the thing and giving oneself to it, allowing it to communicate its essence, allowing it to say what it will, reveal what it will, rather than trying to bring it into the confines of self, altering and changing it by the possession of it, was one of Thomas Merton's profoundest orientations. These photographs do not need to be studied, they need to be contemplated."

A Hidden Wholeness was the only book about Merton that Griffin saw published during his lifetime. *The Hermitage Journals*, Griffin's diaries kept during visits to the hermitage researching the "Official Biography," became Griffin's first posthumous book (Andrews-McMeel, 1981; Doubleday paper, 1982). Elizabeth Griffin-Bonazzi directed the release of *Follow the Ecstasy* a biography about Merton's final years (Latitudes Press, 1983; Revised Edition, Orbis Books, 1993). Griffin's *Epilogue* to *Follow the Ecstasy* speculates about what may have happened to the monk.

Had Thomas Merton returned from the Far East alive, he would have become more and more silent. He would have gone on writing forever—for he was a true poet as well as a faithful monk and priest—but he would have published less and less. He would have continued taking the authentic risks necessary to live his vocation without compromise. He had lived in an absolute way. This is courageous because he had every chance for taking the easy way out. He never did. He never wavered from his true vocation: to be always leaping over the cliffs of the spiritual life.

Griffin and Merton shared a fraternal dialogue, a symbiotic exchange that was never a double monologue. Whenever it became apparent that real resolution of the issues that concerned them (war, civil rights, the need for change in the Church), they left the mysteries in God's hands, taking off on another jaunt through the woods to photograph the objects of their contemplation.

A Hidden Wholeness is not a traditional book to be judged or possessed, because rhetoric means nothing to a vision. While Griffin hoped for a "silent book," his unobtrusive, insightful text guides the reader, while never intending to be a skeletal key to Merton's interior vision. "We don't have to rush after it," the monk remarks about prayer. "It was there all the time, and if we give it time, it will make itself known to us." Merton answered the call to emptiness by becoming a solitary hermit. It was *not* a call to fill up that spiritual emptiness with illusions but to illuminate Being.

Scriptures of the Body

The powerful poetry of Vassar Miller (1924-1998) maintains a tenuous balance between aesthetic form and ravaged shape, tenaciously negotiating a tension between the freedom of her lyrics and the limitations of physical reality.

In *Wage War on Silence* (Wesleyan University Press, 1960), we find an archetypal text of Miller's thematic concerns. "Offering: For All My Loves" is a 22-line sentence in search of an apt symbol. The narrative voice offers itself ("This vessel take—"), and then weighs her body against a litany of more aesthetic forms.

> No chalice and no goblet,
> Nothing so picturesque as a gourd
> Or an oaken bucket,
> But more like a rusty can
> Kicked up from the dirt

Her vessel does not pretend to be an honorific chalice or an aristocratic goblet, and not even 'so picturesque as a gourd." Instead it takes on the ravaged shape of "a rusty can," symbol of urban modernity, evoking the poet's own body forced into its conforming clothing and, then as a child being, "Buckled and bent and warped," like an discarded object. Throughout the poetry, Miller selected a rich variety of images for the rejected body. In "Slump" she writes that "The body, God knows why creeps/along, some crazy creature/half an insect, half a tumbleweed."

This calls to mind Kafka's notion of *smallness*. He wrote in *Dearest Father* that there are "Two possibilities: making oneself infinitely small or being so. The second is perfection, that is to say, inactivity; the first is beginning, that is to say, action." Miller's version of *smallness* in her early books is one of action. In "Subterfuge" from *New and Selected Poems, 1950-1980* (Latitudes, 1981), she writes of her own father, who gave her a typewriter. He enters, "bearing it in his arms like an awkward bouquet"

for his spastic child who sits down
on the floor, one knee on the frame
of the typewriter, and holding her left wrist

with her right hand, in that precision known
to the crippled, pecks at the keys
with a sparrow's preoccupation.

Again we encounter the diminutive figure, "Falling by chance on rhyme" and "pretending pretense and playing at playing," realizing that her fun is "a delaying action against what she knows." Although it was a tentative beginning, she takes up language "in that precision known/to the crippled," as an instrument of transformation. The child like the "hunk of corroded tin" will endure and prevail because words are "Yet filled with the liquor of lightning,/The same as distilled from the flowers of children," and "With the web wax of words,/The same and no different,/Only shaped to misshapenness". . .

The child and vessel are "the wild grapes of martyrs, trampled for Christ," discovering them as "The same and no different." The poet juxtaposes philosophical acceptance of the ravaged form, but with bitterness at how this body is misperceived by others. At this point in "Offering," she issues a warning.

Hold me with care and decorum
For a little but not too long
Lest my jagged edge cut you,
My acrid drip scald you,
Etching a crooked shadow
On the lip of your proper love.

Yet she believed that her God would accept any transcription of her body, even if the "proper love" of others outside her circle of parental affection recoiled from the effects of her cerebral palsy.

Miller entered the garden of poetry as a child in the title poem of her first book, *Adam's Footprint* (New Orleans Poetry Review Press, 1956). There she discovers the first steps of experience in a primal image on the floor of Eden, knowing that "The foot of Adam leaves the mark/Of some child scrabbling in the dark." Adam's signature is that of the child in a new world, one that must be named and learned. Like Adam, the poet was a child of wonder, passion, and paradox. But she did not accept the fate of the "Spastic Child," whose mind is a "bright bird, forever trapped in silence." The footprint, like the trapped mind, resides in the silenced body.

In "Without Ceremony" Miller writes, "We find ourselves where tongues cannot wage war/On silence (farther, mystics never flew)/But on the common wings of what we are,/Borne on the wings of what we bear, toward You,/Oh Word, in whom our wordiness dissolves,/When we have not a prayer except ourselves."

By her third book, *My Bones Being Wiser* (Wesleyan, 1963), experience returns to the body as silent prayer. The title poem, subtitled "A Eucharistic Meditation"—or a meditation upon the transcended body of Christ—begins with

> At Thy Word
> my mind may wander
> but my bones worship
> beneath the dark waters of my blood
> whose scavenger fish
> have picked them clean.

Again the bones are picked clean, offering a blank text for the imprint of God. But here she replaces Adam's footprint with God's in "Loneliness": "This silence, this crying,/O my God, is my country/ with Yours the sole footstep besides my own./Save me amid its landscapes/so terrible, strange/I am almost in love with them!" Rather than waging war on silence, the bones being wiser *become* silence, and the poet touches the ineffable within. In the poet's "country" the paradoxes resolve into oneness, silence cries, and "wordiness dissolves" into one *Yes.* In silence she hears a "Belated Lullaby," "Where flesh and spirit dance,/Shadowing, bound yet free/Bach's ordered ecstasy." Yet in that temporal body, she writes in "A Bird in the Hand" that "I do not feel the peace of the saints,/light fusing with darkness,/passing all understanding."

Except for instants of spiritual ecstasy she responds through the senses. While the mystic must transcend the body, Miller's verse grapples with it. Whereas the mystic hears incantations of ineffable silence, her religious verse measures its music and clarifies its meaning. In "A Dream from the Dark Night" (based on an anecdote about St. John of the Cross burning the letters of St. Teresa of Avila), Miller finds herself in "the desert of darkness/where Your silence speaks so loud/I cannot hear You." At that point of ecstatic transcendence the mystic becomes spirit but the poet returns to the flesh. Miller's scriptures reach toward that transcendence, then become a painful reshaping of experience into beautiful poetry.

In "Introduction to a Poetry Reading," the narrator is "born with my mod dress sewn into my body/stitched to my flesh/basted into my bones." However she "could never, somehow, take it all off/to wash the radical dirt out." Her tone remains unapologetic, even defiant. This poem also concludes with a warning.

> So bear me
> as I bear you,
> high in the grace of greeting.

Similar withdrawals occur in other poems from *If I Could Sleep Deeply Enough* (Liveright, 1974), Miller's darkest, most naked book. From "Tired" comes the book's title and another variation on the body's language.

> If I could
> sleep deeply enough,
> I might touch the eye
> of dark, life.
>
> Yet the way
> I sleep, men drink salt.
> Always wearier
> upon waking—
>
> I have written
> these lines without book,

> thumbing the thesaurus
> of my bones.

Her very bones, one inner text of the body, defiantly thumb their own variations, breaking the skin of form. "Insomniac's Prayer" sketches a "body knotted into a fist/clenching against itself," as she plaintively asks, "Oh, who will unsnarl my body/into gestures of love?" Will it be her lover, her God, or will it be death? "Who will nudge the dreams back into my head,/back into my bones, where rhyming with one another/like wind chimes,/they will make music whenever I move?"

Miller's silence would be music if her body were touched by "gestures of love." Yet it was not to be, and the lyrics of silenced music are broken open by despair. "Read my face and my hands," she cries in "Fantasia"—"stripped raw like Jesus" —or the body sanctified by pain.

In "Posthumous Letter to Thomas Merton," she discovers an ideal counterpart in the Trappist monk as a poet of intense spirituality. The work of Merton reflects a similar reading of liturgy, theology, and the saints. Both were superficially labeled "religious" because of the spiritual content in early books, and virtually ignored later when their poetry opened in form and intimacy. Miller closes this letter-as-poem to Merton ("less poem than presumption") with a long interrogatory that could stand as her poetics. Never pious or certain, always she asked truthful questions.

> I ask you, self-styled marginal man,
> Does not each sufferer always inhabit
> The edges of the world as pioneer
> To prove how much humanity can bear
> And still be human, experimenter in
> The bloody laboratory of our lives.
> Taking and testing every pain tossed from
> The cosmos, fragments we reshape
> As best as the materials allow,
> To buttress God's cathedrals built from chaos?

The question is answered lucidly in the statements of her poetics. "Poetry is creative in that it makes an artifact where none was before, only a mass of thoughts and emotions and sensations; it is redemptive, since in makes art out of non-art, something of beauty and value; it is sanctifying in that it confers order upon chaos. These three functions are one."

Miller mastered and then broke from the traditional forms of poetry she loved (Gerard Manley Hopkins, Edward Arlington Robinson, Emily Dickinson), weaving questions into the textured fabric of her bony work in the manner of a skeptic, but always shaping poems into passionate scriptures of the body.

When Wings was under the editorship of Joanie Whitebird in Houston, she brought out Miller's later work in beautifully designed chapbooks. In *Approaching Nada* (Wings, 1977), Miller's longest poem of 133-lines, she asks the Abbot of the French Academy (concerning "Pure Poetry") about the meaning of his statement that "*le poete, c'est un mystique manqué*," speculating upon his words.

> An aborted mystic,
> a frustrated mystic,
> or did you mean,
> simply, a sorry one?
> Doubtless the latter, since
> the poet like the mouse will scuttle
> clean to the border
> of the ineffable,
> then scurry back
> with tidbits of the Vision.

Miller's "tidbits of the Vision" are appropriate to the diminutive nature of the poet as mouse scuttling or as "child scrabbling" or as "the meanest grub/struggling to swim on concrete." These utterings are not like those of the mystics, who "leap once and for all/headlong into darkness." Yet she was not one of "These poets of the *nada*." She was closer to E.A. Robinson, who wrote that "Poetry is trying to say what cannot be said." In *Approaching Nada* she becomes one of the "mystics of/the bruising thing," who "climb up bloody concretes/to leave nailed high/white pieces of themselves." Like Christ, the poet offers the body of the poem as sacrifice to the word. In this powerful work where she does "take it all off/to wash the radical dirt out," Miller discovers that "Somewhere between silence and ceremony" there "springs the Word" of God. It was that same word in her subtle ascent toward silence in *Approaching Nada*, which becomes "the wellhead of all hush feeding the roots/of tongues, whether of men or angels, interchange/between us and Your world. Listen, whoever/tunes an ear."

Miller listened but with "wings clipped by busy book and body, still in You/my Phoenix!" Only in "Phoenix" could she rise from the body's cage. Otherwise she was grounded by the limits of flesh. No longer was she "content with the pseudonym/of my name, with the disguise," says "Encounter," but "awakened astonished in the streets/ of my identity." (*Small Change*, Wings, 1976).

As Miller approached that dark hemisphere, bound as one with the hemisphere of light, she knew that "Every poet knows/what the saint knows/that every new day is/to retake the frontier of one's name." That is one of the differences between the true mystic and the spiritual poet. The poet names what he or she loves on the human level, including one's identity. But the mystic does *not* name and erases all identity in God. The poet enters silence in order to return to the senses with words to evoke it, shaped into fragments, and, "As best as the materials allow." According to Evelyn Underwood in her seminal study, *Mysticism*, "mysticism is no isolated vision, no fugitive glimpse of reality, but a complete system of life . . . It is the name of that organic process which involves the perfect consummation of Love of God."

For Miller there had been a glimpse of the Vision, and during the last years of Thomas Merton's hermitic existence, there were several prolonged mystical encounters, as documented by John Howard Griffin in *Follow the Ecstasy* (Latitudes, 1983).

Miller's subject in *Approaching Nada* is neither a clarifying mysticism nor the dark luminosity of *Nada*, but the search for these fleeting realms in language. Her searching became her subject, both in life and in poetry. While the mystic gradually becomes purified, illuminated, and transformed at the root of Being, the poet moves inwardly toward "roots of shifted waters/shifting toward *nada*." These movements navigate through the passionate experiences perceived by creative intuition, sensory pleasures, "altered states of consciousness" (and somatic nature itself). These "peak experiences" are the secondary mystical phenomena—essential to spiritual poetry, but transcended by true mysticism. Even as Miller breaks old forms in *Approaching Nada*, she remains a tortured body, wandering "down hallways of my body, ghost/prowling passages of my blood/to my most hidden corners/" where "still/I know my name."

All of Miller's poems form a beautiful arc from innocence through experience to second innocence. The early books, lathered with a distant fear, become washed with wisdom in her later work. "Of some child scrabbling in the dark" led to her willingness to "trace footprints/of princes, rebels, martyrs"—all images for Christ—two decades later in *Approaching Nada*. It was her courageous tracing that signified this new child in the wilderness of the modern psyche.

A decade before Vassar Miller was gone, Stephen Ford Brown published the only collection about her work, *Heart's Invention: On the Poetry of Vassar Miller*, in 1988. The book of literary criticism includes essays by Larry McMurtry, Paul Christensen, Frances Sage, Thomas Whitbread, Sister Bernetta Quinn, Kenneth MacLean, plus an interview with Karla Hammond. *Heart's Invention* reached a national audience, standing next to a few others on a short shelf of critical books on poetry in Texas. The most significant, Paul Christensen's *West of the American Dream: An Encounter with Texas* (Texas A&M Press, 2001), brought further attention. Two books by Dave Oliphant—*On A High Horse: Views Mostly of Latin American and Texas Poetry* (Prickly Pear, 1983), and a memoir, *Harbingers of Books to Come* (Wings, 2009)—are certainly important additions to this little library of recognitions.

Vassar Miller struggled for 74 years with cerebral palsy, and became known nationally, due to her elegant poems that received critical acclaim. Two of her books were nominated for the Pulitzer Prize, and she was the first Poet Laureate of Texas. The grace of her finest poems proclaimed her to be a poet of the first order in American poetry from 1950 until her death in 1998.

Ultimate Borders

I

In *Some Recognition of the Joshua Lizard*, poet Robert Burlingame (1922-2011) transforms experience into genuine awe in more than 100 subtly shaped poems in a shrewdly organized collection, his final book (Mutabilis Press, 2009).

Burlingame's intense wonder weaves humbly into the fabric of his West Texas habitat (specifically, the Guadalupe Mountains and Chihuahuan Desert region), while never stooping to mere gloss or landscape tourism. Best known as a nature poet, this desert scholar shaped many varied subjects, including splendid homages to a pantheon of artists and thinkers from ancient China and Greece and forward to the last century, a lovely gathering of tender memories about family and friends, plus a sheaf of the most lucid lyrics on the art of poetry.

The title poem suggests identification with a "sleek saurian" of "stealth gemmed inside that tense/Sanctuary" in "an Old Testament stance//this chameleon faith solemn/At the foot of a desert king with God-shaggy head."

Burlingame celebrates solidarity with all life forms "in harmlessness" and profound respect. Stunning hymns praise various trees, including Plato's "Sycamore" for the "half-beneficent, half-tutorial, shade it casts."

> Shade we don't wish to waste since it recalls
> the broad-shouldered philosopher,
> prophet of the changeless unseen.

He ponders the "Netleaf Hackberry," that "vague unimpressive tree/doomed to be infested/as it holds to stingy soil," which stands as "noble" and "loved for its berries that float/into the next life of a common glory," although we consider it a trash tree. His homages also bear tints of lamentation.

In "Marsden Hartley (1877-1943)" the painter's hands "moved in spasms of color,/how they praised the roughness of sea cliffs."

Later the homage laments: "We need you still, wise spokesman of the cliffs." Near the end of "Late Twentieth Century Remarks on an Early Painting by Monet," he writes, "Your world's ease, its joys, will not come again.//We used to be rich. What has happened?/Where, graceless and unspent, will we journey?"

His explorations gather an edifying anthology of insights into the works we once studied: W.B. Yeats and D.H. Lawrence; Thoreau, Melville, Dickinson, Frost, Poe; Dostoevsky, Pushkin, Chekov; César Vallejo and James Wright; Basho and Li Po. A long, varied list of approaches to literature read by a clarifying intelligence.

Divided into four sections, the book begins with personal histories. Among the loveliest yet simplest poems in the first part is "A Clean, White Handkerchief," which begins with "I sit in my study/writing these/words. Not for-/ever will I do/this." The folded handkerchief is in a pocket. "Linda washed/and ironed it/for me.//Not forever will/she do/this."

After "Stalking the poem,/the half-wing fear of failure/plunging like a beak bright/through innocent sky," the poet reaches near mystical meditation in his final poem ("That Stillness Which Pleases the Mind"). There the narrator has "decided to give up on traveling anywhere/he's gathered up and burned his gaudy maps/he has stopped gazing beyond the tufted furrow." Instead "he sits and listens in his one friendly chair/& rinses out the glistening bright thought."

As for the simple elegance of his poetics, Burlingame writes:

> I am a celebrant of the universe as I see it. I am also an elegist. I cannot imagine being one without the other. I have no rigidly formulated views about poetry. I would agree with Mayakovsky: Let us have as many poets as we can and as many different kinds as possible. I do not consider my residency in Texas to be much of an influence. I do hold strong feelings toward the desert, especially its plants and rocks. I live in the desert's heat and light. I feel my aloneness in this world to be more or less inevitable. I shall write poems in this world of light until the day of my final breath. If I ever work out an esthetic concept of my own, it will be in the blaze of the desert, in its silence.

This volume appeared in the poet's 88th year, recalling the authenticity, intensity, and depth of poetry by Vassar Miller, although their styles and subjects are entirely different. Both have influenced generations of poets, editors, and students.

This collection includes a fine introduction by Joseph Rice (1944-2009), the poet's devoted student. Mutabilis Press has produced a handsome trade paperback that amounts to a cultural service of this astounding and long-overlooked poet.

II

The personal voice of Jack Myers (1941-2009) evokes tremendous life force in the conundrums of dying that he contemplated in this final book, *The Memory of Water*, from Western Michigan University Press (2011).

The beautiful title poem for his wife, Thea Temple, opens

> After I am gone and the ache begins
> to cease
> and the slow erosion I felt,
> being older than you, invades you too,
> you'll come to see that an image of the desert
> is the memory of water, like remembering
>
> when we were walking in beautiful Barcelona
> and you said you thought the trees were gods
> because they were rooted in earth
> and flew in the air and magically made food
> out of light and made the air we breathe.

This breath-taking elegy reveals lyric flowers on narrative stems. "I was stunned how you could open up a God-space/just like that. Like when my two-year-old dug holes/in the yard and fit his face into each of them to see,/as he explained, if he could find where the darkness/came from. Then you asked me why I never prayed."

Then Myers' thoughtful response becomes the third stanza. "I believe whatever disappears or survives/or comes into being is a prayer that's already/been answered, and that we feel alone/because we won't let go of what is gone/or changed or hasn't happened yet."

The final stanza of "Desert is the Memory of Water" strikes a sweet spiritual tone rather than one of religious dogma, promising an unselfish and humane prayer for his wife. "Waking this morning with my arms around you,/the dogs snoring, and a mourning dove cooing,/I felt I awoke in a peaceable kingdom/where the fear of death turned inside-out/into a love for life. If I prayed, I'd pray that for you."

Myers' mentor in the conversational narrative was Richard Hugo, a student of the American poet Theodore Roethke (according to the book's excellent Foreword by Mark Cox). This New England transplant created a lasting body of work—ten highly praised collections, eight books on poetry (including a portrait of Hugo), dictionaries of poetic terms, and anthologies of American poets from the 1980s and 1990s. His many awards included the prestigious National Poetry Series, selected by Nobel Laureate Seamus Heaney, who described Myer's poetry as "wise in the pretense of just fooling around."

Myers' autobiographical scenarios dramatize the daily lives we all experience, but he spices his wisdom with a self-deprecating wit. In "Unstable" he realizes "that he turned not understanding/into an art for the anonymous few throwbacks who shared/a similar malady while the movers and shakers of the world/played craps with electronic signals and facts." In "My Life" which "was never large enough even for a B-movie," he observes that during childhood, "Fate sat and watched from the empty bleachers/as surely as our shadows on the ground were having fun/parodying us." Replete with hilarious lines and clever verses, the book remains backlit by mortality. The elegies for his son lost to suicide (Jacob, 1985-2009, the book's dedicatee) are as powerful, painful, and free of sentimentality as any contemporary poem could be.

Myers took his "Calling" as teacher seriously, yet without any grandiose sense of accomplishment. "You must realize/what I keep/bringing you/are separate pieces/of the same insight.//Carrying what/I can't express/from one darkness/into another/is a trade//so simple/the tools given me/are still nailed/where the walls/have fallen in.//Each day/is an empty house/with its one word/over my mouth/like a call."

His lucid texts about poetry are effective by way of indirection. "Each day only a sliver or two of awareness/flies into my amorphous consciousness," begins "The Archer"—as close to perfection as poetic intuition can deliver us. "I sharpen my face into a third eye,/pull back everything I am,/then let go and vanish/beyond an invisible point of no return." The poem returns to these final two exquisite lines: "I've lived my whole life this way./There is no target." Jack Myers will be missed. As a Texas Poet Laureate he brought enormous wit and sagacity to that regional station. We are privileged to have this wonderful last book.

III

"Ideally, a book is the record of a mind at work," says poet Lorenzo Thomas (1944-2005) in an interview. His last book, *Dancing on Main Street* (Coffee House Press, 2004), brilliantly illustrates this and, since many of his poems are deftly ripped by satirical wit and droll humor, the book *also* records a versatile mind at play.

Dancing on Main Street demands full attention to Thomas' insight about reading at "three levels of attentiveness." He gives us a useful guide. "First, there is attention to the subject matter of a text or an utterance. Second, attention to the shape of the argument or discourse. Finally, there is attention to the entire performance."

The subjects are wide-ranging and his deepest texts integrate all poles of experience—thinking, intuition, emotion, and sensation. There are poems about love, sex, dreams, and loneliness; language games, street rants, and improvisations—from jazz and the blues to rhythm & blues, rock & roll, and hiphop.

His astute "arguments" appear in elegant forms—lyric, narrative, cinematic, polemic, and experimental. His shapely discourse can be visual, aural, or mixed media. The "entire performance" begins unfolding on the first reading of these intense pages, but the book must be reread over time in order to crack its complex code. His poems can be simultaneously personal and political and, as he said, they are more concerned with time than place. Yet they also evoke a visceral sense of place.

"South St. Blues" opens at a saunter then leaps quickly.

South St., you know, is not on any map.
There's just a bending line, a littered street.
It might even be a mental region.
So many faces, black, so occupied with pain and others,
just as painfully, a frozen blank.

"Sentiment" calls ironic attention to "Any place you have ever been" that "still responds/To the rhythm of your illusion." Places change, we change, and that has less to do with place than time—and timing. The brief "Quiet Riot" begins "I'd rather not negotiate/An understanding" and ends with "If you really have something to say/It's worth breaking out the good china/Put the damn tin cup away . . . ."

Longer poems ("Displacement," "Excitation," "Spirits You All," "Sightseeing in East Texas," "Psalm," "The Marks are Waiting," and "Dirge for Amadou Diallo") are vibrant tableaus of social history awash in challenging language. "Songs Without Shadows" ends in defiance. "I don't know what I will shout in your streets." He explores what media ignore, revealing a tension between a piercing perspective and valid sense of black outrage.

"Dangerous Doubts" begins with "The mind invents its own inadequacies/But not the power to erase illusion." The poem ends with a faint hope: "To really live means needing other people/That whatever that means love/Could conquer hate." Commenting on "Dangerous Doubts" in a brilliant expression of critical insight, Thomas calls it "a response to a society that, in the 1990s, became so completely distracted by materialism and self-delusion that even our philosophers have conspired to reify greed by calling it *desire*."

Born in Panama, Lorenzo Thomas was raised and educated in New York City. He authored significant critical works, like *Extraordinary Measures*: *Afrocentric Modernism and Twentieth-Century American Poetry* (2000), and critically acclaimed books of poems, including *Chances Are Few* (1979; reissued 2003). He was a key figure in the Black Arts Movement and directed the Cultural Enrichment Center at the University of Houston during his last 20 years.

Dancing on Main Street is not merely a candidate for review during Black History Month or National Poetry Month, but a major literary event for all our human seasons and humane attentions. Now that we have lost Lorenzo Thomas, this wonderful collection spanning two decades of fine work, establishes a fitting legacy for this remarkable man and brilliant poet.

IV

The late Leonard Randolph's *Wind Over Ashes* (Carolina Wren Press, 1982) opens a book of mysterious visitations from the real world. These poems suddenly transform into the "drunken moths," revealing an inscape, "where our fears/like ashes/turn gray/and rise as dust/and fleshlike/fall away." Randolph's open verses transmit without pretense or bloodless artifice. The surface represents direct experience "until there is nothing left but scars." Yet

> Slowly the top of the mountain
> rises out of silence,
> its snow ridges
> float in the air
> like ghostly promises.

Randolph's art strikes a natural balance between the prose of daily life and the poetry of epiphanies. The characters are personae, yet his poems become the world. The poet is at once the hunter, the deer, and the story-teller in "Kill, Die, Live"—man kills, animals die, but the poet lives to be a witness—"You see the flow of life in him/ You sense the dignity of his life,/the disorder of your own." This graceful victim ("an innocent, a stranger") is sacrificed on "the sharp dull throne of blood," and the masses find their meat "where the obedient lieutenants" are dressed as butchers, who "have committed all your murders for you." This second person is the accused hunter and butcher, but also the reader and poet.

In "Memorial" a woman gets her last wish to be buried among the bed sheets of her passion. Her sister abides by this wish, but with a twist of irony. "These sheets are filthy," she declares and washes them for "fear of dirt. And the root of dirt."

"If" begins as a discourse on alcohol that becomes a meditation on identity.

It would have been enough, after all,
to be a common drunk. (There are no
common drunks.)
Each drunk has a separate story,
something unusual. (There are no unique
stories, sober or drunk.) But, if you listen,
they do not sound the same.

This internal dialogue sees and hears itself, remaining divided. Then the persona mediates on "feeling the grain of good wood," and "knowing, at last, the grain cannot last.//The grain is wrong. As soon as the knife bites into it,/the wood will split./The past will not endure.//Grain, wood grain. Against the grain. Booze./Grain. Could have been./Could have been enough."

Randolph resolves these conflicting voices into a single voice that must accept the horizon of the ineffable. The voice emerges in "The Dream Father": "Whose voice, like light,/Breaks about the room/Of my body." Later that voice becomes a "Waking to my own voice,/Washing out, like light in a dream,/Lost, half-lost, half-life of light/In early mourning." His play on the words "morning" and "mourning" is *not* gratuitous, since it refers back to what is "half-lost" (that mourning for the wrong grain, those laundered sheets, and that loss of dignity). Another morning arrives in "The Visitation" and "he knows, at last,/what he must do."

Leonard Randolph was astutely aware of the crucial role independent presses play in our literary culture, since he directed the literature program of the National Endowment for the Arts. He was supportive of young poets and struggling publishers. Leonard Randolph did not publish a book for a long time and, when he finished his tenure at the NEA, he chose a small literary press (founded by Judy Hogan), to publish this fine selection of poems.

V

Norma Farber's unique memoir contains the most elegant nature poems ever written as an antidote to grief (with interspersed journal passages resonating as prose poetry). Published 40 years later, *Year of*

Reversible Loss (El León Literary Arts, 2012), was composed during the year after the death of husband in 1973.

Envisioning Boston's seasons through 15th floor windows, the text opens with a simple, shocking wound: "Last night you died." Next the first April poem. "Sing your name on the wind./Then I'll know which way/to follow you." For "How silent my body feels,/hush of my shoulders/upholding the weightlessness of loss." Finally the month ends with "In the vast planting under sky,/whether I watch or not,/things bloom and die, or not." Living through the stages of grief, recycling out of sequence and at will, she finds in universal rhythms an understanding of blossoming nature bound to inevitable passing.

Farber ponders the complex contradictions of death in the midst of abundant nature. In May "nature proves indifferent, whether to my reluctance or my rapture." Yet "The weight of love:/measurable/as the ponder of light." By June she observes "How much of nature happens in silence!" She attempts "To make songs of loss,/and lose it,/keeping only the music." Alas, for "Someone I knew/now knows the noise of nothing." July brings a fleeting measure of acceptance. "Knowing that I shall lose it/over and over and over/I accept the universe." Witnessing the river below, Farber realizes that "A certain hunger/wants to be kept/going to sea."

Yet nagging, painful questions persist. "Can there be loss/worn so thin/the sun shines through?" In August, Farber contemplates Rembrandt's anatomy painting in relation to the autopsy report about her husband, Dr. Sidney Farber. "Whatever you were, you are no longer. This is the message of the funerary theater."

Guilt shadows September. "A strange, subtle increase: totality, generality of losses infiltrates my private mourning. Am I already losing you still further in a more diffuse awareness? A disturbing possibility. I have been entertaining my comfortable bereavement: a suspect comfort, focusing upon my single grief. . ." But there remains a "Strange residue: how large a portion of survival/remains in mourning."

By October, Farber withdraws further inward, and "can't help praising a certain fixity. Remaining strictly in residence, I keep my faithful lookout," perceiving "travel as a pilgrimage" with "no desire to wander farther than thought itself can take me—far enough indeed."

However "When I am most filled with the magnificence of these days of my life—suddenly I am most emptied of their meaning." Then "Piercingly I recall an ecstasy shared. Implausibly, I search for a way to draw you back into my continuing time, to remember you vividly into my future."

The prose poem for November turns the multiple meanings of the verb "let"—to admit, to allow, to suffer. "Let daybreak balance on chimneys. Morning's a circus, sun a star acrobat./Let branches discount their leaf-losses, and compensate with buds." And finally: "Let metaphor help me lift your loss on board."

"So long as the rhythm of nature persists, you prevail," she writes in December, believing that "Through the intervention of images I can touch you." January changes the beloved into "dissolving shapes of clouds," and "Longing and fulfillment identical —because ecstasy has merged their outlines in a momentous embrace." February turns on the phrase "without you," as "the melody of the skies continues." March, the last month of this heartbreaking inspiration, discovers that "Now is the moment of reversal," and "What new discoveries are possible in reversal!"

Norma Farber (1909-1984)—poet, concert soprano, actor, children's novelist— authored 35 titles. *As I Was Crossing Boston Common* was a National Book Award nominee in 1975. Her poems were in the finest magazines and the "Poets of Today" anthology series.

Year of Reversible Loss stands as an original work, a seamless tapestry of the essential poetry necessary to experience deep longing and loss at the ultimate border between life and death.

Apertures of Wisdom

I

Glover Davis, Professor Emeritus at San Diego State University and author of three critically acclaimed books of poems—*Bandaging Bread* (1970), *August Fires* (1978) and *Legend* (1988)—opens *Separate Lives* (Pecan Grove, 2007) with a fitting emblem for many of his dark narratives that flash with lyrical imagery.

The opening stanza of "Illuminating Manuscripts" streaks through a brilliant declension from mythology to primitive inscription to modern science. "Like unicorn and dragon, eagle soon/may be an ornate symbol in a book./Hung from a column, wings will be a rune/whose twisted lines, though smeared with carbon, hook/light-swimming potencies in channels shook/by hand through leaves which raise a cottonwood,/first letter in a lost genetic code."

At the book's mid-point, "The Game Keeper" subtly evokes grief, beginning with a descriptive drive through countryside until reaching "the house where I once lived." He recalls vivid conversations with his cousin, gone early "from too much drink." Before the final lines, he writes, "I know internal landscapes," facing his friend's death. "At the end he lived in a blasted field, a charred house/His delicacy, his musical wit are gone/and the world is a stranger place."

Suddenly we realize the depth of the narrator's wound in the poem's closure: "I wander these woods like a game keeper, or the last scion of a ruined lord."

Toward the end of this stunning book of beautifully crafted and metered texts, we encounter a poem of healing. "Tai Chi" moves gracefully in an intuitive dance. "I have tired to move this way and be this way/but I have not lived with such singleness/of purpose, such purity of heart." The next stanzas evoke the struggle of closed eyes thinking "of nothing or one thing" until "one by one anxiety's voices fade." Then to practice breathing and stretching—"my joints behind each slow punch, block or kick." Finally the narrator moves "as though these synchronous and dreaming hands/were emblems of a self united, healed/at last, hands paddling through the tidal air,/

every move cut in the glass of a still pond."

In Davis' most recent collection, *Spring Drive* (Ash Tree Series, Tebot Bach, 2010), poet David St. John provides a useful introduction to this fine poet.

> Glover Davis is a formal master whose lyricism is coupled with a natural colloquial, conversational diction and a deceptive modesty. His poems have a poise and composure, even a kind of stateliness, rare in our contemporary poetry. Yet the urgencies of memory and the immediacies of daily life resonate in all of his work . . . . These meditations are by turns celebratory and valedictory, as he recalls passages and events from both personal and public pasts.

In dark dreams and observations of nature, which call to mind the "underworld" and the ravages of war, a sunnier side unfolds in "Wild Parrots"—a flock that "people inadvertently released," but who have "learned they could live on their own."

> Every year he sees the flock,
> larger, more obstreperous,
> scolding the cats or the dogs,
> flying north or south,
> wherever they go for the rest
> of the year when he'll forget
> them or think occasionally
> of a raucous joy he'd never
> seen before or since.
> As they rise defiantly, they
> let slip a memorized
> word or two, broken
> syllables flowing back
> over their wings into the past
> as though parrots would deprecate
> our Adamic power to fix
> things in a place with names.

St. John makes a point about the poet's awareness of language's limits: "Even as the reader is carried forward by his flawless iambic pentameter lines, across dazzling webs of his rhymes, he acknowledges that the naming he is seeking remains, as it does for all poets, at best provisional." The "Wild Parrots" fly colorfully through the validity of this observation. St. John's final insight accords the highest praise.

> Conversational eloquence is always a given in Glover Davis' poetry. Ordinary men and women are lifted by the clarity and intimacy of their observations to *something* resembling a state of grace. From the carnal meat—both animal and human—that he considers in his sequence of poems based on the paintings of Chaim Soutine to this vision of deliverance in the collection's concluding poem, "Burial Dream," Glover Davis has placed the question mark of mortality, inverted like a hook, hanging before our eyes. Maturity and experience are said to breed wisdom. You are holding a book of profound wisdoms in your hands.

II

Chase Twichell carries challenging themes in her new poems in *Horses Where the Answers Should Have Been: New and Selected Poems* (Copper Canyon, 2010). While similar themes were developed in earlier books, her recent odes on aging are flush with fresh imagery. "Mask of a Maiden" ends with a brief stanza. "I wanted words to contain consciousness,/so I was a child until I was old." There is much more to this and, as with most of her poems, one must read down the ladder and then back up. Not all final images wash back over every poem, but those that do are never merely reflexive and always reveal meditative thinking.

The last stanza of "Good-bad Zazen" reads: "How I feel age coming on me now,/fast, suddenly way too fast,/tremor in my hands typing this,/playing the keyboard like a piano,/puppet bones dancing, clickety-click./My very bones, right here in front of me!/It's a matter of life and death." The view alternates between a childlike puppet dancing with aging bones—suggesting the *second innocence* of an adult mind open to the fearless vulnerability of childlike discovery—and resonating with images of childhood that counterpoint the insights of late middle age. This alternation of imagery infuses the lines with a vital dynamism, a view at the midpoint between the free animal nature of children and the adult resignation before death (yet with hope for a "new self"). The complete text of "From a Distance" lucidly illustrates this.

Of all the selves I've invented,
the ones most fixed in memory
are the horse-child startling,
the dog-child sniffing the still-warm ashes
where the smell of food has almost been erased.
Child-mammals, clothed in dead leaves
that slip right off their shivering,
still haunting the snowy woods of dreams,
the twilit smoke of past and future lives. . .
Not ghosts, although they vanish and reappear.
Not human, for they were never born.
And all the others, their successors,
where have they all gone, my forebears,
my lineage? And where am I now,
bereft of their company? Death will come
and take me to them, and a new self will begin
to ask these questions as if for the first time.

Other poems reveal sightings of what may be these "child-mam-mals." In "Clouds and Water" Twichell writes, "Whether slumming in the ghost-lands/of memory or striving for the pure precincts/that lie before thinking, I chase an animal/I rarely see, though clearly it fre-quents the pond./Sometimes when I kneel to drink where it drank/its face looks back at me." Her "pure precincts/that lie before think-ing" are reminiscent of the intuitions of "pre-philosophy"—not to be confused with naiveté—wherein seeds of poetry germinate before the first word spills out. She points to words in the last stanza of "How Zen Ruins Poets" which are "Stripped of their thinnest selves,/words turn transparent, to windows/through which I sometimes glimpse/

what's just beyond them./There, a tiny flash—did you see it?/There it is again!"

Thought wears the emblem of language, but silent consciousness inhabits senses and intuitions beyond the realm of ideas. Twichell's image evokes this as "The little engine of thinking sputters/and dies in the great silence." ("Playgrounds of Being") Again the childlike "little engine" encompassed by an adult dying "in the great silence."

Other lines in this lovely poem relate to thinking about thinking: "Why can't the mind bear to stay/in the beauties that surround it?" She ends the poem in defiance: "Some people will say that these words/make a dull clopping. I hope they sound/like horses on the road—plainspoken." She has a gift for making the ephemeral concrete. "Things do not come in and out of being/in words. There are no words until after." ("Snakeskin") And as for the words?

"Before I knew that mind/could never marry the words/it loved/ in which it lost itself,/in which it dressed itself/in which it sang its most secret/tender and bitter hymns,/I also loved the thrill of thinking." The next stanza of "How Zen Ruins Poets" takes us toward it by way of lyricism. "I lived inside language, its many musics,/its rough, lichen-crusted stones, its hemlocks bowed in snow./Words were my altar and my school./Wherever they took me, I went,/and they came to me, winged and bearing/the beautiful twigs and litter/of life's meaning, the songs of truth."

Yet in this school or on that altar: "the question arose in me:/ *What language does the mind/speak before thinking, before thinking gives birth to words?*/I tried to write without embellishment,/to tell no lies while keeping death in mind./To write what was still unthought-about." Her italicized question hears the Dogen in "Good-bad Zaezen": "*If we're all born Buddhas,/why seek enlightenment?*"—hints that even after speech, a mind can perceive consciousness although one cannot articulate it. Immediately reality wakes up to observing animal-nature. "The dogs know. Look at them,/wrestling the ancient eternal questions,/play-crouching, mock-fighting over a stick." This follows three narrative stanzas that tell the tale: "For years I sat zazen intermittently/while reading fervently, a form of bullshit." But "Sometimes I still go swimming secretly/in the joyful garrulous river,/the delicious white water of thought,/or play on the ladders of logic,/re-asking Dogen's question. . ."

Always questioning from first language until last. In "Math Trauma" we discover horses where the answers to those questions are supposed to be written.

> Mrs. X, drunk the year we did
> multiplication and division,
> never checked our workbooks
> so no one ever saw the horses
> where the answers should have been.
> That's when I first wandered off into
> the white pastures on my own,
> with nothing but a spiky quiver of words
> and an urgent question.

Yet her most compelling questions are about consciousness itself. In "Zazen and Opium" she implies the classic question without asking directly why consciousness is interrupted by thought. "I realize, then forget, then realize that mind/is an ax that splits the one continuous moment."

Chase Twichell's clarifying poem then returns to a natural, serene image of consciousness, ending the book. "My eye goes home to the pond,/the bluestone slates I laid in the low places,/rain-shining their way to the water."

III

It has been more than two decades since Jim LaVilla-Havelin's last book of poetry appeared—the critically-acclaimed *Simon's Masterpiece* (White Pine, 1983)—a fictional narrative about a black prisoner, who "pitched as he always did, against both sides," and once "no one on either side got a hit." That powerful American narrative stands as the finest serious poem about baseball ever published.

The only poem about baseball in *Counting* (Pecan Grove, 2010) is the wry "Centerfield, New York," which jingles the town's name with the three Hall of Fame center fielders from New York City's golden era of 1950s baseball—Mickey Mantle (Yankees), Willie Mays

(Giants), and Duke Snider of the Brooklyn Dodgers. But it evolves into an elegy for the aging amateur ballplayers who might actually live in Centerfield—"not far from Cooperstown, but not so near," being his witty rejoinder on happenstance. Perhaps baseball was a first system of metaphors, which taught Pastoral Romanticism, the ethics of fair play, and the possibility of grace (beyond the obvious lessons about winning and losing, power and speed).

Counting takes a critical view of this Empire's war dead and uncounted civilians among our "enemies"—famished children, slaughtered animals—a very long list. His cleverly camouflaged list poems are an ingenious kind of counting. "Red" focuses on San Antonio's library across from the Southwest School of Art. "I work across the way, and our white stone/catching the light/looks like blushing." It ends with an uncomplicated line replete with sly literary references— "color of the wheelbarrow, balloon, riding hood, badge/and letter." In "a red leaf falls. . ." he offers a diverse mix of images until the last line unlocks all in one key word.

Counting begins with a lyric prelude called "what we can't know," revealing some of his themes—"the number of the dead/the stretch of an hour" and "what our hands do while we sleep/a lie's uncurling," and finally "how we are remembered."

We remember poets by their books, by individual lines, by original metaphors, and perhaps even by "The Limits of Metaphor"—a terrific 60-line text that begins "can vegetarians look at cows with more ease? less guilt?/look more closely?" Later it turns sharply to a scene of "a trailer crowded with brahmas to the slaughterhouse."

> the cow at the back, squashed in had turned its head
> in terror, caught, knowing what was coming
> blood on his neck from scraping against the bars
>
> we had the windows closed and the radio on so we
> would not hear its terrified bellow
>
> head turned on itself, like Guernica
>
> a bouncing, bounding, big animal's movement

across a large space
brings me out of this reverie

This heart-breaking elegy ends with a deep query about empathy.

is this the limit of metaphor
the skin itself
breathing a rhythm unlike those of us on two feet
sniffing with large nostrils for the smell of a meat-eater
and then calming

is understanding
the limit of metaphor
                    is reconciliation
is helplessness?

Counting includes exquisite explorations into the realm of language, yet always with significance ("Cracking the Metaphoric Walnut," "The Hopeless Dictionary and Three Thing," A Scholar Considers Primitivism: A Compendium," "Last Speaker" and "The Face of Translators")—plus wordy-playthings, like "drivel. . ." and "The Gloss" and "dada—disco—nnect" that are wildly witty and savagely pointed rather than pointless. This virtuoso writes insightfully in varied forms, styles, and tones on nearly anything—shoes, busses, road kill, fighter jets, lost artist-friends, moonlight, and galaxies—alas, too many fine lines to quote.

One of three poems inspired by photographs ("Into the Davis Mountains") opens with "the crack in the windshield" that keeps the poet "focused"

on the peaks beyond
it is the plumb line present between
imaginings of movie crews shooting classic
            westerns in this tame
                    west
and paranoid plots in box canyons
        of a breakaway republic.

Yet that crack "holds me/and holds me back," marking "a line that leads us forward/out of dream, out of chance/a line on a map of intention/on no map.//the world we break between our breaths/ remains whole." However life does *not* remain whole for everyone. His meditations against violence ("Strategies of Light," "Under the Cone of Silence," "The Lost Art of Empathy," and "An Interim") bring this reality home, while "A Bomber's Moon" asks

> how much light does a bomber's moon give?
> more than a crescent, as much as a harvest?
>
> enough to tell a hospital from a munitions depot
> enough to know civilians
> enough to leave a shadow of a doubt
>
> and send the mission home
> with bombs still
> in their bays

Before emigrating to Texas to become Director of the Young Artist Programs at the Southwest School of Art and Coordinator of National Poetry Month events in San Antonio, this New York poet published *Rites of Passage* (Charon Press, 1969) and *What the Diamond Does Is Hold It All In* (White Pine, 1978). *Simon's Masterpiece* was read at Joe Papp's Public Theatre in New York City and performed at the State University of New York (SUNY, Geneseo). His "Silver Nights" is included in *Diamonds Are Forever: Artists and Writers on Baseball*, a luxurious 1987 art book (Chronicle Books of San Francisco), published with the Smithsonian Institution Traveling Exhibition Service and New York State Museum of Albany.

Jim LaVilla-Havelin's chosen words float rhythmically over illuminating pages, resonate through textual bodies, connecting elegantly in our imaginations. *Counting* touches deeply as a painful elegy that lucidly observes a disappearing world.

IV

The labyrinth appears as a dynamic image in Rosemary Catacalos' stunning poetry from *Again for the First Time* (30th Anniversary edition) and *Begin Here*, a new limited edition chapbook (both from Wings in 2013).

Again for the First Time weaves the classic mythology of Catacalos' Greek heritage into the daily resonances of her Mexican ancestry. The first poem leaves childhood in "La Casa," where "All the mothers are inside,/lighting candles," down on their knees, "begging the Virgin's forgiveness/for having reeled us out/on such very weak string." Like Ariadne's string for Theseus to escape the labyrinth after slaying the Minotaur.

Communal homages follow—old Sam Katakalos, who "braved the maze of Ellis Island," Dog Man with his trusted pack, and the shadow-Boxer, "who is quite mad and remains faithful," all searching for safe passage along streets and alleyways. Later the empathetic witness confesses that "love has gone out of my seeing./Now because I have lost my way,/lost what you taught me to celebrate."

The book's second part unpacks the dangerous luggage of heartbreak, yet her mythological narrators erase any sentimentality. "Psyche To Eros" exclaims, "I must have my myths, I tell you. And my games/that I would rather call ceremonies.//Confusion is only the smallest/price we pay for so much dream./Terror only the longest.//I want to grieve if I have to.//I want to stride/alive into the widest aisle of heaven/and call out the names of all our dead/and have them answer proudly."

The lyrics dance and sing, but often bleed. From "Demeter Speaks After a Long Silence"—"Who are you, gardener?/You dig deeply into me,/into the dark home of the old/woman who is a childless worm,/an imperfect memory of grace.//The blood you bring out of me/is sweet, guileless, ready,/laid open to the sky/with amazing ease./I who have been angry for so long.//Under your hand I am again/the simplest of soils,/clean, accepting of seed,/throwing up roses that are/thornless and unashamed." The open labyrinth of healing rose petals.

Begin Here evokes a similar narrative ferment, chiseled in long, elegantly looping lines. Alluding to artists rather than to Greek myths, the title of *Begin Here* evokes a carnival maze. But this "labyrinth needs grout," declares "Double-fractured Sonnets from Subway and Ferry," offering a vocal map, but without a crucial string. "When in doubt, be calm. Shout, and be calm." The intimate "Pumpkins by the Sea" contains a refrain of lamentation ("We wander, we choose."), which suggests navigating the experiential labyrinths of memory.

In the absolutely delightful "David Talmántez on the Last Day of Second Grade," the jubilant boy escapes the school maze for a few liberating moments, while crossing out the teacher's critical red marks on his papers, crafting airplanes he sails around the barrio, proclaiming, "Yes, David, yes!"

"Memory in the Making: A Poetics"—a critique of "what some call, without irony, the American Century"—is dedicated to Lorna Dee Cervantes, who also resides "on the purple lip of the *cañon*, telling and telling, and/there's no such thing as going too near the sun." Both have been labeled by the Academic Poetry Establishment as Chicana or Latina, whereas Cervantes is Mexican-Native American and Catacalos wittily characterizes herself as "an east side Meskin Greek." Yet both poets eclipse all the stale dichotomies—major/minor, national/regional, male/female, white/*other*—by simply writing powerful poems.

Catacalos was a Visiting Scholar at Stanford's Institute for Research on Women and Gender and the executive director of San Francisco's Poetry and American Poetry Archives. For a decade she directed Gemini Ink, putting it on the national literary map. She has received Stegner, Dobie Piasano, and National Endowment for the Arts Fellowships. *Again for the First Time* won the Texas Institute of Letters Poetry Award. Her work has been published in textbooks, literary magazines and anthologies, including in *The Best American Poetry*, and translated into Spanish, Greek, and Italian. *Begin Here* honors her election as the Poet Laureate of Texas for 2013.

The labyrinth as metaphor holds its classic shape, while being as supple as the intuitive leaps throughout Rosemary Catacalos' graceful poetry.

V

Jane Hirshfield's new poems in *The Beauty* (Alfred A. Knopf, 2015) emerge as fiercely strong yet tender, drawing on supple intuition and clarifying intelligence to evoke the richness of her authentic inner life. Hirshfield sees beyond self, perceiving fresh perspectives flowing through our permeability and interconnection. Her intense alertness to the subtle music of poetry articulates the site of natural silence, becoming a flashpoint for intimate spirituality.

The Beauty contains lovely hymns for the aging body and astonishing strophes of Being. These reflections in solitude are not mere texts of aloneness and, even though personal, the poems never parade the egocentric details of some "confessional" poets. Instead, she is "Like a cello/forgiving one note as it goes,/then another."

"An hour is not a house," begins "My Eyes," and "a life is not a house . . .//Yet an hour can have shape and proportion,/four walls, a ceiling./An hour can be dropped like a glass.//Some want quiet as others want bread./Some want sleep.//My eyes went/to the window, as a cat or dog left alone does." "My Memory" turns the quotidian metaphysical. "Like the small soaps and shampoos/a traveler brings home/then won't use,/you, memory,/almost weightless/this morning inside me."

Being opens a solitary journal of fragmented perceptions, similar to the sequence "Works & Loves": "Rain fell as a glass/breaks,/something suddenly everywhere at the same time." It has charming wit: "However often I turned its pages,/I kept ending up/as the same two sentences of the book://*The being of some is: to be. Of others: to be without.*//Then I fell back asleep, in Swedish." It can be epigrammatic: "A sheep grazing is unimpressed by the mountain/but not by its flies." Or insightful: "What is the towel, what is the water,/changes,/though of we three,/only the towel can be held upside down in the sun." But it must be truthful to be convincing: "'I was once.'/Said not in self-pity or praise./This dignity we allow barn owl,/ego, oyster."

In "A Cottony Fate"—a complete meditation in three couplets— Hirshfield writes: "Long ago, someone/told me: avoid *or.*//It troubles the mind/as a held-out piece of meat disturbs a dog.//Now I too am sixty.//There was no other life." In the last poem ("Like Two Negative

Numbers Multiplied by Rain"), she approaches the conundrum of "*Yes, No, Or/*—a day, a life, slips through them,/taking off the third skin,/ taking off the fourth.//The logic of shoes becomes at last simple,/an animal question, scuffing.//Old shoes, old roads—/the questions keep being new ones./Like two negative numbers multiplied by rain/into oranges and olives."

This final equation could be a Zen koan, entirely metaphorical despite the simile, its intuitive wisdom hidden from explanation. In a PBS interview with Bill Moyers, Hirshfield says she did not write while living for three years in a Zen monastery. Many reviewers have noticed the Buddhist focus. Yet "I've always feel a slight dismay if I'm called a 'Zen' poet. I am not. I am a human poet, that's all." Neither are the poems political rants nor romanticized odes to nature, although her compassion reaches out to all, acknowledging the preciousness, uncertainty, and brevity of life.

Hirshfield's declaration of being "a human poet"—and certainly one with a distinctive voice and an honest vision—suffices. Her humanity includes self-criticism, genuine humility, and a penetrating interest in the sciences. "What did I know of your days,/your nights," she asks in "My Skeleton"—"I who held you all my life/inside my hands/and thought they were empty?" Her discreet questions, immersed in moments of inspired creation, are suspended on grace notes of memory. The questions are never answered, because metaphor remains partially hidden from explication.

Jane Hirshfield stands with the finest contemporary American poets. *The Beauty* reveals a poetics of Being that inhabits mysteries, essences, and beautiful lyrics. In previous books of prize-winning poetry, translations, and essays—we realize her works are apertures into wisdom.

Such apertures are especially evident in *Ten Windows: How Great Poems Transform the World* (Knopf, 2015). Hirshfield, a passionate advocate and resourceful explicator of poetry, evokes the "mysterious quickening [that] inhabits the depths of any good poem" in this brilliant collection that follows *Nine Gates: Entering the Mind of Poetry* (1997). Her essays ask: "How do poems—how does art—work? Under that question, inevitably, is another: How do we?" Admitting it cannot be answered, she has searched 30 years for "some sense of approaching more nearly a destination whose center cannot ever be mapped or reached."

All ten essays are probing and insightful, while several are deeply illuminating. In "Language Wakes Up in the Morning," Hirshfield discusses the etymologies of image and statement, the foundational "modes of attention and their prolific offspring," then reaches the concept of musing—"no accident, that word used to describe the ways in which thought's more fluid transformations occur." She considers the nine Muses of the arts, interprets "The Stillness of the World Before Bach" by Lars Gustafsson, and "Music's self-aware re-orderings" that "bring experience out of randomness and into the arc of shaping direction," as it is contrasted "not to silence but to 'noise'—sound that lacks structure, intention, and meaning."

Hirshfield makes a convincing case for the artist's life not being the source but the servant of a poem. In reading Czeslaw Milosz's "My Faithful Mother Tongue"—she notes that "the Polish language and the condition of exile can be read as addressing also the place of poetry itself in Milosz's life." This becomes even more apparent in the longest essay about Basho ("Seeing Through Words"). "When the space between poet and object disappears, Basho taught, the object itself can begin to be fully perceived." Basho's mature haiku are like the "fidelity of Zen is to this world and its moment-by-moment expression of things as they are," in effect, "discovering what can be known when the world is looked at with open eyes." Basho's haiku accomplish a clarity of perception, although complexities of his imagery suggest several interpretations, until one discovers the naked vision of the poem free of projections.

In "Poetry and the Hidden," Hirshfield understands how "meaning" hides in metaphor. "Mystery, secrecy, camouflage, silence, stillness, shadow, distance, opacity, withdrawal, namelessness, erasure, encryption, enigma, darkness, absence—these are the kaleidoscope names of the hidden, each carrying its particular description of something whose essence eludes describing."

"Poetry and Uncertainty" is a far-ranging discussion in the context of Keats' "Negative Capability"—that sense of doubt that does not depend on fact or reason. Hirshfield cites her translation of Izumi Shikibu's Japanese tanka from a millennium ago: "Although the wind/

blows terribly here,/moonlight/also leaks between the roof planks/of this ruined house," commenting that "poetry comes into being by the fracture of knowing and sureness—it begins not in understanding but in a willing, undefended meeting with whatever arrives."

In the "Close Reading: Windows" essay, Hirshfield examines poems that do not shift perspective and those which "have a kind of window-moment in them—they change their direction of gaze in a way that suddenly opens a broadened landscape of meaning and feeling." The explication of Emily Dickinson's deceptively simple "We grow accustomed to the dark" is one of the book's memorable highlights.

Later essays concerning surprise, transformation, and paradox in poetry are equally thoughtful, building on what has been established. While chapters stand alone as essays, the collection's effect is progressive and cumulative. Hirshfield's original excursions take no short cuts, subtly integrating image, statement, experience, and understanding into lucid, imaginative musings. Most of us were taught to find literal or logical meanings, but *Ten Windows* reveals fresh awarenesses and ways that transform consciousness. At one point she opines that "Art can be defined as beauty able to transcend the circumstances of its making."

Jane Hirshfield knows how to make poems and knows how to read them.

The Artist and the Neurotic

Just say that the report of my death has been grossly exaggerated.
—Samuel Clemens (1835-1910)

I

William Dean Howells called his friend Samuel Clemens the "Lincoln of our Literature," but also he would have been justified in calling him America's Beethoven. Beethoven's last years—when he composed his final piano sonatas and the starkly prophetic string quartets—were filled with his deepest and most enigmatic visions, producing the most purely humanistic music in western culture.

Mark Twain's last years were filled with work of the same originality, value, and concern—work that has been derided, ignored, or suppressed until Maxwell Geismar's *Mark Twain: An American Prophet* (Houghton Mifflin, 1970).

Geismar (1909-1979) covers Twain's last 25 years, from 1885 until 1910. It was during this quarter century that Twain wrote his most outrageously caustic political and social criticism, a period that has not been given full attention. It is this radical Twain who interests Geismar, not the days of Tom Sawyer and Huck Finn.

During this final period, when newspapers of the day gloomily portrayed him as being deserted by everyone, drunk, and dying, Clemens issued his famous quip to a newspaperman. Geismar establishes that the popularly accepted collapse of Twain's talent has been similarly misrepresented. This view was completely opposed by all the major critics, beginning with Van Wyck Brooks' study, *The Ordeal of Mark Twain* (1920; revised 1933), "which set the style," Geismar points out, "for the whole school of Twain criticism, which in a different Freudian form, has been revived and refurbished in the contemporary period." Geismar establishes it was Twain's "depth realization of life's pain and evil," never losing "the central source of his artistic virtue: that untouched spring of pagan, plenary and endemic innocence, that full sense of joy and pleasure in life, which sprang up even more freely in his final decades."

The Brooks study was controversial, but as Philip S. Foner writes in *Mark Twain: Social Critic* (1958): "Not all of Brooks' followers, however, accepted his thesis uncritically." Carl Van Doren regarded suspiciously "a good many details of his psychoanalyzing." Bernard DeVoto flatly rejected Brooks' view in *Mark Twain's America* (1932), questioning the "pseudo Freudian method." Brooks was often accused of humorlessness, which would be problematic for approaching Twain.

An interesting example is a funny and perfectly consistent remark by Twain that Brooks found so "*revealing*": "I came in with Halley's comet in 1935," Twain writes, "and it is coming again next year, and I expect to go out with it. It will be the greatest disappointment in my life if I don't go out with Halley's comet. The Almighty has said, no doubt: 'Now here are these two unaccountable freaks, they came in together, they must go out together.' Oh! I am looking forward to that." Brooks counted this as a precise piece of evidence revealing Twain's "malady" and that this "dualism" was a rather ungrateful aspect of personality, which others had failed to recognize. It seems that Twain's humor had gone too far, as Beethoven had gone too far in allowing the sonata form inherited from Haydn to change under his pen.

Geismar's different view is so radical that a synopsis only serves to devalue the book's enormous body of evidence. It is the kind of provocative study that sends one back to the sources—to Twain of the last period, as well as to earlier studies by Brooks, DeVoto, Charles Neider, and Justin Kaplan's popular *Mr. Clemens and Mark Twain*. Geismar objects to these critics for their outright rejection of the radical Twain. There is a chapter each on DeVoto and Neider, primarily focusing on their respective editions of Twain's *Autobiography*. Geismar is most critical of Neider, since this critic (as late as 1959) simply deleted most of Twain's biting satires, while claiming that *his* edition considered all of the later manuscripts. In fact, the Neider volume turns out to be the most streamlined edition, while DeVoto (in *Mark Twain in Eruption*, 1940) at least offered the material, even while criticizing it.

The most significant critical battle is waged against Justin Kaplan. It is Geismar's conviction the Kaplan book is flawed by employing traditional Freudianism, because its structures are too limited for such a large figure as Twain. This section is particularly significant because Geismar is not only debating Kaplan's version of Freudianism, but as a critic who used similar schemata in earlier literary studies, he is also reexamining his former self. This "battle" is central to *An American Prophet* and to its author. Geismar explains how he read Kaplan's *Mr. Clemens and Mark Twain* (1966) "with increasing reserve."

> To use, as Kaplan does, orthodox Freudianism on Twain's talent and work alike is simply to reduce all that was original, bold and best in him to some trivial personal maladjustment. The Freudian symbols have a sometimes interesting but usually minor significance. They cannot define a culture hero such as Twain; while Rank pointed out that the artist is not a cured or sublimated neurotic— but an artist.

II

Geismar's refers here to Otto Rank's pioneer work, *Art and Artist*, translated from the German by Charles Francis Atkinson (1932). Along with Adler and Jung, Rank was one of the intellectual giants in Freud's inner circle. His book on the relationship of art to the individual and society pursues a broader cultural context that had a deep influence on 20th century writers, beginning with Henry Miller and Anaïs Nin. In *Art and Artist*, Rank makes clear distinctions between the artist and the neurotic, revealing a significant distance between these two personality types, and certainly much greater distance than Freud was willing to acknowledge. Rank believes the artist, in his "continuous rebuilding or building anew," manages to create

> an autonomous inner world, so different and so much his own, that it no longer represents merely a substitute for external reality, but is something for which reality can offer in every case only a feeble substitute so that the individual must seek satisfaction and release in the creation and projection of a world of his own.

In the psychoanalyst's scheme of the average man, the neurotic, and the artist, Rank elevates the artist to "the highest creation of the integration of will and spirit." He disagrees with Freud's notion that artists are very close to neurotics, because it is the neurotic and *not* the artist who fails to resolve his conflict. This occurs because "the neurotic no matter whether productive or obstructed suffers fundamentally from the fact that he cannot or will not accept himself." The neurotic—unlike the average man who accepts what he is with a sort of dull social ease—can neither accept what he is or what he is not. Only the artist, Rank says, "by accepting his personality he not only fulfills that for which the neurotic is striving in vain (and that the average man has ceased striving for), but goes beyond it." The artist becomes who he is, evolving his idea of himself from himself and not from society.

Freud was harder on artists, even while acknowledging his large debt to art. At his 70th birthday celebration, he was introduced as the "discoverer of the unconscious." Freud corrected the speaker. "The poets and philosophers before me discovered the unconscious. What I discovered was the scientific method by which the unconscious can be studied." In Rank's view, Freud did not study the unconscious nature of the artist in depth. Instead, Freud saw all expressions of individuality as explainable as reactions to social influences or as responses of biological instincts, depriving the artist of genuine autonomy or power or initiative toward selfhood. For Freud, the artist becomes a passive reflex for forces beyond his control. Art becomes, "substitute gratification," and as such is "an illusion in contrast to reality."

Lionel Trilling's insights in "Art and Neurosis" (1945-47), an essay published in *The Liberal Imagination* (1950), was written long before Geismar took on Twain's later writings and before Geismar applied Freudian notions to American novelists. Trilling's essays are the most penetrating examinations of Freud's views in the American canon. In "Art and Neurosis," he writes:

> The reference to the artist's neurosis tells us something about the material on which the artist exercises his powers, and even something about his reasons for bringing his powers into play, but it does not tell us anything about the source of his power, it makes no causal connection between them and the neurosis. And if we look into the

matter, we see that there is in fact no causal connection between them. For, still granting that the poet is uniquely neurotic, what is surely not neurotic, what indeed suggests nothing but health, is his power of using his neuroticism. He shapes his fantasies, he gives them social form and reference.

The activity of the artist, we must remember, may be approximated by many who are themselves not artists. Thus, the expressions of many schizophrenic people have the intense appearance of creativity and an inescapable interest and significance. But they are not works of art, and although Van Gogh may have been schizophrenic he was in addition an artist. Again, as I have already suggested, it is not uncommon in our society for certain kinds of neurotic people to imitate the artist in his life and even in his ideals and ambitions. They follow the artist in everything except successful performance. It was, I think, Otto Rank who called such people half-artists and confirmed the diagnosis of the neuroticism at the same time that he differentiated them from true artists.

Nothing is so characteristic of the artist as his power of shaping his work, of subjugating his raw material, however aberrant it be from what we call normality, to the consistency of nature. It would be impossible to deny that whatever disease or mutilation the artist may suffer is an element of his production which has its effect on every part of it, but disease and mutilation are available to us all—life provides them with prodigal generosity. What marks the artist is his power to shape the material of pain we all have.

III

Otto Rank points out that "the creator-impulse as the life-impulse made to serve the individual will." Here is the key insight into the shortcomings of previous critics, whose views were psychologically outdated and politically cautious. Geismar says, "like all great writers found his opiate and his salvation and his resurrection in the creative act itself." Or, as Twain writes in a letter to Howells: "I don't mean that I am miserable; no—worse than that—indifferent. Indifferent to nearly everything but work. I like that; I enjoy it, & stick to it. I do it without purpose & without ambition; merely for the love of it." Like Beethoven who retreated to a solitary forest cabin to compose (after losing hearing), Twain dropped out of his social circles, and retreated to write some of the most lethal satire in the history of letters.

Geismar pays tribute to these radical satires, which he considers Twain's most powerful work, like "The Czar's Soliloquy" on the tyranny of conventional Christianity or the genocidal racism in "The United States of Lyncherdom." Then Twain's justified screed against "the damned human race" that we read in "To the Person Sitting in Darkness," relating the history of the German Kaiser in China, "who lost a couple of missionaries in a riot in Shantung, and in his account he made an overcharge for them. China had to pay a hundred thousand dollars apiece for them in money; twelve miles of territory containing several millions of inhabitants and worth twenty million dollars; and to build a monument, and also a Christian Church; whereas the people of China could have depended on to remember the missionaries without the help of these expensive memorials." Twain asks: "Can we afford civilization?"

In the most shocking essay, Twain condemns the United States invasion of the Philippines in the "Killing of 600 Moros," a slaughter that included the murder of every woman and child (and of course every man).

> The official report stated that the battle was fought with prodigious energy on both sides during a day and a half and ended with a complete victory for the American arms. The completeness of victory is established by this fact: that of the 600 Moros not one was left alive. The order had been, "Kill *or* capture those savages." Apparently our little army considered that the "or" left them authorized to kill or capture according to taste, and that their taste had remained what it had been for eight years in our army out there—the taste of Christian butchers.

In addition to these denunciations, we are not deprived of his satiric glances at the racist policies of President Theodore Roosevelt. While Twain was courted by the "aristocracy," he was the most outspoken critic of the nation's capitol. Twain became our first culture hero on the strength of his public personality, the humorous travel books, and later the successful novels. These are the periods we read so much about and upon which his popular career is based. But after these times, when Twain began to strafe and bomb the "wrong" targets did the critics bail out. But Geismar stays aboard to report Twain's entire mission.

Twain once lamented to his friend and initial biographer, Albert Bigelow Paine, that "I shall never be accepted seriously over my signature. People always want to laugh over what I write and are disappointed when they don't find a joke in it." This was a definite critical handicap for a writer, who was *not* joking, knowing that U.S. imperialism was no guffaw.

According to Geismar, Twain "did not have the split-personality which is commonly attributed to him."

> He had a soul both pagan and civilized, but a civilizational soul which did not repress or replace the pagan one, but lived together with it harmoniously or acridly, as it may be, but together, always fused and joined in Clemens' central artistic vision: the double awareness of its loss and rejoicing in its heritage.

Rather, Twain had "the double soul of a great artist," and the "primitive and animistic 'I' of an organism which does not even recognize its own separation from the world around it, which is that world, while being most clearly itself."

Critical Thinking in America

I

John Updike's *Odd Jobs* (Alfred A. Knopf), a 930-page collection of essays, reviews, and speeches, was published in 1991. It presents a dazzling global review of challenging texts, a set of fresh reconsiderations of established artists, and a charming confessional ("Fairly Personal"). The verbal self-portrait, painted in the opening and closing sections, holds up Updike's wide critical shelf like personal bookends and flashes its vivid colors throughout this useful sourcebook.

Updike's essays are replete with connections, examining work in the American grain—Melville, Emerson, Howells, Franklin, Edmund Wilson, E.G. White, and John Cheever. He also lends perspective to the international influence of Kafka, Tolstoy, George Bernard Shaw, Isak Dinesen, and Graham Greene. The expansive center shelf—some 90 reviews covering over 500 pages—maps a fascinating literary world and, simultaneously, charts the genesis of an open mind.

He constructs a Modernist context for fiction (Flaubert, Joyce, Proust, Mann, and Pound) and discusses Postmodern works by Borges, Beckett, García-Márquez, Nabokov, and Calvino in relation to more recent books by Mario Vargas-Llosa, Umberto Eco, Robert Pinget, Patrick Suskind, and Julian Barnes. Never pedantic or doctrinaire, his criticism reveals smooth erudition, precise knowledge of craft, a poetic sense of wonder, and an uncanny instinct for the essential in art.

Updike believes that "a work of fiction is not a statement about the world," but "an attempt to create, out of hieroglyphs imprinted by the world upon the writer's inner being, another world." This creative intensity "feels holy," and if the wonders of "another world" seem in decline, "it is because we have lost faith in the capacity of the individual to venture forth and suffer the consequences of his dreams."

Confiding that Joyce, Nabokov, and Calvino meet the standards of his critical taste, Updike questions the Postmodern "books made out of books," wondering "are they what the future holds?" In a continuous dialogue with the authors he reviews, and utilizing the resources of comparative literature, he asks insightful questions and makes pertinent observations. "Since the death of Vladimir Nabokov, no writer has been more agile than Italo Calvino—and there was something gruff and abrasive about Nabokov, something modern as it were, which the Italian postmodernist has smoothly shucked. Calvino's prose, though ingenious, is never difficult; though colorful, never opaque." In a tribute, he writes: "The sudden death of Italo Calvino, scarcely into his sixties, deprives the world of one of its few master artists, a constantly inventive and experimental writer who nevertheless brought to his work a traditional elegance, polish, and completeness of design."

Updike sees Peruvian Vargas-Llosa as taking the torch of South American literature from Columbia's García-Márquez, believing that his later work fails to match the originality of *One Hundred Years of Solitude*. Italian Umberto Eco's fiction does not measure up to the work of Jorge Luis Borges in a convincing analysis. Juxtaposing the styles of Borges and Eco, he observes the Argentine master ("the first self-consciously postmodern writer") "wrote with a poet's ear; his own blindness and reclusive habits gave his mental explorations a peculiar and inimitable resonance, an earnest sorrow and uncanny repose."

In contrast, he sees Eco in *The Name of the Rose* as "a postmodern intellectual as animated as he is intelligent, a mental extrovert whose cerebrations spill over into a number of disciplines." He judges *Foucault's Pendulum* as "a monumental performance, erudite beyond measure," but as "a tale of human adventure, it totters and sags, and seems spun-out and thin."

Pondering more recent novels by Suskind (*Perfume*) and Barnes (*Flaubert's Parrot*), Updike asks if it is sufficient for a novelist to research "an area of geography or history and then be clever and cool about it?" He points out that Joyce and Mann did their research also, but left a palpable weight of personal impulse if not confession in their constructions. Their fictions have a presence and a voice that are humbly human." In a thoughtful welter of ideas he discovers Russians Benedict Erofeev and Yelena Sergeyevna Ventsel, Albanian Ismail Kadare, Dutch novelist Harry Mulisch, Japan's Junichiro Tanizaki, and Nigeria's Buchi Emecheta.

Updike's view of North American writers is mixed but mostly critical. His tributes to the late John Cheever trace a personal rather than critical line, and contain the embarrassing disclosure that the older writer did not share Updike's enthusiasm for their friendship. In his book of letters, Cheever wrote: "Updike, whom I know to be a brilliant man, traveled with me in Russia last autumn and I would go to considerable expense and inconvenience to avoid his company . . . his work seems motivated by covetousness, exhibitionism and a stony heart."

Odd Jobs, published two decades after Cheever's chilling assessment, does not leave these impressions. While Updike displaces some covetousness toward his own creations in marginal pieces at the end of the book, he became more self-critical in later years. As for "a stony heart," Updike's portraits and his great love of literature do not seem to bear out this opinion.

The Preface makes clear that Updike expects no one to read "this collection straight through," but he has "tried to arrange is over 160 items along an encouraging curve." Following this shapely arrangement, our perceptions are sharpened in subtle ways that a random sampling would obviate.

His essays on Benjamin Franklin and Ralph Waldo Emerson are models of research and reassessment and, in fact, excellent introductions to these seminal writers. The speech ("Should Writers Gives Lectures?") turns out to be a masterful study of an author's public persona. However the prolific John Updike (1932-2009) said he preferred solitude.

Odd Jobs serves such varied food for thought that most readers will find it too rich to digest quickly. But it can be a leisurely banquet if one savors one course at a time over a long winter. We could *not* find a more serious or fascinating overview and companion of literature with whom to converse.

II

During the 1950s when the dusty academy had a death-grip on the voice of American poetry, an intense vanguard of young poets performed at the Six Gallery in San Francisco. Allen Ginsberg premiered *Howl* that first night in 1955, along with readings by Philip Whalen, Gary Snyder, Philip Lamantia, and Michael McClure. The spiritual elder of the mini-Renaissance and master of ceremonies that night was the great poet-critic-translator Kenneth Rexroth.

In his first public reading, McClure felt an unprecedented energy flowing into our culture, and his memoir, *Scratching the Beat Surface* (North Point Press, 1982), testifies to it. "In all our memories, no one had been so outspoken in poetry before. We had gone beyond the point of no return—and we were ready for it." The evening created a stir. Eventually we would know about the Beats from San Fran, despite that *Time* magazine splashed a headline like BEATNIKS OF FRISCO.

By way of William Blake, Walt Whitman, Ezra Pound, William Carlos Williams, and Charles Olson, these younger poets intended to create a new poetic consciousness and to resuscitate the body of American poetry. Ginsberg began *Howl* "in a small and intensely lucid voice. At some point Jack Kerouac began shouting '*GO*' in cadence," and as the chant ended, everyone was left "standing in wonder, or cheering and wondering, but knowing at the deepest level that a barrier had been broken, that a human voice and body had been hurled against the harsh wall of America."

That unique generation of poets—from Black Mountain to the Beats, from the New York School to the San Francisco Renaissance— drew on different sources than had the straight line of the "New Critics" (T.S. Eliot, Alan Tate, John Crowe Ransom, Robert Lowell). Breaking academic form, they invented organic shapes in Olson's *Maximus*, Kerouac's *Mexico City Blues*, Snyder's *Regarding Wave,* and in the poetry of Denise Levertov, Robert Creeley, and Robert Duncan.

"We wanted to invent it and the process of it as we went into it," writes McClure. Their poems became extensions of the body, animations of the human animal, and the flesh of intellection in expanding consciousness. McClure draws directly from biology (as Olson drew from geology), envisioning the poem as a seed, a cell, an evolution. "The new scientific vision sees life creating itself *outward* from the physical level to the macroscopic world of muscles, organs, perceptions of the sense and animal activities." The poem becomes a field of possibilities, according to McClure's lesson from Duncan, insisting "on truth without the mask of formal art—on the poem being true to itself first of all."

Scratching the Beat Surface is true to itself as a "living bio-alchemical organism," evolving out of its historical context through an interesting analysis of the "shape of energy" to the forms themselves.

In Part II, McClure evokes his aesthetic freedom in poetic prose, based on the notion that "When a man does not admit that he is an animal, he is less man than an animal." He illustrates this deftly in William Blake, as a mammal in continuous revolt, because his religion was "*being* itself." McClure is also in revolt. "A creature in revolt can conceive that there is NO solution and there will be unending construction and destruction. REVOLT perceives the continuance of action and energy from multiple sources . . . . *Revolt* perceives that life is a flow. . ."

In McClure's view there are no answers, no meaning, except for a dance of poetic light around words, and the epiphany of graceful bodies in motion. Resurrecting the naked body made the "New Critics" seem old, dusty, and out of touch. These younger poets found liberation in their exuberant voices, opening the cages of the spirit and letting all the animals go free.

In a series of dialogues (via voices of a giant panda, a herd of sea lions, a female snow leopard), McClure creates a new Romanticism of Beats dancing with the beasts. The leopard's language finds understanding in the human animal, hearing her "rage, anger, anguish, warning, pain, even humor, fury—all bound in one statement." He calls it "music-speech," which is even "more beautiful than any composition by Mozart" (although not all of us would agree).

McClure ends with a long text—"HAIL THEEE WHO PLAY!"—a dazzling dance of capital letters and exclamation marks, as a spirited expression of joy to the Muse. "I AM MY ABSTRACT ALCHEMIST OF FLESH/MADE REAL!" In statements rather than imagery, he lives the credo: "Communication was not as important to me as expression. To speak and move was the most important thing."

III

Anne Waldman—among America's most accomplished performance poets—feels uncomfortable with the term "performance poetry," maintaining that "It suggests a rehearsed entertainment," and "good poetry shouldn't need the actual voice of the poet; the voice is additional."

Waldman begins with poetry and evolves to performance, but not everything she composes is meant for the stage. "I have texts which I could not read. They are in the books of poetry." She began quietly and privately, struggling with the silent words. But she received early encouragement from Allen Ginsberg and Kenneth Koch. "In the early seventies, Allen suggested I push my voice farther. Kenneth wanted me to write longer works and develop my vibrato—he liked my vibrato!"

Waldman has read with many of the best writers in the country—Gary Snyder, William Burroughs, Ginsberg, Koch. She toured with Bob Dylan's Rolling Thunder Review during the mid-70s. Her first six books were published during that same decade. Fellow poets have celebrated her. Aram Saroyan writes that "Of all the poets of my generation, none has done more than Anne Waldman to bring poetry before the public at large." Ted Berrigan said "Ann is brave. She is experimenting as the most exciting poet of her generation."

In the 1980s Waldman moved to the forefront with *Skin Meat Bones* (Coffee House Press, 1985), and her recording of "Uh-O Plutonium" ("We'll all be glowing for a quarter of a million years!"). *Skin Meat Bones* uses three body elements as a random refrain, coming down the scale of tones with screeching skin, modulated meat, and deep-bass bones, as she recites the intervening text. These elements edge their way into wild variations and word play. This sense of immediacy and experimentation make her performances resonate with excitement.

Waldman, on stage with musicians, dancers, and actors, sees performance poetry as "a hybrid art, which can reach out to the other arts in an attempt to make them one, as they once were." She feels it possible to create both forms of poetry, and often, "a performance will lead one not usually interested in poetry at all to read the performance texts and go on to the poetry in print."

During this period Robert Peters (1924-2014) became the most influential critic of poetry in a series of books, beginning with *The Great American Poetry Bake-Off* (Scarecrow Press, 1982) and the *Black and Blue Guides* (Cherry Valley Editions, 1987). Peters projects an image of fearlessness, of being unconcerned with the reputations of the poets he reviews. He warns in his first *Bake-Off* book: "As a critic of these goings-on, I continue to see myself as a Big Bad Wolf. I am not averse to nipping the heels of the sows, boards, shoats, rams, and ewes of poetry whenever they deserve it."

But this wolf is also a comic persona, who huffs and puffs as often as he bites. Unlike Robert Bly, cited as one of his mentors, Peters will try for "a catholicity of taste, and find room for a variety of verse modes and poets." While Bly condemns the eclectic in criticism, Peters extols it. Both critics expose the false and the shallow with insight and wit, while explicating the authentic work convincingly. No recent criticism can match Bly's for leaping insights or Paul Christensen's for imagination and depth. But Peters has the widest range, a necessity for the immense diversity in our poetry. Peters expresses it this way.

> Poetry is many-faceted; and there is much aborting of original talent for the sake of sanitized deliveries. The critic must declaim against mediocrity wherever he finds it—in the National Poetry Series, the *American Poetry Review*, the Wesleyan series, and the Pulitzer, Lamont, and similar competitions, where prizes, reportedly, are awarded to the friends and protégés of former winners. Critics must shake the scented gauntlet at mindlessly revered poets who have come to write badly, or who ape their former selves.

What Peters looks for beyond all qualities is energy, displeased with "work that reports in enervated and boring fashion the interminable prosaic actions of 'I'." What he desires is brought to his criticism—energy that opens fresh dialogues of feeling and thought. His strengths are knowing how to listen, and not being afraid to speak his mind. To critical readings of texts, he brings a casual erudition, imaginative schemata, and a lively intensity. Considering that he turns out hundreds of pages each year, the quality of writing stands tall and repetitions are few. Robert Peters is an essential critic for serious readers of American poetry. His wolfish stance is literary engagement only, for he wants to be taken seriously. As a guide who leads us into the kitchen, he concocts a complex stew, stirring it deftly.

The message of Steven Ford Brown, publisher of useful editions in the American Poets Profile Series, is the rediscovery of poets of real achievement, who have been neglected or overlooked in a larger critical context. The book's heart seems to be the poetry itself—texts carefully selected, reread, assessed. *Earth That Sings* (Ford-Brown Publishers, 1985), is a collection about the work of poet Andrew Glaze (edited by William Doreski), revealing an exciting rediscovery.

Originally from Birmingham, Glaze lived in New York for 31 years, creating an idiom neither New Yorkish nor Southern. With an entirely original voice, he entered a great dialogue with the outsiders who had ignited his poetry—South American giants Neruda and Vallejo, Russian masters Mayakovsky and Mandelstam, and the classic French poets Baudelaire and Rimbaud—poets he translated in a *Masque of Surgery* (Menard Press, London, 1974).

Like Lorca in New York, Glaze goes to the streets, listens to the microcosmic cacophony, sidestepping the enormous lips of a faux Marilyn Monroe, poised "to eat/a nameless art student looking somewhere else in a timid beret." This vision of a city out of control became "Fantasy Street," viewing a traffic jam as "Stupid, enormous, brutal,/meaningless" beneath a sky "overwhelming us like a wonderful painting." Glaze blends the reality of bicycling Manhattan avenues of kitchen ducts that "snuffle over the marquees like commercial noses." This blending opens a cavern of horrors. "Why is it I am slowly encroached upon by I don't know what?/The immense trenches of something going to happen/are about to swallow me." Yet, "I go home like this every day," with heart pounding "like a riot policeman's feet, rapidly, gloomily."

"Fantasy Street" recalls Whitman, the poet Doreski calls "Glaze's most vital source," but with a comedic touch unlike the grandiose bard. His lists are more like Neruda's, to whom Whitman was also a central source, although these lists are entirely urban. Doreski comments on this. "The particulars of the urban scene, through sheer accumulation, resolve or blunt the terror and passion of the imagination."

As a venturing urban naturalist, Glaze inverts the surrealist canon—imagination terrified of itself in a world of random phenomena. "He has spent his life confronting the trash of living with the fantasy that is the hidden core of the language-act," writes Doreski of Glaze's "The Trash Dragon of Shensi." These poems reveal variations at adaptability. Even his dragon adapts, since "he is too full of old watermelon rinds/and millet straw to pay any attention/to his wings." The dragon remains as grounded as the "army of illuminated penitents," Glaze observes on Eighth Avenue.

Earth That Sings contains 40 pages of poems and 70 pages of critical matter, including a dialogue between Glaze and Ford-Brown, a personal essay by the poet on growing up in Alabama, and two perceptive critiques by younger writers (Carole Kiler and Theodore Haddin). In a fine piece by Robert Wilkinson, we learn that Glaze studied ballet (at age 43) just for the love of it. Born in 1920, Glaze describes himself as "an intellectual born in an athletic, dancer's body." His poem on Nijinsky makes clear he did *not* take himself seriously as a dancer, yet dancing lives in that poem of the body. "It signals a momentary victory before the slide back into rhythmless torpor," writes Wilkinson. "As Blake discovered, the New Jerusalem must be reached over and over in the condition of fire, and the struggle can never end." Kiler takes her clue from the urgency in Glaze's poetry: "I cannot recall any poem in which Glaze fails to exhort, challenge, unsettle, and finally heal the reader."

Except for *Damned Ugly Children* (Simon & Schuster, 1966), Glaze's subsequent collections were issued by independent imprints. That first book received wide critical acclaim from established poets—Richard Eberhart in *The New York Times*, John Ciardi, Maxine Kumin, Karl Shapiro, and even Robert Frost recommended it. The book was the subject of an essay in *The New York Review of Books* and his work appeared in *Poetry*, *The New Yorker*, *Atlantic Monthly*, and *New World Writing*. He also wrote plays, libretti, and a limited folio of poems with lithographs, but did not publish his second book of poems until *The Trash Dragon of Shensi* (Copper Beach Press, 1978).

Andrew Glaze had gone to New York with his family in 1957—partly as a career move, but also because he had written scathing articles about police brutality as a courthouse reporter for the *Birmingham Post Herald*, testifying against a deputy sheriff in defense of two innocent black men. The experiences eventually evolved into poems in *I Am the Jefferson County Courthouse* (Thunder City Press, 1981).

V

NewSouth Books of Montgomery, Alabama, publishes quality regional works of national interest with a strong emphasis on African-American history and memoirs of the civil rights movement. What is new about NewSouth, as opposed to Old Dixie's cultural segregation, has been its openness to multiculturalism, to the eloquent voices of silenced minorities, and to marginalized progressive authors.

John Beecher (1904-1980), whose radical lineage went back to Henry Ward Beecher and Harriet Beecher Stowe, was one such voice. He wrote powerful protest poems against war, injustice, and prejudice for 50 years. With a Studs Terkel forward and an introduction by Stephen Ford-Brown, *One More River To Cross: The Selected Poetry of John Beecher* (2003) represents the humane depth of his work.

Beecher was lauded by Pete Seeger, John Howard Griffin (who photographed him), and William Carlos Williams, who wrote that he "speaks for the conscience of the people," since many narratives directly concerned victims of racism. Beecher's voice is direct and uncompromising. "You ask me/what would I do if I were a Negro?/ And I keep thinking of these two/who died/one on land and one at sea/murdered.//If I were a Negro/I would swear the same oath I am swearing now/to avenge these men...//Being a Negro would change nothing/the same men would be my brothers/for brothers are not known by the color of their skins/but by what is in their hearts/backed up by their deeds/and by their lives..."

VI

In constant nightmares, Claude Eatherly saw himself on the ground after the atom bomb had fallen on Hiroshima. This vision emerged gradually, after the morning of August 6, 1945, when Eatherly had given the weather clearance signal to the crew of the "Enola Gay" to drop the first atomic bomb on Hiroshima. None of the members of that crew or Eatherly's "Straight Flush" crew experienced after-effects. The general attitude toward this event of historical devastation (including Nagasaki) was that it had been a necessary job well done. Recent historical accounts make it clear that we dropped the bombs on Japan *not* to end the war but to warn Russia of our atomic capabilities, which was poised to invade Japan at our request.

"I'd have to stretch things real far to see how he could arrive at a guilt complex. He didn't do anything but look at the weather," said Paul Tibbets, pilot of the "Enola Gay" that dropped the bomb. "His imagination would have to be pretty broad to tie himself with responsibility with all the people that were casualties." But perhaps Eatherly was the only sane person, who took on this responsibility. His post-traumatic behavior took him through a series of heavy drinking bouts, continuous job changes and attempts at passing bogus checks—and finally to the edge, spending time in jails and mental hospitals. Eatherly has been the subject of poems and books, including a collection of his letters to psychologist Günther Anders (*Burning Conscience*, 1961). Questions shifted back and forth until William Bradford Huie's popular book appeared, pretending to answer all the questions (*The Hiroshima Pilot*, 1964). Huie admonished Eatherly for his self-pity. It was Huie's book, admits Ronnie Dugger, who made him decide to finish *Dark Star: Hiroshima Reconsidered in the Life of Claude Eatherly of Lincoln Park, Texas* (World Publishing, 1967).

Dugger's reasoned yet sympathetic portrait offers an important document in the story and a statement of man's history of grotesque ability at war, and the ways in which we all become victims. "Claude's special experience was midwifing the worst abortion of moral standards in the history of war. He has taken his stand with the victims and offered himself to us, that we may examine him. Because we are afraid and fascinated, we have accepted."

Few of us have accepted so passionately as Dugger, who went farther—he and Eatherly became friends. "In the new situation, he no longer a patient, I no longer an interviewer, we were two men in a coast town. We sat in his room for long spells, talking. I feel that I can say that Claude has seen an ideal and has sought to give it voice through his experience. The fact of Hiroshima stares, children running out of the flames. . . . I can see, in the retrospect, how having given the signal that consigned them to their laceration, his feeling that others, perhaps (perhaps not!) even his mother, thought of him as a party to the slaughter of innocents."

Dark Star contains personal identification, but also clear, precise reporting. Certainly there are times these views overlap, times we cannot feel as strongly as Dugger does. But the honesty of one man looking into the heart of another—rather than an author researching hospital records and newspaper clippings—surges forth. Dugger's portrait evokes a complex Eatherly, who "lived a rootless life of dames, liquor, apartments. . . .One can see how a fellow who is so open-handed with money and enjoys being this way could become depressed if he didn't have it. Claude is not all kindness!" The matrix of events presents a crippled and confused man.

Eatherly lived Hiroshima every night. "In a dream he told me," Dugger writes, "he is flying a propeller plane, a fighter. It is in trouble, and he pours on power to lift over some highlines. . . He's about to make it, but there's some trouble somewhere; he feels it in the plane. It sputters. . . sinks. . . bumps on the street. . . rolls and tumbles, rolls and tumbles. . . he claws out and runs. . . he sees terror on his face as he is running." Ronnie Dugger has come closest to seeing Eatherly as a man, but he points out that "Respecting a person means admitting he is a mystery." Claude Eatherly (1918-1978) was that and more. There were no boundaries to his nightmares. His star remains covered by shadows.

VII

Anti-War Poetry was forced to make a "comeback" because of the unnecessary invasions in Iraq and Afghanistan but, as in all millennia, war continues despite poems written about particular atrocities or against the madness.

Even before these books about the Bush-Cheney wars, especially Iraq, both David Ray and Palmer Hall wrote powerful critiques of the Vietnam War. Ray was one of the founders of American Writers Against the Vietnam War and Hall authored *From the Periphery* (Chile Verde Press, 1994)

David Ray's *The Death of Sardanapalus* (Howling Dog Press,

2004) contains over 200 texts that are comprehensive in argumentation and varied in form, including lyrics, narratives, haiku, as well as Spanish translations by Lilvia Soto. Ray's strongest poems exhibit a restraint that intensifies their horror. "To A Child of Baghdad" discusses "smart bombs" with an innocent victim. "If you knew these bombs you would love them./We draw smiley faces on them. We keep them/spit-shined and give them pet names. . . ./And they are *smart*— that's how they found you."

The title poem, based on Delacroix's painting after Lord Byron's play, recalls the last day of Sardanapalus, who reigned as king before the fall of Ninevah in the seventh century BC. In a gory scene, the despot, "tired of holding out against a siege,/lay back upon his crimson bed/and with indifferent gaze. . ./observed the massacre/around him—all prearranged/as tribute to his greatness." He slaughtered concubines, slaves, swordsmen, and finally himself (by fire), to foil an enemy who would find little loot. The final stanza projects a billboard of Saddam, "tall and proud/in a golden chariot and spoke/of himself as the reincarnation/of ancient kings, but in texts/inscribed in clay it is not/an easy task to say which one."

Hall's anti-war poems are deeply meditative and compassionate. In "An Old Story" we "roll across Euphrates, approach/Tigris, eye the hanging gardens in/that old cradle of Mesopotamia./Eve reaches once more for the fruit/and Adam wonders, agape, watches/precision bombs. . ." Then to Baghdad, where "crossroads/of armies for ten thousand years, of/traders, conquerors, squabbling kings."

Perhaps David Ray, H. Palmer Hall, and Robert Bly, along with those who have published poems against our so-called war on terror, wish that their poems had *not* been necessary. But the perversion of language-into-propaganda and the loss of logic and truth always will be the earliest casualties of deadly conflict, especially when rationalizing a pre-emptive attack. Nonetheless keepers of the word will protest and anti-war poems will be written and read.

The media blitz that continued to whitewash the lies and gross miscalculations of a pre-emptive war and a presumptuous hand-over of a sovereignty not ours to hand over, we watched the Bush administration scurrying to deny their rationale for war, to repair gutted infrastructure, to remove evidence of torture, and to reattach puppet strings to Iraqi bureaucratic heads not yet decapitated. What has become cannon fodder for sanctimonious preaching and smirking assurances from bully pulpits volleyed across the net in Michael Moore's film *Fahrenheit 911* and in droll political cartoons from the left, would be hilarious if not unceasingly tragic.

Robert Bly takes a refreshingly different view—philosophical, poetic, critical as well as self-critical, in response to the madness in *The Insanity of Empire* (Ally Press, 2004). As one of the most effective literary voices against the Vietnam War, he became an early public critic of the Iraq War with his poem ("Call and Answer," written in August 2002 and published in *The Nation*). "Tell me why it is we don't lift our voices these days,/And cry over what is happening. Have you noticed/The plans are made for Iraq and the ice cap is melting?" Then Bly writes, "Go on, cry. What's the sense/Of being an adult and having no voice? Cry out!"

> We will have to call especially loud to reach
> Our angels, who are hard of hearing; they are hiding
> In the jugs of silence filled during our wars.
>
> Have we agreed to so many wars that we can't
> Escape from silence? If we don't lift our voices, we allow
> Others (who are ourselves) to rob the house.
>
> How come we've listened to the great criers—Neruda,
> Akhmatova, Thoreau, Frederick Douglass—and now
> We're silent as sparrows in the little bushes?
>
> Some masters say our life lasts only seven days.
> Where are we in the week? Is it Thursday yet?
> Hurry, cry now! Soon Sunday night will come.

One should not have expected the Bush Administration to appreciate the poem, since it demands that citizens take responsibility for a war perpetrated under the guise of self-serving patriotism, the symbol upon which the tea baggers and even angels fear to tread. Instead of compassion for the victims of our war and occupation, we hear paternalistic platitudes about raising a democracy from infancy, casting "Eye-rackis" into *Otherness* along with *enemy* combatants, *foreign* insurgents, and Muslim *extremists*. The effect of our silence has been to rob our own houses of the free speech and privacy we claim to be giving generously to Iraq.

When Bly wrote this poem we were "silent as sparrows in the little bushes" of homeland security, while the loud hawks soared. In earlier crises, literary voices were *not* silenced by fear. Lack of imagination prevents the merchants of endless war from understanding the masters of peace to whom Bly refers. "What did Whitman say a hundred years ago?"/'Let sympathy pass, a stranger, to other shores!'" The poem "Let Sympathy Pass," ending with the question of why we voted to lose everything.

> All for the sake of whom? Oh you know—
> That secret Being, the old rapacious soul.

But what does Bly mean by this and "the greedy soul" to which he refers often? While we tend to associate soul with ancient spirituality and ego with modern greed, it seems we demand heavenly comfort, even if violence leads to apocalypse.

> More and more I've learned to respect the power of the phrase "the greedy soul" . . . We all understand what is hinted at with that phrase. It is the purpose of the United Nations to check the greedy soul in nations. It is the purpose of police to check the greedy soul in people. We know our soul has enormous abilities in worship and intuition coming to us from a very ancient past. But the greedy part of the soul—what the Muslims call "the nafs"—also receives its energy from a very ancient past. The nafs is the covetous, desirous, shameless energy that steals food from neighboring tribes, wants what it wants, and is willing to destroy anyone who receives more good things than itself.

Bly does not stop there, which would be merely a more honest sort of piety, but goes on to include self-criticism. Of this ancient greed he admits: "In a writer, it wants praise," he says, and "I live very close to my greedy soul./When I see a book published two thousand years ago,/I check to see if my name is mentioned." No one in the current Bush administration has come close to self-criticism, except to say that the resistance to occupation in Iraq was underestimated. The intended effect was not to admit a mistake but to create greater fear, because this fiendish enemy turned out to be *even more evil* than fundamental Christians imagined.

The Insanity of Empire contains recent poems, a final commentary, and six poems from *The Light Around the Body*. The first lines of "The Executive's Death" from the earlier poems read like a precursor to "the rapacious soul" and the Bushites in a desert landscape. "Merchants have multiplied more than the stars of heaven./Half the population are like the long grasshoppers/That sleep in the bushes. . ." Even though this alludes to Vietnam, Bly's consistent response strikes as prescient.

No one agrees today, because the debate has been contextualized by extreme positions and remote controls, ignoring the substantive middle registers struggling to be heard. We were awakened by the magnitude of "the biggest mistake any American administration has ever made," which is the collision between "20th century capitalist fundamentalism and 11th century Muslim fundamentalism." The extremist shouting—a double monologue but never a dialogue—only increases confusion, destruction, and bloodlust, which neither side admits. When monotheistic cultures are controlled by madmen only a monolithic apocalypse can result. Bly's humane antidote serves as a sane cry for us to take responsibility for our complicity.

> Four times this month I have dreamt I am
> A murderer; and I am. These lines are paper boats
> Set out to float on a sea of repentance.

The Bushites would call this bleeding-heart-liberalism, since they label everything according to their self-interests. Thus occupation becomes freedom, global capitalism means equal opportunity, empire equates to democracy, and endless war leads to lasting peace. But without true self-criticism, like Robert Bly's, there will only be false self-righteousness.

VIII

Lawful Abuse: How the Century of the Child Became the Century of the Corporation (Wings, 2013) stands as an assessment of U.S. history, each chapter covering key subjects in chronology, interspersed with Robert Flynn's nakedly honest "Personal Notes," revealing the viewpoint of a thoughtful Christian focused on the human cost of political decisions. The humanitarian views of presidents—Lincoln, both Roosevelts, LBJ, Carter, and social leaders of conscience—are contrasted with presidents who enabled Wall Street and international corporations to control our economy, while eroding human rights in the name of Homeland Security.

"There has always been class warfare in America," writes novelist Flynn, "a war by the ruthless and greedy, often with the help of the government, sometimes with the help of the church, against those least able to fight back . . ." If one merely reads the historical facts, it becomes clear that some in power did come to the aid of children and women, the ill and disabled (war veterans among them), while others ignored the plight of those at risk. Flynn's chapters discuss public battles for family and workers' rights, education and health care (from hunger to early epidemics to climate change). But governmental responses have been inadequate, despite promises.

Reagan's two terms of "progress" stand as the strongest chapter. "It was the kind of America that Reagan, the Bushes, rich Republicans and the 'Religious' Right dreamed of. If the federal and state governments had been parents, they would have been guilty of child neglect, child abuse, child endangerment, and depraved indifference." Such commentary will be dismissed by some as liberal rhetoric, but the sad facts of Reagan-era of deregulation brought us the Savings and Loan bailout and the collapse of Enron, while "allowing the contras in Central America and 'freedom fighters' in Afghanistan to finance their wars through drug smuggling" fortified the enemies in the failed war on drugs. While the GOP views Reagan as a hero (and ignores the secret Bush years), Flynn does not spare criticism of the Clinton or Obama presidencies, interested only in historical realities, particularly in children's issues, for which he becomes the ultimate fact-checker.

Flynn's fiction is often witty and charming, but *Lawful Abuse* is not, and by intention. Yet some "Personal Notes"—particularly a 10-page reminiscence of growing up on a Texas farm and attending a primitive country school—are engaging. It was a hard scrabble era, but he attended university, earned advanced degrees, and taught. Flynn's acclaimed novels, *North To Yesterday* (1967), *In the House of the Lord* (1969), and *The Sounds of Rescue, the Signs of Hope* (1970), were published by Knopf, while subsequent titles appeared from university and independent presses. Flynn's life and work can be characterized as a truthful search for morals and ethics. As a sincere Christian, he does not fail to critique religious institutions.

In *The Devil Finds Work* (1976), James Baldwin writes, "Dreadful indeed it is to see a starving child, but the answer to that is not to prevent the child's arrival but to restructure the world so that the child can live in it: so that the 'vital interest' of the world becomes nothing less than the life of the child." Robert Flynn would agree.

IX

Early on Robert Jensen's cogent guide, *Arguing for Our Lives: A User's Guide to Constructive Dialog* (City Lights Books, 2013), claims that our arrogant denial of the planet's demise reveals our limits, calling for humble acknowledgment of our ignorance in attempting to understand nature's complex dynamism.

Jensen sees this as the first step toward "critical thinking"— that maligned search now absent in the contentious double monologues of current public discourse. "Critical thinking should lead us to evaluate all claims, including 'traditional values,'" Jensen points out that "The world came to abandon the traditional values that justified slavery and defined women as the property of men, and most of us agree that was a good thing. But critical thinking can not only lead to challenges to tradition but can also help us understand the strength of some of those values." While some work requires specialization, we need not "be specialists to develop viewpoints we can defend in dialog," concerning issues we gloss over with bias or avoid entirely.

Jensen establishes basic guidelines as questions to encourage critical thinking (compressed here as): What are the assumptions of a claim, are the terms defined favor a position, what is the evidence given (or unstated), and does the evidence lead logically in establishing that claim? It sounds simple, but rarely are these questions clarified. He then discusses specific issues about politics, religion, and news media in subsequent chapters, revealing that both sides of any argument are entrenched in opinions that do not meet the test of analytical dialogue.

Jensen examines paradoxes, metaphors, and aphorisms, quoting Bruce Wright's provocative remark, "The universe is an undifferentiated whole. About that we can say nothing more." Jensen comments, "the whole is more than the sum of its parts, and considerably more than the sum of the parts we can observe. The process of scientific analysis—of studying the parts to try to understand the whole—is powerful but limited . . . . Once we see the world as a living system, our attempts to know it through analysis of the parts is, by definition, always an incomplete project." Our tiny planet, not to mention the universe, "exceeds our capacity" to understand.

In "Thinking Courageously: Reframing Ourselves and Our World," Jensen makes the salient point that "Critical thinking can lead us to take risks when that thinking results in a challenge to widely held beliefs among friends, family, or community. The even greater risk in rigorous critical thinking is that we might have to abandon a position that has been central to our sense of ourselves . . ."

These are points that lay bare the all-knowing Ego, making certain that real dialogue emerges only when we are willing to be self-critical (without false modesty). He also makes it clear that "This willingness to take intellectual risks doesn't guarantee that we will come to the correct answers, but cultivating the courage to think critically even when it is unpopular with others or unsettling to ourselves is important." How easy to avoid the hard work of critiquing another's argument, when a simple dismissal will suffice; the same applies to being satisfied with our viewpoint.

Jensen makes a convincing argument against our falling back on the cliché that our failures are just human nature. "For the first 95% of our evolutionary history," we lived in manageable "societies defined by solidarity and cooperation, with high degrees of equality." Any future will be different from what we have known. "We can accept the world into which we are born, or we can accept the challenge to remake the world. Such a project requires all of us—our passion and our critical thinking, each tempered by humility. The world as we imagined it during the days of unlimited growth is not the world in which we live or ever will live."

X

Clifford Thompson's eclectic collection of personal reflections and in-depth responses to books, music, film, and art (*Love For Sale*, Autumn House, 2013) reveals clarifying perceptions about cultural complexity in a compelling voice of enthusiasm, honesty, humility, and literary balance.

Thompson's essay "A Confession About Jazz" begins: "Years ago, as a young(er) man, I struggled to define my identity as both black and American. In the end I turned to jazz, whose sound I loved, as a symbol of black Americans' inventiveness and as a basis for a sense of cultural identity. That decision both helped me to relax and launched a music-buying addiction that hasn't gone away." He accomplishes this "identity" most effectively in serious yet casual essays about listening to jazz. By evoking characterizations of jazz artists and allusions to their voices, we hear a mimetic translation into the language of feeling. His rare gift for making connections between seemingly dissimilar ideas resembles the action of metaphor.

After discussing the great jazz trumpeters—Louis Armstrong, Dizzy Gillespie, and Roy Eldridge—Thompson turns to Miles Davis, who "was the exception to the trumpet rule," because he "accomplished in spite of that"—his inability to match Gillespie's "agility or range on the trumpet"—"the complete channeling of himself into the instrument," and "his playing was beautifully, heartbreakingly mournful, to the point where he sometimes seemed to be weeping through his horn."

Thompson's complex title piece does the same in words. "Love for Sale" is a touching essay about his mother's dying, seamlessly integrated within intimate and artistic realms. It leaps from her joking with him "on her deathbed," and singing some favorite tunes, to evoking a Miles Davis version of "Love for Sale."

"Like a host, Miles—on muted trumpet—introduces the song's theme at the beginning and plays it again at the end, taking subtle, supple liberties with the bent-note wistfulness of the melody . . . Between those passages come solos by alto-sax luminary Cannonball Adderly, who had not only the sweetest sound in jazz but one of the fastest, and the tenor-sax god John Coltrane, whose signature wails are all that separate his bursts of breakneck virtuosity."

Thompson continues at "breakneck virtuosity" to discuss host Johnny Carson, then moving on to his visit with college friend Tracy "to conquer Manhattan." After various stops, they attend a jazz performance, where Thompson hears the words of "Love for Sale" sung. "I have a passing familiarity with the lyrics of some of the songs that inspired my favorite nonvocal tunes; there are others I don't know at all. And so it was not until [Niranjana] Shankar began to sing that I learned . . . the actual subject" of the song. Since this unpleasant revelation happens on his mother's birthday, he recalls having "had the damnable luck" after leaving her deathbed, "to glance through the doorway of my mother's room. The expression on her face was sadness itself, and she seemed to be looking right at me." Both lasting impressions would stay with him in this masterful and unsentimental portrait of mother and son.

Thompson's penetrating evaluations of the works of black artists are necessary—not only fresh takes on icons Ralph Ellison and James Baldwin, but illuminating assessments of younger writers Colson Whitehead, Paul Beatty, and Zadie Smith. For most of us, his essay on Rudolph Fisher, forgotten author of the Harlem Renaissance, will be a true discovery. He is equally astute in views of American cinema, from being critical of black exploitation movies to appreciating the way John Sayles depicts black characters in his films. Other essays on film, often written for *Cineaste,* discuss popular movies by observing what we may have missed, while discovering little-known films that most have not seen (but will want to see after reading).

Thompson has been an editor at various New York publishing houses for over two decades. He won a 2013 Whiting Foundation Award, and his acclaimed first novel, *Signifying Nothing*, appeared in 2009. Thompson's engaging dispatches that often evolve into brilliant essays for *The Threepenny Review, The Iowa Review,* and other fine magazines, can be read on his tellcliff.com website.

Throughout this vibrant collection Clifford Thompson examines "controversial" subjects in ways that expand our understanding and sense of communal humanity. He views the arts with critical acumen and never hides from self-criticism. *Love For Sale* peers into our cultural mirror and into his own with insight and equanimity.

Borderlands Literature

Literary historian Leticia M. Garza-Falcón articulates a critical challenge to the "Anglo American worldview of exclusion," and narcissistic myths of Manifest Destiny. *Gente Decente: A Borderlands Response to the Rhetoric of Dominance* (University of Texas Press, 1998) rescues fascinating Mejicana voices from oblivion, recovers a powerful novel by Américo Paredes, and opens a dynamic dialogue with the institutionalized echo of the dominant white male monologue.

Garza-Falcón's fresh view of inclusion synthesizes Latina/ Latino literature and criticism into a wider spectrum of thought beyond multicultural clichés, illuminating the psychological subtexts of borderland stories in cultural and historical contexts. She prefaces her inquiry with a definite purpose. "With this work I question a certain dominative history of the U.S. West and Southwest and explicate a number of literary works, hitherto little known, which challenge that history."

Among the women writers examined (precursors of the Chicano Movement's male authors) include María Christina Mena, Fermina Guerra, and Jovita González, "the last two of whom are descendants of South Texas land grantees and students of J. Frank Dobie."

The "history" against which Garza-Falcón argues is typified by the work of the late Walter Prescott Webb, author of *The Great Plains* (1932) and *The Texas Rangers* (1935), who had pervasive influence on history teachers and textbook adoption in Texas. Her study assails Webb's racist histories, which have "done their damage to American thought, particularly as regards the way 'the other' is viewed and continues to be constructed." Webb's version of how *his* West was won would elicit valid charges of racism, if published today.

Passages from *The Great Plains* will suffice to reveal this.

> What is true of the 'Indians' is in a measure true of wild animals. The Great Plains afforded their last virgin hunting grounds in America, and it was there that 'the most characteristic American animal' made it's last

stand against the advance of the white man's civilization. The Great Plains region presents also a survival of early American stock, the so-called typical American of English or Scotch or Scotch-Irish descent . . . .But once we go into the arid region of the plains, particularly the 'Southwest,' we find or did find until very recent time, the pure American stock. . . .

Webb writes that "Negroes did not move west of the ninety-eighth meridian," and "women were few; and every man was a self-appointed protector of women. . . ." He reserves his deepest hatred for the people of Mexican descent.

> Without disparagement, it may be said that there
> is a cruel streak in the Mexican nature, or so the history
> of Texas would leave one to believe. This cruelty may be
> heritage from the Spanish of the Inquisition; it may, and
> doubtless should, be attributed partly to the Indian blood .
> . . . The Mexican warrior is inferior to the Comanche and
> wholly unequal to the Texan.

These obvious prejudices that Américo Paredes exposed in the seminal scholarly work, *With His Pistol in His Hand* (UT Press, 1958), are not the primary focus of her devastating critique of Webb, who invented convenient "facts," while masking the inconvenient truth, thereby codifying his monologue. Central to Webb's myth-making resides an omnipotent narrator who sanctifies Holy Conquest and a ghostwriter who insinuates himself into the pioneering saga. Garza-Falcón lucidly summarizes the elements of Webb's stylistic schemata.

> The narrative elements and linguistic devices in
> his romanticizing rhetoric—the metaphors, euphemisms,
> adjectives, juxtapositions, quasi-poetic language, mytho-
> poetic frames, epic bard stratagems—all invite the reader's
> assent to the "truth" in a peculiar story replete with the
> images of the "rough set's" freedom gained at the expense
> and denigration of others. It is important to isolate these
> elements, for they reappear in various forms and especially
> in times of economic hardship to affirm the "rightness" of

the domination of a particular group over the "others" who make up our nation's diverse population.

Anglo American "history" flourished after the West had been colonized. The consciousness of the majority was ripe for the codification of its collective myth that persists to this day, especially in mass media debates about immigration. Her critique forms a necessary context for understanding a chorus of "polyphonic 'voices' still unheard and unrecognized."

The real heart of *Gente Decente* examines the writings of borderlands women, and none more extensively than Jovita González. A Texas-born Mejicana, a prominent folklorist and president of the Texas Folklore Society, González was one of the leaders of the bilingual education movement (spearheaded by her husband, E. E. Mirales). She was a novelist who wrote about Mexican culture in *Caballero* and *Dew on the Thorn* (published posthumously in 1996 and 1997, respectively).

Garza-Falcón's portrait of González traces the life of a complex personality, negotiating between Anglo society and the Mexican community yet identifying herself as one of the *gente decente*. But what is its meaning beyond the literal translation of "decent people"? According to the author, *gente decente* distinguishes "social rather than economic status in the life of South Texas to this day."

For González it meant a heritage of land ownership and lineage, though not necessarily financial wealth, signifying a woman was educated, cultured, proper, and chaste. Paredes characterized his student as "a young woman traveling alone, acting as an independent professional and at the same time being a traditional model of propriety," while she was researching the borderlands for a master's thesis at the University of Texas. Garza-Falcón's view differs from González's.

> Given my own South Texas and northern Mexican origin, I find her depictions of this highly stratified south Texas system suspect; they are views of someone who aspires to high-class status and 'imagines' the rich condescending to the poor . . . . I believe that rather than from claims to Spanish nobility or inherited class background, dignity in South Texas comes with more down-to earth practical concerns.

While the author admits Jovita González lived during an earlier era, witnessing "what none of us today can testify to," because no matter how "identified today's scholars of Mexican-American literature, culture, and history may be with their 'Chicanismo,' we are all inescapably products of Anglo American dominance." To whatever extent González behaved aristocratically toward the uneducated poor, she broke with her own class on equal education, advocating this enlightened attitude through her fictional characters, and decades of teaching that all Mexican-Americans could become *gente decente*.

"Her story of negotiation, the cognitive dissonance of her psychology, so evident in her writings," states Garza-Falcón, "informs even present-day views of aspiring youth in our educational institutions. The split in González's intellectual environment, her aspirations, and the climate of the times demanded that she leave her more blatant outcries against both the Anglo and the Mexican patriarchies and the elitist/racist views about 'her' people to future generations."

Exploring the border crossings of González's novels in rich detail reveals a feminist focus and a subtle awareness. Garza-Falcón's central theme of awakening the cultural unconscious to fresh aspects of our nation's narrative (through the fictional perspectives of the silenced) adds texture to the plain, depth to the linear line, and coloration to the white noise of historiography. Through these narratives of *otherness*, we begin to hear the emerging chorus of genuine diversity.

Garza-Falcón turns to other early Mejicanas, explicating a clever short story by María Christina Mena and historical sketches of ranch life on the border by Fermina Guerra. These writers also came from a Mexican elite who knew the Anglo elite, but the author contends that this "picturing of their worlds, from their however privileged perspectives, provides and more complex picture which illuminates the dialectics of today's Chicano/a struggles."

Mena was born in Mexico City to wealthy parents and was sent to New York as a teenager when the Mexican Revolution erupted. Her first stories were published when she was just 20, becoming the only woman of Mexican descent to have fiction in the leading literary magazines during the 1910s-20s. Her witty satire ("The Education of Popo") tells of an encounter between Popo Arriola and Alicia Cherry, a blue-eyed blonde, who appears younger and more innocent than she actually is. In fact, Alicia is a 25-year-old divorcée on a trip with her rich parents as guests of the aristocratic Arriolas of Mexico City, and her flirtation with the love-struck boy is an exercise in vanity that ends when her ex-husband appears on the scene. The story reads like sophisticated fluff on the surface, but it carries the subtle irony and critical bite of Dorothy Parker's early social satires.

Fermina Guerra's "Rancho Buena Vista, Its Way of Life and Traditions" was her master's thesis at the University of Texas, where she studied with J. Frank Dobie a decade after González. "But unlike Dobie's quaint paternalistic portrayal of the Mexican's," writes Garza-Falcón, "Guerra's stories record the hard work and struggles of her people, which can be seen as a parallel to those of Webb's pioneering settlers." But Guerra "does not romanticize or mystify the story of her people," making "the lives and struggles of women just as important as those of men."

Garza-Falcón's impassioned reading of Américo Paredes' great historical novel, *George Washington Gómez* (completed in 1940, published in 1990 by Arte Público Press), evokes his radical spirit of protest, resistance, and solidarity. This "Mexicotexan Novel" concerns the complex lives of real people in the Rio Grande Valley and it is not merely a precursor to the Chicano movement, as Garza-Falcón points out. In fact, it stands as the most edifying and truthful novel ever written about the borderlands. The conclusion to her 41-page chapter on Paredes follows.

> Both Webb and Paredes draw from living memory for the strength and uniqueness with which they infuse their historical narratives. While Webb's history is imbued with romantic, literary features, Paredes's narrative is definitely marked with the very spirit of struggle and survival that Webb attributes to his pioneers. Webb's simplistic hero/villain story is countered by Paredes's resistant stance on multiple layers against the dominant word of a tainted history for the benefit of a dominant society. Along the lines of property, labor, education, gender, and class struggles. Américo Paredes recovers through the narrative the banished history of a decent people. He thus provides

a powerful response to the rhetoric of dominance which continues to inspire present-day writers.

Gente Decente fast-forwards in the final chapters to the works of contemporary Chicanas, a reality-check for the way Mexicans are perceived in the media and in historical textbooks. In the harrowing stories by María Viramontes, the misperceived actions of two elderly female immigrants prove violent reactions from their neighbors, who cannot square such "alien" behavior with the media's "falsely unified view" that they have internalized as reality.

The short stories of Beatriz de la Garza concern the effects of displacement upon women who must take on leadership roles. One story is about a Mexican-American soldier who returns to Austin, Texas as a hero to his family, but without fanfare in that segregated society. "The Kid from the Alamo" features a boy, who "had learned to outsmart the system at an early age by claiming an important ancestor with his own last name, in order to make a point in the face of bigotry."

Garza-Falcón ends her critical work with an engaging epilogue of growing up in South Texas, as one of the few "who managed to squeeze through the window of opportunity before the Nixon and Reagan eras closed off what had finally become available during the Johnson years."

This courageous scholar has drawn on her own experiences and the untapped literary and cultural sources of the borderlands to offer an expanded view of the past, which enlightens our present. It is crucial to an understanding of the borderlands that her study *not* be dismissed, as most of the literature it illuminates has been.

Leticia M. Garza-Falcón's significant academic inquiry must *not* be ignored like the profound issues she clarifies so often tend to be.

In Search of Meaning

All is familiar, everything is strange.
—Elroy Bode

Like earlier books by Elroy Bode, *In A Special Light* (Trinity University Press, 2006), evokes a tactile sense of place in Texas and a poetic sense of awe in nature. "To see with new eyes is to look around," he writes, "and where another might see a familiar morning, you are astonished to see creation itself emblazoned on the air."

Best known for vintage vignettes that ponder wilderness and small withering towns, ordinary people and daily mysteries, Bode has been glibly characterized as a nature writer and a minimalist. Most pieces are brief, yet they are layered with significance beyond their vivid settings.

The first 18 texts, set in and around El Paso (Part I), provide examples of this depth. In "Upper Valley Night" the daylight consciousness of trees is contrasted with their immersion in darkness.

> I stood beneath them, and it was as if they had somehow taken on more weight—as if they had undergone a metamorphosis, had lost their bright, leafy daytime simplicity and had been joined with brooding nighttime forces, belonged now to another world. It was as if imperceptibly, after the sun went down, the placid elms and cottonwoods and sycamores shed their familiar daytime identities as stolid harmless givers of shade and were now their looming after-dark selves: not hostile, not threatening, just more mysterious, more secretive and profound.

Here we encounter Bode's most pervasive theme of questioning the unknowable. In "Rhythms" he recognizes the peaceful "essentials" in a barnyard scene, yet feels "a vacancy, an expectation, a curious longing" rather than completion. In "Essence" a leaf does not reveal its "meaning" after "attempting to read in the neat, symmetrical shape a clue that would let me penetrate, somehow, nature's invisible hieroglyphics."

An illustration of his philosophical theme emerges on a walking meditation "in a place of timeless desert air" at 106 degrees. The "nagging need for answers welled up again. It was against common sense, but I had never given up on the idea that one day I could simply stop, be still, and know the world . . ." He searches for "the Authentic Place and the Authentic Moment" in the "heat-hazed clouds that rose in godly fashion above the horizon" and in "the sky overhead, pure and blue and impersonal—but there were no epiphanies there, no messages, and no voice from a Burning Bush . . ."

We leave these recent solitary mediations on desert environs (lyrics very near to prose poetry), moving to a different era and focus in Part II. Bode writes of teaching experiences in a dozen pieces. The longest—"Requiem for a WASP School," which won the Stanley Walker Award for journalism from the Texas Institute of Letters (1970), stands as one view of the shifting demographics and circumstances that changed an all-white high school into a social experiment in diversity for Latino students. There are other pieces concerning his peaceful resistance against the conservative bigotry of colleagues that festered during the 1960s and 1970s. Yet he felt "at home" in El Paso's Austin High School, where he taught English and creative writing for most of his 48 years in the classroom. The freshest pieces are not journalistic, but charming object lessons about the strategies he utilized for stimulating the imaginations of creative writing students, experimenting with thematic challenges, music, and humor (in one instance, inviting students to adopt clever pseudonyms, which turned out to be the most liberating exercise).

Part III contains 40 pages selected from his journals—including some brilliant takes on observation and perception, of meditating on a cosmos of atoms, and of tracking imagination in the writing process. These solitary reflections are expressed with clarity and humility, admitting that he views the mystery of existence with "the compulsive desire of the observer to observe" and with "a certain temperament that responds strongly, continuously, to the aesthetics of the earth."

Bode's witty definition of style "is simply the shape a writer's personality takes after he has been forced to twist about, here and there, trying to find the most comfortable position in which to survive." He believes that his "whole purpose in writing" from the very first "has been not merely to describe but to see through experience, to present it, always, as phenomenon, and then have words become the thing itself rather than words about it."

Bode quotes Albert Camus' regal statement that could stand as an epigraph for the entire book: "A man's work is nothing but this slow trek to rediscover, through the detours of art," wrote the French Noble Laureate, "those two or three great and simple images in whose presence his heart first opened."

In Part IV, *Central Texas*, Bode returns to childhood images about his parents in Kerrville, where his father owned a feed store, and to the ranch of his grandparents. Among these 33 pieces are a half dozen intimate essays, revealing vulnerable and tender moments. "Home town, 1943" and "Home at Sundown" are nostalgic memoirs of a disappearing small-town-world, of growing up in "a place of unspectacular and satisfying contentments." Instead of listening to country music on jukeboxes or radios, he tuned in Stan Kenton and other swing orchestras of the 1940's Big Band Era, when popular music was an art form. He recalls that Duke Ellington's "creations were so new to my small-town ears that they seemed like exotic calls from a rain forest. The singers sounded like instruments; the instruments sounded like voices." Perhaps through these musical innovations, he began to discover the true originality of his own voice, which "cannot stop focusing on the ordinary and the everyday because the ordinary is the essence of life's mysteriousness."

When Bode explores primal experiences—from a brush with death based on a medical misdiagnosis to the tragic loss of his son—these tropes of grief are not for readers in search of easy emotions. The final work ("Looking for Byron") tells the heartbreaking story of his 30-year-old son, Byron Bode, who suffered from a bi-polar condition that led to cocaine addiction. After the author and family spent a frustrating six-month search, the young man's body was discovered in his pickup truck hidden at the back portion of the family ranch. The autopsy indicated that Byron had committed suicide within weeks of his disappearance. Bode's loss "is so profound I cannot process experience anymore . . . and I have lost the sense of who I am."

"A writer must lift a thing out of the steaming jungle of experience and place it on the high, dry plateau of art," he writes, and the extraordinary pieces collected here illuminate this creative transformation.

Bode's tenth book, *El Paso Days* (Wings, 2013), which he characterizes as a "journal of thoughts, scenes, happenings" although "not a record of a specific year but a kind of recent generic year," may also be his final book. "It will be obvious to a reader," says the Preface, "that these pages are occasional offerings of a person with a rather bleak state of mind; mainly a series of personal moanings and groanings dealing with the end-of-things interspersed from time to time with presentations of certain beauties and delights and daily satisfactions of the here-and-now." Fair enough, since we find a balance throughout his journal between "the end of things" and "certain beauties and delights" discoverable in lovely homages to nature, wonderful memories of family (especially of his mother as avid reader), and succinct remarks on writing. The book opens with a cosmic view and a touch of humor.

> Today the Earth is, as usual, solidly in place: meaning, revolving in air in the middle of nowhere.
> My life on Earth is equally solidly in place: meaning, suspended for a while between my origin out of nowhere as a dot-sized sperm-and-egg and my end into nowhere as a decaying mass of flesh.
> So it goes in the life of a sentient being.
> But despite it all—the uncertainties, the unknowns— what a remarkable interlude it is, this strange human sojourn. . . . We just keep moving about in our daily routines, accepting as normal—as ordinary—the infinite and incomprehensible orchestrations of the natural world.

This award-winning writer, now in his 80s, faces what we must all face. "It should be so simple—to do what I have never done: accept my own mortality." Yet it is not just *his* mortality but the suicide of son Byron that makes acceptance so difficult. Bode laments that "I would like to be the Dad of a Boy again," offering this simple, tender scene that can no longer be his.

> I saw such a dad, with his boy, in an aisle at

Albertson's last night. A smiling boy, 13 or so, in a Packers' jacket, he pushed a shopping cart and listened with genuine attention to what his dad was saying. . . . At 6:45 on a Tuesday night the boy was at his dad's side, attentive to what the tall man with the loose shock of hair was saying about an experience of his in Nicaragua.

They walked on down the aisle, comfortable with each other, the boy slightly behind, still listening closely, the man half-turned, his head lowered toward his son, almost touching the boy's shoulder as he kept on with his tale of military intrigue. Other customers passed by, maneuvering their carts around them. The boy and his dad walked on, isolated within their father-son space.

Bode tries to recapture that "father-son space" in a final piece (ADDENDUM: "Looking for Byron: The Complete Account"), and in this heart-breaking passage.

I still try to reach him as I drive country roads. Sometimes I stop and get out of my car and yell out to the sky, "Byron, where are you?" It is still hard to accept that he is gone. I carried him around on my shoulders across the living room when he was a child. He stood beside me at night on a lighted pier at Port Aransas and we looked together into the dark waters of the Gulf. We fished. We went camping. He sat beside me in the car, and each year that he grew older we were still father and son.

But now there is no son; there is no father of a son. Father, son—such words are meaningless.

His death cancelled out much that was me, and the house of my life sits on a bedrock of bleakness.

Often we turn to books for meaning, but in Bode's journal we discover an ongoing argument against meaning. "Traditions give people meaning, making them feel comfortable in a world *without* meaning," but he finds none in traditions.

Many people believe that the Bible contains the Word of God. I find that impossible to accept. . . . For the Word I go to the Earth itself—that constant, visible testament to the beauties and truths of creation—and to me it is better than any Bible, any organized religion. I go where there can be no human distortion, where the wonders of the world are constantly on display. . . I am able to read them in their awesome original script.

Since there was never meaning for Bode in traditions—even before the loss of Byron—was there *ever* meaning? "I think my despair is just the flipside of my passion for life—the inverted other half." But that "despair is really a wild cry into the silence of the universe, protesting the loss of all that is good and remarkable and beautiful."

Teaching held a central place in Bode's life for decades, and he admits to missing it. "There was a kind of glory in teaching nine months of every year—seeing them come in, semester after semester for 30-plus years, all of them, those sons and daughters from the modest homes of central El Paso. . . . Could there be a better place to spend one's time and energy. . . ." A longer passage recounts the experience.

> The teaching years: They won't let me alone. To be there again, in room 169, at Austin High, would be a *life* for me once more, bringing words and ideas into the room and helping to give significance to those words and ideas so that the 15-16-17-year-olds . . . just kids of the neighborhood who might never have cared for books, would find a significance in them in that room. . . . I had brought books into their lives for a while, those sons and daughters who came from houses and apartments near Austin High and went through the motions of signing up for yet another English class because they had to: There was no other choice if they wanted to graduate. But as they filed into the room with their notebooks and pens they found the larger world waiting for them: a world created and sustained by words.

Bode's disclaimer ends this nostalgic reminiscence. "But such a classroom is probably not possible anymore. . . . My age, the old one, has been superseded by the current fascinations to be found on a screen, not a page." Yet in counterpoint to this disclaimer, he later writes that "I believed in teaching. I believed in writing. Those two." Are these beliefs gone now? "I don't teach anymore, and I don't really write anymore. Instead I look out the window frequently. I take walks. I drink coffee. And I read—oh, I read like a monster. But that's not work. Reading is Taking In. I need Giving Out." Teaching was a "giving out," but those chapters are finished. Yet writing remains at hand for a working writer. "I have always needed work. I am a worker. I thrive on having work to do that I believe in doing."

If teaching had *not* conferred meaning, perhaps writing did. "I do not believe I would have lasted this long if I had not begun writing words on paper. I had nowhere else to go except the page. Words were my salvation. They recorded the passage of my life: In essence, words *were* my life." In one passage he reveals his secret aesthetic. "Write as if you are simply describing the ordinary things of life to someone who has never seen them: how a day is, what the streets look like. That's the key: getting the everyday down on paper—but in such a way that the writing has the specialness and the timelessness of life itself." But how to make the commonplace radiate for those who have not encountered it?

In another entry, Bode claims to be unable to follow this advice: "I cannot create any of what I see, and I have no words that will do the scene justice. I am inadequate for the job of reporting on paradise. All I can do is stand and look, paralyzed with awe." In yet another strophe, he declares that "I am alone, museless. I simply wander around, fascinated by the sights of the already created world and wanting to put down words commensurate with its wonders."

Among several other paradoxical notes on writing, these two stand out.

> I don't want to *describe*—write *about*—the natural world. I want to capture it precisely and place it on the page as it actually is in reality and I don't want my words to get in the way. Over the years I have stubbornly tried to make words do the impossible and recreate a scene in its "perfect state." Occasionally, though, I have accepted the fact that nature is beyond the reach of words.

Yet there is this passage.

> It is strange: Sometimes I will make half-hearted, uninspired notes—pretty much just a straight description of a few observed things: notes lacking point, focus, grace. . . . But once they are *down*—actually there on white paper—they begin to perk up with a kind of unexpected significance. The mere fact that they exist, these barest wiggles of life—that they are now tangible instead of unrealized, unthought—makes them begin to hint at the specialness of the moment I first had in mind.
>
> Such notes are like organisms of a culture in a petri dish which, with time, with nurturing can perhaps grow into proper shape—can gain their weight and meaning.

On one hand "nature is beyond the reach of words" but on the other Bode suspects that *some* of his notes "can gain their weight and meaning." He asserts that "Sometimes I think a few of my unfinished, fragmented bits and pieces cut closer to the bone than the more polished ones. They give the jagged edge of essence." These contradictions create a deeper paradox because Bode observes ongoing existence with a double focus.

> In every ordinary, daily act—cutting an apple in half, closing the refrigerator door, answering the phone—we are in the middle of life. We will never be *more* in the middle. If we do not know this, if we ignore the importance of the passing moment, we are lost. . . .
>
> Life is in every unheralded space. Every bit of it is at our elbow—our constant, patient companion even as we scan beyond it for signs of Drama, some astounding *aurora borealis* that will illumine us, overwhelm us, make us glow with rich significance.

Elsewhere Bode concludes that "Humans and the natural world are in parallel universes." Yet he keeps confronting what most ignore, and such observations have been the staple of his autobiographical prose. He carries this same double focus into his backyard, sitting with wife Phoebe, observing their cats and turtles interacting with natural visitors, especially birds. These vignettes become a resonant microcosm of nature during all the seasons. When not at home or driving in the country, he is a walking paradox in the city. "I was in a bad way. A really bad way."

> I walked it, this mood; took it onto the neighbor-hood streets on this late, cold, Sunday afternoon with the wind making it colder. I had on a wool cap, jacket, overcoat.
>
> Hands in my pockets, I moved along the sidewalks. The Sunday cars kept passing in their Sunday isolation. I kept walking. . . .
>
> I picked up half a dozen of the acorns, put them in the pocket of my overcoat, then took one out and looked at it. What a remarkable, pleasing thing it was, this single acorn, smooth and symmetrical, taken from the scattered hundreds: its light-brown middle fading to tan fading to white at the top, with its nipple point at the other end: an acorn as its own completed universe, just one among the many identical to it, all of them destined to rot on the ground or be crushed beneath the wheels of the pediatric patients' wheels: wonderful little unnoticed beauties.

Life hidden in the perfection of an acorn! Vintage Bode. He is not the first to reveal such naturalness. He credits several authors with having done so. But the horde of humanity that moves about without noticing fuels his disappointment and despair. Simultaneously Bode insists that "I long ago understood that I was not a *Me*, a special some-one, but an Everyman. In all I have written I have tried to show that my concerns, no matter how personal, were not about me but about any human alive on the Earth."

Readers may find this contradictory also, for not *only* does Bode record what others overlook, he claims to be like everyone else. How can one be both Author and Everyman? When writers are self-criti-cal, realizing that we are all humbled by life and death, there must be a way to reconcile what seems contradictory on the surface with what remains inherently paradoxical. Or even *absurd*—a word he does *not* use—although hinting at it. "I have long had a sense of the 'greater context' that surrounds our lives, that makes everything we do seem vaguely unsubstantial, incomplete, unreal. Thus reality has never quite been real enough. Something is always missing."

What is missing is *meaning*—and *meaninglessness* is at the root of the absurd.

> It is, of course, the riddle of existence that haunts me, that blurs reality, that casts the shadow of mortality over each given moment: For what can be comfortably solid and real if it is always in the process of dying, gradually disappearing?

Other notes inscribe his double focus in world-weary laments. "I do not know where to stand. I have no center, no equilibrium, no balance. I have one foot beside the pomegranate bush in the backyard and the other in a galaxy." He believes in "human greatness but it is meaningless to the universe." Without common traditions, without teaching, and perhaps even without writing, he faces his son's premature death and his own mortality with a sense of meaninglessness.

> I have enjoyed the world around me; I have been highly responsive to it. But I have not enjoyed just being me.
>
> I must be *in relation to*. I can't just *be* as, say, children can; I must *do*. Simply existing—having the world flow in to me without my "flowing back," giving back, responding—is not enough.
>
> As I get older, as I edge toward becoming less and less of whoever or whatever I have been—as I get less productive—my sense of self-esteem grows less and less.
>
> I don't look forward to the days when I just *am*.

That time of just being himself—now without work—arrives in *El Paso Days*. "I am an ant; I thrive on industry; I lack the butterfly's philosophic grace," he writes, but simple wonder and lucid awareness dart like a butterfly in these pages.

> I happen to look down at my hand. It is a fortunate glance.

As I look at it—this suddenly focused-on part of my body—I think, "This hand of mine: I have not created a single cell of it—not a wrinkle or callus or shiny nail or knuckle or vein. It, and the rest of me—every bone and organ and sinew—is wrapped inside a skin called Me, and it is not of my doing. I have made no part of the Me that is sitting in this chair."

It is a freeing kind of experience.

Hereafter I will have my hand *handy* just to glance at from time to time—a constant reminder of the moment in the chair when I realized, once again, that my hand, my life—all of me—is a gift.

This "gift" of the hand and that "fortunate glance" are the essence of Bode's perceptions. While many may not share his world-weariness and disconnection, it is difficult *not* to appreciate his sense of awe, and clarifying images of the commonplace afloat in the mysteries he writes about. He finds that "Mysteries occur in hidden places." Walking in the valley beside the Gila River in New Mexico, he discovers "a perfect place" (as he eats an apple, while waiting out a rainstorm).

After a while the rain passes on, and I stand outside my car watching the junipers drip and smelling the wet fields. The sky has turned a wintry gray, and a cool aftermath remains. The hawk still sits in his tree.

Standing there, I have no answers to any of my basic questions. All I know is that I am very lucky. I continue to have the land in my life—to walk on, to be next to. The Gila is not an answer, but it is the next best thing.

As long as Bode is alive—despite both bitter and tender losses—he will view existence with a double vision that sees humanity adrift in the inexplicable universe, and a writer searching for meaning in it. Bode's search in this journal of wise bones ("Words have carried the weight of my life; they are the bones of it.") connects us with the heart and tributaries of our own search. He expresses his prose writing poetics in this direct way: "A writer must give the ordinary, the everyday a good shake—to get rid of the dust that has settled on them—then set down on the page again the ordinary and everyday, so that they now seem to a reader to be something fresh and unique, deserving of close attention, even curiosity and wonder."

Elroy Bode's search creates "curiosity and wonder," good signs that he remains on watch for such moments. For others the search itself *is* the meaning, and readers will find their own meaning in this heart-rending book.

Foreign and Domestic

H. Palmer Hall (1942-2013), editor and publisher of Pecan Grove Press, left an impressive legacy of books from that independent imprint, as well as ten books of his prose and poetry. In this posthumous collection of powerful, beautiful elegies, we have "Hall's last book of poetry, as he conceived it," wrote editor Luis A. Cortez.

And so now we come to it . . . (Pecan Grove, 2013) enters with a remarkable *Preface*, in which Hall talks about the decades of chemotherapy he endured in order to stay alive. He reflects on Albert Camus' essay, "The Myth of Sisyphus" (*Myth of Sisyphus*, Knopf, 1955). "In the very first sentence, Camus asserts (and then defends) the notion that "There is but one truly serious philosophical problem, and that is suicide." Neither Camus nor Hall took their own lives. Camus (1913-1960) died as a passenger in an auto accident, and Hall succumbed to cancer.

Looking back at a few of Hall's earlier books, the poems in *Foreign and Domestic* (Turning Point, 2009) are divided into two sections. The foreign focus is on war's madness (specifically Vietnam), and the domestic explorations offer remarkably varied subjects. Throughout the book Hall reveals tenderness toward individuals, mixed with disgust for "all that puffing display of destruction" abroad and violent behavior at home, illuminating the deepest humane response one can evoke. In his well-balanced book, foreign and domestic are not so different after all.

"I have been dreaming lately in Vietnamese," begins "To Wake Again," listening to "the people around me speak quickly, tones rising/ and falling./I listen slowly, still remember all//the words, recall their special meanings: death, old wounds./I learned them with Whitman in wards in the old Armory. . ." The allusion to the bard, tending the wounded strikes a chord in Hall's peaceful psyche, since the wars he writes about (Iraq, Afghanistan, Vietnam) were *also* civil wars as countrymen killed each other.

In a lament about the wall of the 58,000 dead ("Not All the Names Are There"), Hall wonders: "They say the Wall brings healing, peace,/understanding. They never mention rage./I knew I should not write about the wall.//A boy named Bao lay dying on a hill,/his body burned with napalm, his death my call./I know not all the names are there." He taught English to Vietnamese children, learning from them about grace.

"A Sonnet for Napalm"—what an idea, writing of a 20th century weapon in a 13th century form—presents a dialogue between a woman, pointing to napalm on a TV screen, then asking the soldier, "Do any flowers look like that?" The narrator cannot answer but remembers "one space of time, dark green/turned to some color it had never meant to be and the smell/of the morning changed to nothing anyone could love,/a smell of heat and decay and green things turning gray."

War is not Hall's only subject. The section also includes two heart-wrenching elegies about his father, who was lost at sea in 1963. It was not during a war, and it was "no trip to find and kill a mythic whale." His family needed money, so his father substituted for a sick seaman on a tanker that disappeared without a trace.

The next section brings "Big Thicket Requiem"—an elegy for James Byrd, Jr., the African-American who was tied to a pickup and dragged to death by white racists near Jasper, Texas, in 1998. The narrative embeds this horrific tragedy of "dragging terror" within a timeless evocation of the Big Thicket where Hall was born.

"Suburban Blues" sets a contemporary urban scene about being robbed and stabbed in a parking lot. The criminal was caught that night and all goods were reclaimed, but the serenity of "quiet walks on moonlit streets, sitting silent on front law chairs on calm purple nights. . . not searching in the dark" were lost.

Yet other realms are rediscovered, including a charming love poem to his wife Susan. "Camping Out at Fifty" begins "uncomfortably, hot and forced,/knees rubbing against rocks and dirt, mosquitoes biting, the possibility of ants." Then all transforms. "I saw your face,/hair mussed, wild, the arch of your back,/Orion framing you and a thousand stars,//Pine trees standing stiff and tall, the wind/and sweat made my body cool, discomfort vanished/and all I knew was you and the night."

Essentially a narrative poet, Hall tells personal stories, sets scenes and characters in deft sharp strokes, composing on the poetic side of the border from prose. His themes are not always deadly serious and he ends with light-hearted poems. In "Last Night" he enjoys "a cheap cigar" and the "smoke keeps/mosquitoes, my wife and/all other beasts away." Reading love lyrics, he savors the quiet until frogs, "croaking in delight/over the evening rut" and an opossum running across the patio, divert his attention. "Amorous frogs and/skittering possums. They know/before I do. Large rain drops//land on an apt image" and "blot a key letter."

Hall's poems about war rank with the best written by an American and the same is true of his essays about Vietnam in *Coming To Terms* (Plain View Press, 2007). Vietnam and the Big Thicket of Texas are worlds apart, but he has been a careful observer and astute scribe of both places. The 30 personal essays in this collection are chronologically sequenced, read like a memoir, beginning in and returning to the Big Thicket in southeast Texas. Even before he became a poet, he remembers rowing a boat alone at age seven. "Poetry is like this for me much of the time," he writes. "I am alone in a large body of water and I put the oars in the locks and pull the water past me," perceiving "that single moment of awareness" when "pushing yourself and your words out there into water so deep that a single wave can drown you."

The next ten essays touch upon growing up, including a charming portrait of his parents ("Dancing in the Thicket") and an embarrassing tale of becoming a Baptist ("Washed in the Blood"). He confesses to being "an insufferable little prig, snotty and devout at the same time. I was, in short, a true believer and, paradoxically, proud of it." He traces his growth beyond the limitations of East Texas rural culture, gradually withdrawing from religion, honing speech, graduating university, and becoming an English teacher and a librarian. Hall writes a quietly conversational prose with insight and self-criticism. He extols the natural wonders of the Big Thicket, while criticizing clear-cutting loggers, deftly characterizing the charm of small Texas towns while admonishing their racism.

After these early years there are 40 pages about Vietnam. He got a draft notice after he quit teaching high school and before he got a student deferment for graduate school at the University of Texas. Hall could have "gotten out, but what the hell, I figured it was fate and I was so apolitical I don't recall even having thought of Vietnam at that time." But once he had served a year's tour—as a linguist who spoke Vietnamese but rarely left a large military installation—he began to publish essays and poems about Vietnam. Later he was involved with veterans groups protesting that war. What distinguishes these essays are his honesty and humility about interacting with Vietnamese civilians, especially the wounded children. There are also humorous takes about his own part in the war. "The whole time I am in Vietnam, we are mortared only three times. I get a small scratch on one of my toes, and that's it. I don't report it, don't want a Purple Heart for a tiny cut on my big toe."

The final third of *Coming To Terms* features of variety of essays on relationships with women, getting married, and raising a family. "Driving Through Milwaukee" is a fascinating dreamscape about a city he never visited. Two others—"Coming to Terms with Dad" and "A True Story about an Old Woman and Poetry"—are the most lyrical pieces. Throughout *Coming To Terms* are sentences and paragraphs paralleling the immediate text with thematic anecdotes, flashbacks, and reprised details from earlier essays—all weaving threads from the past into the present and providing a sense of an evolving continuum. The book also embeds excellent poems in appropriate contexts, as the poet tells his remarkable story in splendid prose.

But Hall's story is incomplete without this truthful last book. "Elegy 26" begins with an essential contradiction: "This poem is not about Vietnam or war./It is not about the Central Highlands:/ that place where three countries touch/and where blood spilled over a small hill/and nothing lived save through chance." Hall was naïve when he enlisted as a soldier, but the experience awakened him to the suffering of those who died (especially the Vietnamese children he knew).

Near the edge of unbelievable violence, the poet emerges. "This is a poem about love in a time/when love could no longer bloom,/ about affection and what we might call/grace in a time when grace had fled. . . .//This poem contains lotus blossoms/and tigers in dense jungles and elephants/and mountains and streams without end/and villages and paddies filled with water/and two people embracing behind bamboo. . ." Love during war despite always living near death.

This poem is about soft passion
In the midst of drenching rains, small fires
And empty houses. It contains no free fire
Zones or carpet bombing. Only, sometimes,
A hint of passing currents, of raw nothing.

In a beautiful country decimated by bombing and the death of innocent children, H. Palmer Hall was transformed into the sensitive, truthful writer he became.

Human Conditions

Paul Christensen earns high praise as a Charles Olson scholar (*Call Him Ishmael*, UT Press, 1979), as a chronicler of Late Post Modernism (*Minding the Underworld*, Black Sparrow Press, 1991), and as an essayist of lucid insights and sweeping cultural metaphors. Emigrating 30 years ago from Philadelphia with a doctorate in English to teach at Texas A&M, he held the outsider's perspective in *West of the American Dream: An Encounter With Texas* (Texas A&M Press, 2001) and in his memoir of Provence, *Strangers in Paradise* (Wings, 2007). The term "academic critic" applied to his work would be tantamount to calling a crow a large blackbird.

Christensen's poetic voice in *The Mottled Air* (Panther Creek Press, 2008) reveals world-weariness, penetrating "The Crow's Brain" where "There is no exile, only blackness." Despite immense sophistication, his poems are *not* obviously experimental, and he rarely plays with language or visual form. The long sentence has been his template from the beginning, wandering from the left margin, standardized in syntax, grammar, and punctuation. However these masterful prose lines nest hidden images, lush lyrics, and epiphanies nurtured by an earthier, politically radical irony. The internal innovations are subtle reshapings of a wounded psyche and their content creates its own logic of thematics, continuity, and form. There are no easy modes, no stylistic topologies, no sequences of fragments. Each text seeks its own intuitive aesthetic, evoking a surprisingly fresh mood from a series of conflicting ones, while often shifting tone abruptly from poem to poem and even from stanza to stanza.

The book begins with "The Mottled Air of April," which is a perfect illustration of his poetics. Eliot's cruelest month becomes Christensen's smudged image of a lost rite of spring, and also a declaration of its break from Eliot's conservative politics. The first line is direct, "The sun is a pulse on my arms." Change immediately threatens by "parting the gloom with jags of cobalt/heaving with that dark body of light." Inward turbulence comes under "swirling currents/ blowing in clouds from the Gulf" storms to the end of a long sentence until "I read my thoughts in what I see."

Suddenly his voice is "gasping for air/out of that mire of wronged emotions/grabbing hold of a slippery post/tilting in the waters of your sympathy." From sun through storm to sympathy, yet the turned page offers a final strophe. "I'm better now; compromised but better." How far the cloud-shifting, mood-changing voice travels! Can we trust it? Listen to an epiphany of the *I* at the calm eye of storm.

> I sit out when it's not too hot, on
> the white chair of a yard strewn with
> dandelions and fists of weeds, accepting
> what I am. I see myself in that ever shifting
> sky above me, going almost dark and
> then, wrenched by the corkscrew air
> of coming rain, burst into light again.

What can follow after metaphysical drama and metaphorical weather? Only a menu for "Dining At Midnight" that has "no taste on the tongue," but opens its mouth to ask unanswerable questions of naked immediacy.

> The dark is edible, a meal
> of shadows and memory.
> What soul is not famished?
> What spirit can withstand
> the ache of a vanished sound,
> or smell, a door slamming forever?

From that final "burst into light"—a dark questioning regresses to a "childhood bed, stuffed with dreaming/floats in the dark under-world . . . /points its battered face toward oblivion," ending with

> Invisible nurture, coming to the mouth
> as words, no taste on the tongue.
> A closed eye, long, uneven breath
> and we are done.

"Invisible nurture" in the primal scene "as words" of a tasteless meal feed to a poetics of consciousness. All becomes one journey, not always seamless, yet mapped. "Imaginary Travels Through Arizona" illuminates a challenge to lingering shadows, where "the lights are on in the pueblo," and "the red earth glows/and drains its starlight/from the hills/the path of the sun/is lit by what vanishes." Here the "bodies stir, giving up/old fathers and the arms/that held them/when they fell/out of the named places/into the unnamed." Yet the narrator has more to say.

> something must emerge
> with the waking, a flowering
> of amulets and tokens
> spells cast by the breath of gods
> carried into light
> as if the world were heaven

This ends *without* closure, sounding a new variation ("Rites of Spring"), which returns to childhood, earthiness, and "all things fertile," reprising the tone of "the waters of your sympathy" in "The Mottled Air of April."

Reading this carefully composed book becomes a process of discovery. Each poem attempts to be *the one poem*, but pours over its margins into another. "Summer Opera at the Cincinnati Zoo" introduces animals, totemic and real. Initially a comic relief, it slides a bolt on "a caged wilderness" as animals "rage at being/dragged from paradise to this iron ghetto/where humans mocked their rank despair."

"Eating in the Woods" turns toward pastoral, this time with animal prints. The narrator's "eyes have an eagle's/look of anger, and hope." It ends with "the sap of darkness running/over speech into the heart." Three later meditations on nature continue "a muttering/ribbon of water tracing the parched landscape,/like a thought roaming among a heap/of syllables, never to be spoken."

Following "Meditation at Lick Creek" and "Road Kill," he lands on the outskirts of Manila in "The Whores"—an off-key variation, except as political critique of women imprisoned and treated as animals. Visiting a grocery store "Late One Tuesday Night," the narrator finds no real food and riffs on William Carlos Williams, asking "Who will comfort us when the pure,/unblemished products of America/ drive us crazy?"

"After Love" returns to dreams, lamenting, "Once, you thought I was something/brighter than heaven," ending with a signature of love, "thinking of you, thinking of nothing else." The first movement turns everything into a text of awareness, then slips away on a night note of relief.

The undesignated second movement locates this voice in Texas places, beginning with an expansive discourse on "Big Bend National Park":

> That monstrous theater of eternity lies in ruins
> where the road wanders, climbing out of
> a gorge carved by Jurassic rages
> to catch its breath in this Homeric underworld.

But here the fluidly articulate voice turns mute, while the mind stares at sheer cliffs and vanished seas since "nothing explains the roar, the warfare. . . of this land shaped by an angry god" where dry wind "weathers our lips into stark silence."

From this unimaginable geological edifice lies the ledge of "A Family History"—equally unimaginable, yet demanding comment. The poem features a feared father finally laid to rest beside a loving mother, a mentor-brother done in by war, a surviving brother, and the narrator, who "were a family once, gathered under the dining room light to eat in silence." Muteness before Nature and silent before nurture.

"In the Dark Room"—a purposeful exile of a photographer spying negatives that "hang like scrolls on the drying line" in an "underworld" that reveals not only a father with "his impotent emotions," but a son distant enough to include him "among the shadows/I have captured and drained of blood."

The deepest passions leave one empty when they are absent, when absence becomes grief in "A Poem Without Blackbirds" that ends

And then it passes. We are strangers
under love, hardly speaking the same
language. My desires are like a foreign
city in which you fear to lose yourself,
so many dark, twisting alleys where
love would lead you, and leave you.

Loss will not rhyme with *win* or *find* and, several pages later, this dichotomy of being led and left reappears in the metaphorical windows of "Marriage"—in one summer flowers and in the other leafless stalks of winter. Between these nests a loving poem of marriage ("Admiring Your Hands"), which traces a scar's accidental history toward the wisdom of a cicatrix.

A scar on your hand
tells me the soul
of the tree that died
entered you.
Its branches rise
and follow the veins
of your tender skin.

May I kiss the place?
I smell soap, I smell
labor and love, humble
ways of living.
The hand is as light
as a leaf, and the scar
now blue, now silver
against the fan
of small blue veins
is a landscape of gods.

This is the miniature
Navajo sand map
of the soul's aspiring.
A tree on a broad plain

with blue leaves
and the mellow sun rising
in the glow of your skin,
the fruitfulness of your hands
that have broken beans
and kneaded dough, and stirred
and offered, and accepted

this cicatrix as the bud
accepts the rose.

Christensen's other poems about Texas landscapes are among the most cerebral, evocative poems written about this vast, varied place. They work as correlatives to the interior mindscape and the world-weary tone. But they also represent slides of a decaying America, our battered biosphere and the poet's own aging, all set against the quest to uncover hidden beauty in the things and spirits of the earth.

In the most stunning poems, Christensen re-invents the wheel as a dynamic image of simultaneous change, continuity, and decay. While both a cartoon of progress and a crude symbol of human invention today, before that "A wagon wheel is the mandala/of parched ground," declares the first line of "The Wheel" that "It turned once under the groans/of a wagon loaded with grain/bound for the rutted hills of Eden.//It broke against the silence/and was pulled from use, given/to the weather." Now the wooden wheel "concedes roundness/to the leveling earth, and slides/gracefully under the vines/like a word forgotten among/old languages."

While the poems do not experiment with language-as-plaything, they suggest metaphorical equivalents. Everything becomes a page of text, a continuing invention projected on reality, imposing a linguistic stamp upon the natural world. The poetry's originality emerges from the psychological tension between poles: conscious culture against unconscious nature; the cold father as functionary-destroyer lying next to the warm mother as mystic-creator; artificial academic structure smothering poetic freedom. These dynamics operate everywhere at once.

Christensen poems re-awaken the experience of creation while re-creating the experience of awakening, as in "Night Journey"—

> If you are quiet
> and unprepared, left
> at the border of the wild
> and the human,
> the mild dark of forest
> will begin to speak in small rivulets
> of air. You will feel
> the breath of the ground
> lifting you, and the whole
> tilting forest of wind create
> a body around you.

Once again the world has uttered its words "in small rivulets/of air," inscribing a sub-text that struggles to endure. "Inside every pain is an Eden/pooled like glitter/waiting to be found." "The Mist Over Lake Somerville" ends with an egret "in a crook of cypress," becoming "a soul/caught in the clutches of the flesh, white and unused." If egret and soul are one vision, where are we? "I'm out there somewhere, wandering around" begins "A Prayer" in response. "I can hear my own/footsteps coming through the wall," establishing a false division between inside and outside.

> I am sealed behind the landscape,
> in a corner of daylight where nothing
> is possible. Soul-like and silent
> as time, I wait, leaning on the shadow
> of God, which has built up a pillow of
> grit and dust in the mind. This is the
> stranger who lurks in me, whom I reach
> out to like a desperate child, begging
> to be answered by this prayer.

Split by loneliness, he wants an answer to this conundrum of self.

What you offer you give
to yourself. But you knew that. You knew
all along this was the word aching to
touch your tongue, to ride the nerves
out of your own darkness into love.

Does loving a woman remain impossible without healing the fracture in the self? Three poems cast about in "darkness" for an answer. "One Fine Morning in Saigon" returns in memory to a first marriage and "A Difficult Woman" confronts a present marriage. As "answers" to deep philosophical questions, they will not pass careful scrutiny. But such mid-life questions must be asked by this poet, who painfully evokes a naked process of change that we shall experience *if* we face our own aging.

"The Mechanics of Freezing" suggests longing for a new love.

At a certain point
of afternoon, you look up
and your body is silver
you are no longer young
the glass jar is filled
with an indefinable fragrance
of time, and wind, and memories
with your face in it, smiling back
from a great distance
forgiving what you are

This first stanza forgives the self with a smile—not a smile of rationalization in a mirrored close-up, but "from a great distance" sealed in a glass jar, recognizing the embarrassment of taking the self-pitying ego too seriously. We do not suddenly heal, but stop to contemplate reality beyond the self: "sit a while, think of a meaning/ to all this magic/in the world,/the power of change itself."

In "Above the Weissensee at Obernaggl"—the narrator sees "Past all the problems, all the doubts," and his exasperated voice exclaims.

You wonder what the shouting was about.
Why you couldn't just forgive and
go on, instead of crashing uphill
into whip-crack branches, the webs
veiling your eyesight, the heart
sobbing aloud in your twisted thoughts.

Because these poems feel truthful, the world-weary self-mockery risks judgment in quest of a new poetics. However, under this frozen lake of cynicism—or at least skepticism—swims a cagey Romantic who bumps against a philosophical cliché or strains to forge the mysterious into psychoanalytic or literary theory. These impurities are conscious developments of his sensibility, aspects that validly could be considered weaknesses. They *are* weaknesses when the lines are *not* diving toward the depths or breaking through the skin of thin ice. "Believe in something," the poem concludes, "in this blue length beside you,/this curving affectionate/word filling an old glacial scar." After this sense of acceptance, the reader might expect the last pieces to be songs of celebration, perhaps an uplifting *coda* of light from the darker movements. Not so, because the text has been designed as one flowing commentary, neither relinquishing its complexity nor erasing that "enemy" doubt. Instead of ending it continues, wave upon wave, always wary of an undetected undertow.

In "The Wave" we return to the womb of western literature—not to Greece or France or Texas *per se*, but to myth—where "The old gods fall, new ones make/passage to their place." This attempt—beyond Pound's "make it new" and the impossible "tradition of the new" that Modernism spawned—remakes a mottled mosaic of classical allusion and existential confession, of sexual desire and romantic loss, of our political bloodletting and environmental blunder.

Christensen's latest poetry, *The Human Condition* (Wings, 2011), traverses new paths from Texas to France to Beirut. These walking meditations, mapped by political insight and literary élan, are metaphors for the internal directions we must choose.

"Beyond the Horizon" opens with "The mountains are always near me now./The path is faint, lit by a cloud-draped moon.//I carry nothing with me. I go as I am,/in my sandals and shorts, my short-sleeved shirt.//All my life I wanted to be safe, to dress/for the cold, to protect my feet at night.//Now that I'm free to wander, roads mean nothing." The narrator moves beyond the past to a higher elevation, observing "the future jumbled/in a haze of drifting stars" as "I disappear into the hill's power,/whose silence drowns my chattering soul.// Here at last is the clearing I have wanted,/where the body dissolves into air/and everything lifts into flight." The soul's metaphorical flight? The final couplet evokes our human condition, "Beyond, lies the dim boundary of reality,/and over it, like a waterfall, pours the world."

The deceptively simple sentence has been his template in five books, including Violet Crown Award winners *The Mottled Air* and *Blue Alleys* (Stone River Press, 2001). *The Human Condition* was nominated for the Texas Institute of Letters poetry award. These poems witness a decaying America, a shattered biosphere, the insanity of war, and aging—all set against the quest to discover beauty in our natural world.

In "By the Sea of Everything" he writes tenderly about marriage.

> Our sleep is a journey to oblivion.
> Even a dream is a paper boat.
>
> When we are old and sitting
> in a corner of the room, too tired
> to rise to close the window,
> the wind will remind us we are still in flight.

Nothing could be simpler than a "paper boat"—but what a lucid image for a dream! Conversely, the powerful anti-war poems uncover our ugliness, especially a masterful text on a returning soldier encountering in fantasy an innocent Iraqi woman he murdered in a rage ("The Dogs of War"). Christensen never served in combat, but these violent narratives are devastating, and utterly believable.

Christensen brings a fresh perception to the aging conditions of the human, and we were fortunate to have had his guidance when he lived in Texas for a quarter century. Now he shares time in Vermont and Provence with family, while writing astonishing short stories (recently published in *Antioch Review* and *Agni*). He has been the most eminent "Man of Letters" ever in Texas, and the first literary artist to excel as poet, novelist, short story writer, essayist, and literary critic; as editor of the Charles Olson-Edward Dahlberg letters; as publisher of Cedarshouse Press books; as a professor of literature and creative writing (also authoring guides about writing); and as a radio interviewer and video commentator on the arts. Last but not least, he has also provided some remarkable photographs for book covers.

Known internationally as a literary critic, Paul Christensen's powerful books of poems have been published *only* by independent imprints. Yet a reading of his original poetry establishes him as among the finest poets of his generation.

Archaeology of Inspiration

Bryce Milligan's remarkable *Alms For Oblivion: A Poem in Seven Parts* (Aark Arts, London, 2003), an inspired book about poetic inspiration, explores the lovely—and terrible—realm of the Muses. This long and very rich poem weaves its dynamic inter-connectedness in variations, counter measures, and surprises integrated into a unified thematic whole, illuminating a tale of creative pilgrimage.

Always there is danger when writing poems about poetry for the poet to become merely self-referential, but Milligan avoids this trap by examining the main modes of inspiration (religious, spiritual, scientific, artistic), while questioning the nature of imagination itself. His first of many Muses "arrives as a dim rumbling/at the back of the mind, like distant lightning across the llano . . ."

> She returns long after the old memories
> have weathered, years and years after
> the nights within nights that defined pain,
> only to redefine it, reshape it yet again,
> recalling all for me now in a scrawl
> I could always decipher as easily as my own.

In the beginning we encounter an unnamed "She" or the Muse as generic symbol for inspiration. She also represents the author's *anima* of remembrance, dictating her scrawl to be deciphered "as easily as my own." But in the next stanza, Milligan suggests a counter-discourse to this mythos.

> There is no objective truth but
> mathematics, which relies
> upon observation which relies
> upon perception which is ultimately
> human, and to be human is to err.

Then what does the poet believe in, the subjectivity of inspiration or the objective truth of mathematics? Or perhaps we are approaching a different truth, for this stanza ends with a conundrum: "Perception. Seeming. Neither." Perplexed by the operation of imagination upon which the fictive scrawl and the mathematical cipher seem to depend, what does the poet envision?

Milligan envisions a scene in the following stanza, holding the creative urges in a unique balance.

> a man at a desk in a laboratory
> lost in the maze of his own making,
> drawing illusory lines that cannot curve without
> growing shorter, composing songs subtle
> as the calculus before him yet disconnected
> from his calculations, reconnected to the voices
> that speak to him the seductive eloquence
> of reduction: the monster at the center
> will not ignore the logical thread,
> reducing the many fears to the one.

This maps a labyrinthine underworld—the poet as creator, instrument, and text, disconnecting and reconnecting, composing subtle songs while hearing seductive voices, calculating the passage into reductionism—all characterized as the paradox of the creative process. Or so it seems.

Then in the second part a new possibility for the source of art emerges beyond the romantic voices of muses, the finite equations of math, or the labyrinth of the psyche—a deity of the monotheistic male variety.

> We have seen Him, walking in terse
> magnificence among his mountains
> numbering his sheep on an abacus,
> racking a new calculus to account
> for the numbers beyond infinity.

But this part pauses "at the crossroads/of time and the timeless," closing with an advanced shorthand that suggests further openings:

"All is perception. Constructed illusion. Both. Neither." There are allusions and bold turns of discourse in these two parts, but the remaining sections unfold as a rich, lyric scroll.

We encounter provocative thinkers and esoteric muses in the rich contexts of a pilgrimage. These textured tapestries resonate with lush metaphors and stunning images, going back millennia, as the journey proceeds toward the "idol at this crossroads" where the sensual, intellectual, and spiritual meet. These intersections of the horizontal and the vertical, of time and eternity, bear no sign, no direction, no way up or down. What do we encounter? Muses or gods, utopia or void, relativity or transcendence at "the unsuspected moment/where ages merge, the basic forces/coexist, interlock and/all becomes one"?

This crossing marks the site of the poem, a unity of form and content, embracing his Muse as "the singer within the song."

> Her stylus, like her single kiss, carves
> my sorrow into eternity, shapes
> truth in clay, vitrifies the moment with fire,
> and cast the shards into time's wallet:
> alms for oblivion.

Milligan lifts his title from Shakespeare's *Troilus and Cressida*. "Time hath, my lord, a wallet at his back wherein he puts alms for oblivion." The quest does not end here, assiduously exploring deeper layers of awareness. His many sources, familiar and obscure, will challenge readers, although he wears this erudition lightly, providing a useful glossary. He dedicates the book to Enheduanna, the Akkadian priestess who lived in 2300 BC, noting that she was the first poet known by name, as well as the first to use the "I" in poetry. Who was *her* muse? Inanna, the Sumerian goddess of planet Venus, the first identified celestial muse. These and other delightful discoveries can be mined in this archeology of inspiration and its sources.

Milligan's meditations are as subtle and sophisticated as any poetry published in America, and *Alms for Oblivion* charts a fresh way toward the development of extended poetic forms. Literary critic Paul Christensen declared *Alms for Oblivion*: "An important poem," that "breaks new ground for the contemporary long poem," comparing it favorably to T.S. Eliot's longer poems. *Alms* was originally published in a limited, exquisite hand-bound design with art by Jim Harter and Kathy Vargas.

In *Lost and Certain of It* (Ark Arts, 2005), Milligan *seems* to wander into different subjects, yet when these poems are *not* about poets (the late Jane Kenyon, Joy Harjoy, or a young Latina poet), they concern creators (bluesman Mance Lipscomb and painter Georgia O'Keefe), and the unnamed muses of his poems and songs.

In most of these texts we experience the play of *Either/Or/And*.

"Metaphor" opens with: "I need a metaphor that will transform/ this skeleton of passion into some/thing that breathes fire rather than the still air/of considered conundrums, into some/thing that stands of its own accord against/time and these chill unseasonable winds." Placing "thing" to begin two lines ("this/thing/of/thing/time") can be *no* accident. Mind tosses soul into abyss. "I need a shape-shifting incantation/to turn the shaman's cape into the shape/of the panther it contained, to take in/whole the one mind, the one soul that brought forth/the transforming morpheme, that piece of sound/that like some particle born of theory//remains unfound, unseen, but whose effects/ attend all the invisible powers,/that force all our hours into vectors, pointing to new futures rather than past/cycles."

The abyss of time, if one believes in past and future in the present—but what is this "thing" unnamed? "I need a metaphor to change,/I need a metaphor, a master rune,/a word, a sign unspoken since time/was set in motion. *Deus erat verbum.*/I need to warp this, our reality,/to be the body that bends your body,/to create the pulsar, the double star./I need a metaphor to change, to change." A metaphor of the metaphor for writing itself—shape-shifting, transforming, time disappearing, lost and certain of it? Except for the lovely image of the shaman's cape and the panther hidden in it, this continues the discursive conundrums of *Alms for Oblivion*.

"Between one crack and another," a poem as extended metaphor, presents a deceptively simple narrative of climbing and possible fall (in writing a poem).

> On this rock face, as on every other
> there is a fine line, almost indecipherable

lying between courage and madness.
You discover it between one hand hold
and the next, between one loop of rope
and another, and you find it alone.

Faith in finger strength, in the assurance
of internal balance when all that matters
is down, faith in the ability of a foot
to test through leather and steel
the stability of a two-inch ledge, itself
a product of ice and sunlight,

faith in these is suddenly one with one's
faith in the ability to fly, to free fall
in full control, as if will alone could turn
splayed fingers into wing tips guiding
your hawk-body's slow descent, tying
time into Gordian conundrums.

Alone in this December rain, I watch
a sidewalk of bobbing umbrellas,
stare at the fine line between ascent
and free fall, fit my fingers into one crack
then another, sensing the difference
between talon and wing tip.

Again the dichotomies of fine lines between one crack and
another, of courage and madness, of one hand and the next, of ascent
and free fall, of talon and wing tip—all harmonized in the hawk
symbol sailing beyond the Gordian knot by faith in "internal balance"
(even in the way stanzas are balanced). Three breaks the dichotomy
of four and achieves the new balance of *Either/Or/And*. Another
false dichotomy arises in this collection—between poem and song—
five songs are at the back and 14 (including these) appear with his
essay, "Hum Them as You Will: Notes from a Texas Troubadour" in
Langdon Review of the Arts in Texas in 2007.

Reading the excellent lyrics in the context of his claim that "I am in my own mind a better songwriter than anything else," one discerns achievement in the poems, as well as in the "curious hybrid artform" of song.

> To my mind, there is little difference in the creative processes that produce my poems and my songs, except that songs are much more tolerant of what contemporary poets and critics would deem topical and cultural clichés. To me, the craft is far more important than topic, genre, or motive—it is the making that matters, and specifically the quality of the making—the craft. Literature and writing are a great part of my life, but they are not everything. Creativity and craft are the crucial elements, especially as they concern the idea of "making." Not much that is good in life just happens by accident. One makes a family, makes a song or poem, makes a book, makes a guitar, makes a garden, one even makes an old house continue to keep out the rain. This is why writers do not retire—to stop making is to stop living. . . . the heat of the fire depends upon the quality of the fuel. And here I leave the words to defend themselves. . . .

His earlier books of poems, *Working the Stone* (Wings Press, 1993, before he took over the imprint from Joanie Whitebird in 1995), *Litany Sung at Hell's Gate* (M&A Editions, 1990), and *Daysleepers* (Corona Press, 1984)—were praised by Donald Hall, John Gardner, John Nichols, Daisy Alden, and Edward Hirsch, James Hoggard, and Dave Oliphant among others.

Unlike Bryce Milligan's award-winning novels for young adults and children, the major Latina anthologies he edited for Riverhead and Penguin, and his awards as a editor/publisher, book designer, reviewer/essayist, and songwriter, this beautifully crafted poetry has yet to attain the national readership it deserves.

Spiritual Empathy

The selected poems from 1980 to 2008 in Naomi Shihab Nye's *Tender Spot*, published in the "World Poets" series by Bloodaxe Books, touch many tender spots. Whether singing a lullaby for a child or praising wise elders or visiting far-flung places and imagined destinations, Nye feels at home with all peaceful beings.

As a Palestinian-American, Naomi Shihab Nye does *not* speak for the voiceless "Arabs" in *Tender Spot*, any more than John Howard Griffin spoke for segregated African-Americans in *Black Like Me*. She is a reluctant activist, just as Griffin was. Their narratives map the reality of oppression, illuminating authentic idioms of pain at the human level. Today we call such people human rights activists. Yet the universal principles of prejudice *never* change, even as bad actors rehearse indefensible rationalizations endlessly.

Since her earliest published work, Nye has composed elegies and homages for people around the world, as well as her lyrics of daily life at home. Yet her domestic poems are never domesticated and the travel poems are never foreign. The false dichotomies of domestic or foreign, of high or low culture, of evil guerilla terrorism versus benign state terrorism—all claiming intrinsic differences between Self and *Other*—are resolved in that rare dimension of spiritual empathy.

One of Nye's ways of awakening readers has been to narrate from a child's viewpoint, forcing adults to encounter innocence again. These children ask questions that adults do not ask or do not want to be asked—valid queries that spotlight the brutal absurdity of powerful nations waging war for stolen territory and natural resources, while always exacting the price of "collateral damage" paid in blood by civilians. She writes of those living under occupation, but also about the kids on American streets—often through reflections of her own childhood. Nye's books for children and young adults tend *not* to confront these horrors, but nonetheless are concerned with moral imperatives.

In the poem "One Boy Told Me," she strings a series of remarks over time made by her son, Madison (now a university professor), expressed as declarations and retorts. "Music lives in my legs," Madison declares, "It's coming out when I talk." Then he observes adults with this rebuke: "Grown-ups keep their feet on the ground/ when they swing. I hate that." Even parents of gentle understanding still stand as authority figures. "Don't talk big to me," he warns, "I'm carrying my box of faces. If I want to change faces I will." The narrative ends with "It is hard being a person.//I do and don't love you—/ isn't that happiness?"

While even Nye's earliest poems focused on the people of Palestine, especially tender poems about her father (Aziz Shihab) and her paternal grandmother, most texts are not overtly political. Certainly she did not intend to be a "political poet," and has never slipped into ideology. She flatly says in the first stanza of "Jerusalem" that "I'm not interested in/who suffered the most./I'm interested in/ people getting over it," realizing that peace will never blossom at the sites of oppression and revenge. In the second stanza, she relates a charming anecdote told by her father, which shifts from the bold statement opening the poem to

> Once when my father was a boy
> a stone hit him on the head.
> Hair would never grow there.
> Our fingers found the tender spot
> and its riddle the boy who has fallen stands up.

Then she expands the story into a larger context of relative experience. "Each carries a tender spot: something our lives forgot to give us." Near the end, she returns to say: "There's a place in this brain/ where hate won't grow."

Nye's earlier books (*Different Ways to Pray*, *Hugging the Jukebox*, *Yellow Glove*, *Fuel*, and *Red Suitcase*) won prizes—including the 1982 Poetry Series from Josephine Miles, several awards from the Texas Institute of Letters, and recognition as Most Notable Books by the American Library Association. Many of the poems in these books are humorous takes on our social habits, lighthearted lyrics on local characters, and subtle personal meditations, reflecting shades of emotion that have nothing to do with politics. These are the books for which she became known nationally as a poet, containing poems that evoke the unnoticed mysteries of daily existence with fresh perception. In almost every text rests a vulnerable image at the heart of poetry. "Fresh" observes a moment when nothing seems to be happening.

> To move
> cleanly.
> Needing to be
> nowhere else.
> Wanting nothing
> from any store.
> To lift something
> you already had
> and set it down in
> a new place.
> Awakened eye
> seeing freshly.
> What does that do to
> the old blood moving through
> its channels?

It moves mountains when we are immersed in the eternal moment, even if only a pot plant or curio has taken up new residence in the same room. Over and over, Nye turns non-events into splendid poems. "Open House" confesses to "work as hard as I can/to have nothing to do.//Birds climb their rich ladder of choruses.//They have tasted the top of the tree, but they are not staying.//The whole sky says, *Your move*."

Her simple language belies these witty epiphanies. Even in a much earlier poem (*"Adios"*) are variations on "the small alphabet of departure" saying goodbye once the words reach print. "Explain little, the word explains itself./Later perhaps. Lessons following lessons,/ like silence following sound." "Eye Test" views a more fragmented alphabet, beginning with a stanza that puns on letters, then one expressing enthusiasm for stories over eye charts. "How much better to be a story, story./Can you read me?" Even in such brief poems there are outlines of a story beneath.

While there may not be a prototypical text in the academic sense, we hear a similar ironic tone and a sense of serious playfulness at work, befitting a renegade voice. "Fuel" typifies this irony by suggesting that things are not as they may seem. "Once my teacher set me on a high stool/for laughing. She thought the eyes/of my classmates would whittle me down to size./But they said otherwise." Meanwhile our laughing student escapes the intended effect of the punishment. "I pinned my gaze out the window/on a ripple line of sky.//That's where I was going."

In "Always Bring a Pencil" we hear the teacher's voice assuring the students that "There will not be a test." Erasing the tension of unknowing with the soft end of a pencil, Nye tenderly warns, "But there will be certain things—/the quiet flush of waves,/ripe scent of fish,/smooth ripple of the wind's second name—/that prefer to be written about/in pencil." A pointed lesson in creativity, but why a pencil? Because "It gives them more room to move around."

Therefore we have a sensorium at the threshold of naked experience—primal waves, ancient scents, wind as naming music—all in free motion, touching tender spots connected by the undivided attention in an object lesson. We find another lesson of naming in "Hidden": "If you place a fern/under a stone," it begins, "the next day it will be/nearly invisible/as if the stone has swallowed it." The parallel second stanza moves around inside you. "If you tuck the name of a loved one/under your tongue too long/without speaking it/it becomes blood/sigh/the little sucked-in breath of air/hiding everywhere/beneath your words." It ends with a rush that awakens old blood: "No one sees/the fuel that feeds you."

Nye's *You & Yours* (BOA Editions, 2005)—winner of the Isabella Gardner Award and her first book since *19 Varieties of Gazelle: Poems of the Middle East* (a National Book Award finalist in 2002)—includes some of her most challenging poems. What makes this book more difficult are aspects that may surprise loyal readers, but these should gain the respect of the sternest critics, who tend to dismiss Nye's view as too precious to accurately represent today's global reality.

This may seem so in "Fold"—that admits to being "partial to poems about/little ruminations, explosions of minor joy,/light falling on the heads of gentle elders," and even admits to a "proclivity for the words/'small' and 'little,' a diminutive tendency/in a world given often to the sprawling and the huge." Yet if we spent each hour pondering only big questions, we would *not* experience the passing moment.

In "Please Describe How You Became A Writer," Nye does *not* gush about it, but offers a perceptive opinion of the Dick and Jane characters: "Possibly I began writing as a refuge from our insulting first grade textbook. Were there ever duller people in the world? You had to tell them to look at things? Why weren't they looking to begin with?" A few poems examine language directly, a primary task for poets.

"Dictionary in the Dark" protests the violence committed under the cover of governmental *newspeak*. "Why I Could Not Accept Your Invitation" critiques jargon, explaining "that is not the language I live in. . . . /I live in teaspoon, bucket, river, pain,/turtle sunning on a brick." Others concern young victims of violence in the Middle East. "For Mohammed Zeid of Gaza, Age 15" implies a linguistic fault beneath a larger human crime. "There is no *stray* bullet, sirs"/"So don't gentle it, please." Unlike young Mohammed, "this bullet had no innocence, did not/wish anyone well, you can't tell us otherwise/by naming it mildly, this bullet was never the friend/of life, should not be granted immunity/by soft saying—friendly fire, straying death-eye,/why have we given the wrong weight to what we do?"

In "The Day" the narrator wonders about weapons of mass destruction through child's perspective. "I missed the day/on which it was said/others should not have/certain weapons, but we could./Not only could, but should,/and do." Governments would dismiss this as naive, yet unanswered questions have profound consequences. "What about all the other people/who aren't born?/Who will tell them?"

In "The Light that Shines on Us Now" a child asks a pesky question in response to the image of a "strange beam of being right,/smug spotlight./What else could we have done?" Then an adult narrator declares: "Now that we are so bold,/now that we pretend/God likes some kinds of killing,/how will we deserve/the light of candles/soft beam of a small lamp/falling across any safe bed?"

Observing migratory birds as a splendid image for nomadic peoples, Nye spies "the long stroke of hope." It is not gratuitous because the title clarifies the true context: "*I Never Realized They Had Aspirations Like Ours: An Israeli, about the Palestinians.*"

"During A War" reflects on a letter's closure, "*Best wishes to you & yours,*" asking "where does 'yours' end?" In many Nye poems ordinary people are quoted or paraphrased, since they are human concerns. She knows how to listen, and this poem ponders what we have *not* heard—or ignored. "Your family,/your community,/circle of earth, we did not want,/we tried to stop,/we were not heard/by dark eyes who are dying/now. How easily they/would have welcomed us in/for coffee, serving it/in a simple room/with a radiant rug./Your friends & mine."

How far away violence seemed before 9/11, or easier to deny. Since then every Nye poem about the Middle East has been reviewed not only as "cultural enrichment," but judged by right wing pundits as "unpatriotic." Yet by traveling extensively, she has connected with a wide circle of witnesses in war-torn areas, responding by retelling their stories and by editing anthologies from the Middle East and beyond. Earlier books are deftly and quietly composed, although never passive or unconcerned about the pain of others. *You & Yours* breaks free from Nye's carefully controlled rhythms and cunning closures without losing the intense vitality of focus necessary during desperate times. This book contains fractures and persistent questions, ethical anger, and a painful honesty. Its heart pumps with a naked risk, never settling for violent business-as-usual, but always trying to reach the other side of the page.

Nye's side of the page in *Transfer* (BOA Editions, 2011) speaks of losing her beloved father, Aziz Shihab, reflecting on the mysteriously shifting sands of grief throughout this vulnerable book. "Missing him contains moments so intense," she declares, "I don't know how I will continue." Yet these elegies of dislocation, which are as emotionally complex and raw as grief itself, discover ways to continue.

"1935" opens with "You're 8 in the photograph,/standing behind a table of men/dipping bread in hummus.//You spoke inside/my head the moment before I saw it./Now the picture hangs beside my desk, holding/layered lost worlds where/you are, not only the person I knew/but the person before the person I knew,/in your universe, your life's possible story/still smiling."

"Scared, Scarred, Sacred" begins "Daddy! What's that ticket/ in your hand? Our transfer." Later "he felt safer traveling, wanting to be elsewhere,/restless, gone." Yet he "dreamed of doing something great/for peace, international healing,/but argued with people close by." Questions follow without answers. "When do we get there?/That place we are going?/What have we hauled along?/It was too much, wasn't it?" *Transfer* alludes to the journey we all take and to her father's "transfer" after the eviction from Jerusalem by the Israeli government in 1948, which was a subject "we didn't talk about often/because it was like a person who had died in another country/and we had never been able to wash the body."

In the wry "The Only Democracy in the Middle East" we learn that "Israeli soldiers order Palestinians to 'leave your house immediately./Do not call it a home./This is our home not yours./Security demands it.//Stand over there, against the rubble, where you belong.'"

The writings of father and daughter emerge from a rich storytelling tradition, which she combines in a dozen poems, taking their titles from lines in her father's notebooks. One charming text in "his" voice ("When One Is So Far from Home, Life Is a Mix of Fact and Fiction") begins, "No one should hold that against you./It's a means of survival./Sometimes I thought my best talent was/taking a skinny story, adding wings and a tail./Dressing it in a woolen Bedouin cloak/ with stitching around the edges." His touching memories become poems. "Where Are You Now?" opens with "my head on the pillow/ where you told your last folktale,/mixing donkey, camel, mouse,/journey, kitchen, trees,/so the story grew jumbled. . . ."

She "listened from the other small bed//remembering two and four and six/when this voice calmed me every night,/thinking, how will I live without this voice?" But the poem recovers, as his tale returns "to the comforting donkey, bucket of olives,//smoke curling up from twig fire/over which anyone, a lost girl, a wanderer, a dying man,/could warm his hands."

An exiled diplomat for peace, Aziz Shihab returned to Palestine often and wrote a memoir about his birthplace, *Does the Land Remember Me?*, published four months before his death, in 2007. Sharing his nonviolent philosophy, and also recognized as a peace advocate, Nye has included poems about Palestine in every book.

Their voices project sincere calls for peace, while remaining rebellious in questioning blind prejudices and tragic wars.

Nye makes clear in a prose epilogue ("Wavelength") that her father will reappear in cherished memories. "He had been the one person in my world absolutely on my wavelength, since I was little. The one whose humor made us laugh the hardest, whose quirks and commentaries rang the most bells. He sang cheerily in the shower in two languages—something better was always about to happen."

Since Aziz Shihab's "transfer" and his spirit's transference into our lives, Nye has inhabited all the "stages of grief" ever postulated, but never in any conscious, clinical sense. Rather, Naomi Shihab Nye bares this deepest wound without self-pity, tracing its gradual healing in poetry. "There's a way not to be broken"—reads the closure of "*Cinco de Mayo*"—"that takes brokenness to find it."

Border Crossings

I

The Farthest Home Is in an Empire of Fire (Viking, 2010)—
John Phillip Santos' companion to the acclaimed memoir (National
Book Award nominee) *Places Left Unfinished at the Time of Creation*
(Penguin, 1999)—arrives with a longer title, and telling a taller tale.
While *Places* explored his father's *mestizo* roots in Mexico and Texas,
this memoir traces his mother's origins back through the cultural
crossroads of the Iberian Peninsula. Celebrants of *Places* will enjoy
equally vivid characters, scenes, and settings in *Empire*, which is also
brushed in poetic prose.

Among colorful San Antonio portraits, we meet family genealo-
gist, Uncle Lico, who "fancied himself in the ilk of a new urbane Latin
noir slick, a modern American imbued with all the elegance and
nobility of the Spanish tradition . . . his chivalric manner translated
into a persona that was a Norteno amalgam of Hernan Cortez and
George Raft."

It was this uncle who inspired Santos as a young poet fascinated
by family history. Lico's older brother, Uncle Lauro, was another dash-
ing figure, who "looked every bit the part of the man of commerce, less
from the all-American stereotype and more in the style of Marcelo
Mastroianni. Uncle Lauro was lanky, over six feet tall, fair and lean,
balding in a distinguished European sort of way. . . . He and my Aunt
Ruth often looked as if they had stepped out of *La Dolce Vita*."

Their ancestral saga has a long and, until now, unspoken back-
story. Beginning "at the turn of the 19th century as the heirs of con-
quistadores, they began the 20th century transformed into members
of an American 'minority'"—who were "poor denizens of the old
Tejano ranchero life, in a forgotten part" of what we call Texas. The
Spanish "usurpers were themselves usurped, onetime conquerors
themselves conquered"—the eventual fate of every empire throughout history.

But Santos travels further back—to Spain and the Holy Land—
an interrupted trail that charts his Oxford days as the first Hispanic

Rhodes Scholar and two decades in Manhattan as a documentarian for CBS News, PBS, and the Ford Foundation. Shifting from the biographical in *Places* to center stage in this autobiographical narrative, we read a fascinating *mestizo* version of the making of a poet and the writing of this book as a spiritual quest. Santos describes his process as "inadvertentism"—an artistic approach that values only unintended events as significant, and the gambit certainly rings true here. His sophisticated work maps a journey into the past and into a speculative future, yet always with the authentically sensual feel of the present. Not to be confused with genealogies or ethnographies, this inquiry opens fresh possibilities intrinsic to and beyond "the deepest roots of our *mestizo* lineages."

Subtitled *A Tejano Trilogy*, the multidimensional work "was meant to evoke the poignant sense that even as we discover new understandings of our past, we must also reconcile ourselves to the fact that we are becoming something new . . ." Several experiential realms are revealed in the procession of balanced chapters: fragmented processes of terrestrial migrations, diasporas, and resettlements; detailed research into antiquities; clarifying cultural discourses on identity and *otherness;* and a postmodern mirror reflecting the complex evolution of this very project. Parallel to the colorful threads in a flowering fabric, we soon discover either a cosmic connection through Cenote Siete, the author's "ancestor from the future" (overheard as a voice), or we encounter a fantastic fiction that integrates philosophical insights and leaps of poetic fire. Cenote Siete speaks from the *Zona Perfecta*—"a time when humanity seems to have evolved new powers to directly access knowledge through a sort of psychic Internet."

Tejano Trickster or *Santos of the Spirits*, the author believes what he writes. "The truth is that his voice has been with me since I was a kid, and I've tried to be truthful about the way it manifested itself in my life and influenced the way I understood the story I wanted to tell. . . ." Whatever your viewpoint, this mysterious sage's passages are among the loveliest and most profound in *Empire*, a work that leaps beyond the borders of dreary academic genres and prejudicial social hierarchies. Compared to *Places*, a text of lovely resonances, *Empire of Fire* takes ambitious risks, while also revealing greater maturity and poise. It sparks a *mestizo* arc in the direction of global consciousness—

just where we have been headed.

Building border fences along the Rio Grande or around the landlocked island of Israel are not only absurd acts, but also the weird projections of racist paranoia and delusional purist identity. "To be mixed is to be from everywhere," John Phillip Santos points out. "If we are from everywhere we have a right to be anywhere. And if we have a right to be anywhere, no borders will stand."

II

In Alexander Maksik's first novel, *You Deserve Nothing* (Europa Editions, 2011), we encounter a familiar tale—inspiring teacher idolized by intelligent students—thankfully without clichés or a tawdry Hollywood ending.

Will Silver, an American teacher of literature at the International School of France (in Paris, circa 2002), challenges teenage students with his dazzling Socratic method. Not merely deconstructing difficult texts by Shakespeare, Thoreau, Sartre, and Camus, he cajoles them toward critical thinking about eternal questions and cultural prejudices that imprison them. Themes suggested in class play out among the characters in a literary sub-text that enriches this shrewd novel. One prevalent theme—that readers' experiences influence what they read—bears upon perceptions of Silver by the characters.

The classroom scenes are dynamic in Silver's narration, and thrilling from the viewpoint of Gilad, an introverted student in senior seminar, who describes the class dialogues. The novel unfurls seamlessly through three alternating narrators. The third voice is Marie's, an outgoing yet confused student, who pursues the popular teacher. Reluctantly at first, Silver eventually enters into a secret and very tender affair with Marie that advances undetected until she reveals details that lead to campus gossip.

In class Silver displays almost absolute control and élan, but off campus the students' "hero" tends toward ambiguity in decisions about the affair and his less-than-heroic inaction in two stressful public encounters (witnessed and "read" by Gilad). Like Meursault, the absurd anti-hero of Camus' *The Stranger*, Silver does not defend himself when his "crime" of having an affair with a student reaches the administrator's attention.

Even then Marie does not condemn the man she loves, desiring to continue the relationship. Silver remains supportive of any decision she might make—but in ways that reveal his alienation from emotions and a sense of powerlessness. Finally confronted by the administrators and summarily fired, Silver will *not* admit to being "morally" wrong, since he does not accept their judgment of his personal behavior.

We will "read" this dilemma according to our views, although during the affair readers are privy to the unguarded narrations of teacher and student, while the other characters are not. The ambiguities of "judging" are complex, perhaps imponderable. Yet this proves secondary to realizing how truthful and insightful are these pages that unfold in three distinct voices. The narrators—and several minor characters through revealing dialogues—create a compelling chorus that engages our deepest emotions and subtlest thoughts.

While *You Deserve Nothing* explores psychological labyrinths with no easy answers or cowardly rationalizations, the riveting story and literary allusions are lucidly accessible. Maksik delivers a sophisticated novel in simple, vivid prose, evoking the pleasures and perils that abound in the human psyche.

Maksik's brilliant new novel, *A Marker to Measure Drift* (Knopf, 2013), reads with the precision of narrative poetry, singularly focused on Jacqueline, an educated, English-speaking refugee from a privileged Liberian family, now exiled on a Greek island of sparkling resort towns. Jacqueline evokes a courageous, complex human being rather than a mere character or heroic immigrant symbol.

Jacqueline's immersion in elemental reality—with few clothes, no money, first finding refuge in a cave above a tourist beach—is astutely portrayed through detailed observations, vivid sensations, and troubled memories. The novel peers deeply into Jacqueline's solitude as she constantly debates choices, while feeling the presences of parents, a younger sister, and her lover Bernard (a foreign correspondent who realizes the end of the dictatorial regime to which her family was bound).

Mostly we receive the silent voice of her mother, providing cryptic, sarcastic clichés meant as advice. "Time passes, her mother said, peeling carrots. No matter what you do. No matter what happens, she said, crushing garlic, hammering the side of her favorite knife with her fist. Beauty or horror, my heart. Turning on the stove. Beauty or horror, it passes."

Maksik maps Jacqueline's careful movements, paralleling her interior journey into a seamless soliloquy of memory, hunger, and extreme dislocation, during which she resists madness. An indelible sense of horror returns and dissipates, as she moves through survival realms, devising a stratagem to earn money by giving foot massages to women tourists on the beach. She measures existence by the accumulated markers, gauging how far from a once-secure life she has drifted.

After earning enough for a time, Jacqueline walks about the island, ascending to a mountaintop, where she meets a tourist guide, viewing the ruins left after a volcanic eruption and a later earthquake destroyed a civilization. Jacqueline's engagement with the female guide reveals a prideful need to present herself as a married tourist, but since her exposed feet look like a vagrant's, the pose is unconvincing. She spends a night on the mountain, catching a free ride next morning on the tour bus.

Jacqueline finds an abandoned, unfinished building above that village, fashioning a crude home. In town she frequents a pleasant restaurant, having conversations with Katarina, a young waitress with whom she develops a friendship during several encounters. While we witness the exterior action over Jacqueline's shoulder, the real novel becomes a text of the body—her emotions, senses, thoughts, and haunting memories, which are only hinted at until her family's fate is revealed during a hesitant, drunken dialogue with Katarina in the dramatic last section.

A Marker to Measure Drift follows Maksik's debut novel, *You Deserve Nothing*, which included several narrative viewpoints that are here internalized. The novels are entirely dissimilar and the second is a significant advance. *Drift* evolves from the intense lyricism of carefully crafted sentences and fragments that never turn precious. The political background is experienced on the deepest human level, never moralizing about war or romanticizing the immigrant experience. In fact, Maksik virtually erases his authorial voice from Jacqueline's universal story of starting over.

This rare inhabitation of an unforgettable "character" (an

African woman from a distinctly different culture than Alexander Maskik's American male perspective) can only be declared as a feat of literary imagination and extraordinary empathy.

III

Jerry Craven's *Women of Thunder* (TCU Press, 2014) portrays a multilayered journey through the dangerous jungles and waterways of Venezuela—a lushly detailed adventure of wild places, and a plot replete with fascinating characters.

The novel is told in alternating chapters by the authentic voices of Rosa Rojas, a wise Venezuelan beauty trained as a nurse, and Tom Seal, an intelligent American veteran of the Vietnam War. Tom has returned, hoping to find Rosa, and to recreate their childhood adventure of 18 years earlier—wonderfully told in *The Wild Part*, an intriguing prequel (Angelina River Press, 2013).

Both narrators are visited by phantoms from the past and remembrances of their first river run as children. But they are adults now, and what they have experienced during the time apart slowly leaks into the story. The internal monologues in response to each other and in reaction to their remorse about past "sins" are adeptly articulated into an imaginative tapestry that never loses sight of the incredible trip on the jungle river. They encounter real dangers, especially in villages inhabited by a murderous cult leader and questionable mystic healers—arousing suspicion in Rosa's keen intuition or in Tom's outsider intellect, as well as the poisons and cures of local flora Rosa knows from experience (despite her denials of being a *curandera*).

In tense scenes about outwitting the strange villagers, they find intimate refuge from the rain and insects by constructing crude tree houses for the nights. "The women of thunder have arrived," remarks Rosa, "referring to a clap of thunder," as "lightning crackled above the canopy . . . and we move closer together." But it is not only thunder that represents these mysterious women, as we discover later. Deft passages flash forward to raise warning signals without revealing the future and glance backward to summarize the past without losing the intensity of the moment.

Craven's seamless style accomplishes this so subtly that we are never confused about where the narrators are or what they are thinking, but their complex dialogue is dramatic because they love each other, yet are unsure of who they have become. Tom is divorced from a wife who bedded his brother; she haunts him, as do the ravages of war. As a devout Catholic, Rosa blames herself for the deaths of her family during a cholera epidemic. Both try to erase each other's guilt, but cannot ease their own. The past invades their dreams and fits of insomnia and, even as they realize the visitations are imagined, the lyrical prose creates convincing substantiations.

Throughout the novel, Rosa and others relate intriguing and fantastic folktales that carry valid lessons, which at first Tom debunks as meaningless. But since several reveal the validity of truths, he slowly begins to accept their pertinence, while Rosa relates folktales that sometimes vary from other's versions. Their belief systems—Tom's somewhat cynical take and Rosa's emotional view—create the novel's dialectic. This never obviates the exciting quest, which is one of the few "page-turners" to have both a gripping story and a dynamic exchange of ideas.

Tom reasons that the murderous cult leader "came to the jungle with his flock to find Eden like we did . . . Wasn't he burning and clearing part of the jungle for crops? Didn't he build houses? He came here to change the jungle but it changed him and before long all he could think about was death, so he forgot the reasons that brought him to the jungle in the first place and forgot all of the wisdom or else remembered only the words that were hollow to him and needed someone like you to see the wisdom behind the words about forgiveness."

Jerry Craven's *Women of Thunder* reminds of Gabriel García-Márquez's fiction because the literal world and the spiritual realm converse on every page. No other North American novelist has created a better clashing conversation to ponder than this prize-winning author.

Voices from the Margins

Carmen Tafolla's *Rebozos* (Wings, 2012) includes passionate poems by the first Poet Laureate of San Antonio, paired with the haunting paintings of California artist Catalina Gárate García. It is a magnificent art book that recreates the originality of Mexican rebozos in vivid images. "Although a daily part of the lives of Mexican Indians for the last 400 years," explains Hector García Manzanedo's Afterword, "no written evidence has yet been found to indicate the rebozo's pre-Hispanic origin. . . . women in rural and indigenous communities still wear their rebozos every day, not only to cover their shoulders or their heads, but also as a way to free their hands while carrying a baby on their backs, or to support a load of wood or fruit."

Rebozos have been mass-produced in Mexico for over 150 years, but village women still weave them by hand, to sell in markets as utilitarian shawls and as folk artifacts. "In rural areas, the woman wearing a rebozo is invariably present," writes the artist, "seeming to emerge from earth itself, as a symbol of strength and life. . . . It can conceal, it can express," exactly like her evocative paintings.

Ekphrastic poetry celebrates the other art forms—from John Keats' "Ode on a Grecian Urn" to Wallace Stevens' modern masterpiece, "Man with the Blue Guitar" after a Picasso canvas. There are poems and a pop songs about Van Gogh's "Starry Night" painting. Now we have bilingual verses inspired by rich paintings, extending this venerable tradition. Tafolla avoids literalness and pierces the soul of these stories "to unfold our lives as if they were/rebozos/revealing/ our inner colors/the richness of our texture/the strength of our weave/ the history of our making. . ."

The cover painting is based on Agustín Victor Casasola's startling sepia print of women soldiers in the Mexican Revolution, about which Gárate writes: "But while her face, even with its anxiety and anguish, is beautiful, my soldadera is horrorosa . . ." She exposes a frightful mask of a face in a swirling red rebozo, freely transformed into a stunning painting from one detail in an iconic photograph.

The rebozo's uses are depicted by shrouded figures in essential female roles in Mexican culture—dispensing incense to drive away evil spirits, dropping seeds into a "Sweet soft furrow of earthen power . . ." and a currandera's "hands exceed/the boundaries of their bones/ and reach/to make the cure." Another woman with head covered by a rebozo appears like the Madonna (as many do), holding a candle for a loved one on "The Day of the Dead": "You will never die/I light these candles/leave these oranges/whisper these words/into the altar of your ear."

The earthy spirituality is inescapable. In Tafolla's "You Can Tell We're Related," the connection of earth and spirit are clear. "I can see it in your thunder and your rumble/your voracious appetite for sweet newness, for bold beauty/the Esperanza flowers you weave into your hair/the red seeds you hang from your neck/the wanting, the dreaming, the power in your belly." Her corollary is heard in "You can see it in the way I quiver, dream, want, grow/determined to stand strong, free/always building mountains from the crater of my center/erupting revolutions passions transformations/the solid rock of my core the same taste as your soil/I expand I discard I recycle/Everything./As you do.//You can tell we're related, Madre/I wrap the shroud around my dead/to warm them, care for them, memorize them."

Wrapped in mysterious folds, 16 paintings and 32 poems (in Spanish and English) are artfully designed in a 9x11 cloth edition. It celebrates centuries of women on the continent—"Indigenous, Mestiza, Criolla, Pre-Columbian, Colonial, Modern Feminist, Revolutionary—who used their rebozos as creative instruments in their lives," says Tafolla. "The words of these women in the paintings are, like rebozos themselves, both soft and strong. The poetry lies in the courage of their lives." Earthy and spiritual, women and rebozos, poems and paintings—they are inseparable, yet "weaving us together like threads in the larger rebozo of this world."

Jan Seale's *The Parkinson Poems* (Lamar University Press, 2014) concerns the 20-year struggle with Parkinson's disease that struck husband Carl Seale (1936-2014), and includes poems of this caregiver's empathetic characterizations of a dreadful disease. The Seales were married 56 years, raised three sons, and carried on as artists (Carl was a composer, conductor, and professor of music).

Initially called "the shaking palsy" in 1817 by Dr. James Parkinson, this incurable disease is known today due to famous people who suffer with it, like boxing champion Muhammad Ali and actor Michael J. Fox.

The opening long poem is a resourceful and witty personification of the disease as the unwelcome yet demanding guest. "He begged to come in./The husband said he wasn't there./The wife thought she'd seen him earlier." Then "The doctor gave the answer—/His name was Parkinson/and his presence was permanent."

In "The Guest"—and 32 other short poems—Seale articulates encounters with this degenerative disorder of the central nervous system. Gradually the "guest" takes over: "he wouldn't allow conversation/unless it was about him./He dropped silverware, knocked over glasses,/spilt food, complained of dull knives,/awkward fork tines,/ spoons purposely small./The meat was too tough to cut or chew./ Vegetables played tag all over the plate./Lettuce salads went straight for the lap."

"Threshold Initiation Syndrome" portrays the difficulties of patients dealing with common thresholds. "Like a cat, you pause before a doorway,/ancient limbic cells deep in your brain/working overtime with the signal/Caution! Beware! New Territory!//Finally, neurons fire, synapses/snap to, jambs unjam and you/pass from room to room,/sidewalk to café, yard to house."

The last poem talks about what has changed. "You have given me excuses for things I did not want to do anyway./You have given me new skills," like "How to be grateful but brief in phrasing your health to others" and "given me patience I never had before,/with my strange limbic anger calmed into understanding,/with waves of resentment transformed into compassion,/and with permission to laugh with you/ at things that were formerly serious and important."

Texas Poet Laureate for 2012, Seale also brings an astonishing versatility to her expanded edition of *New & Selected Poems (1974-2012)* from Ink Brush Press (2012). As a natural storyteller, her poems are carefully wrought yet wildly free, including wise evocations of nature, satirical takes on teaching, and intimate narratives about family and friends that are endearing but never sentimental.

Arranged in thematic sections, *The Wonder Is* opens windows on our shared humanity. "Sistering" admits vulnerability to a close friend: "I will risk 'hysteria' with you./Also 'no sense of humor'/and being a 'case of nerves.'" On her son's first lost tooth, Seale observes that "The trust of a child has no roots." Among several witty poems on mid-life, "Touring a Well-seasoned Woman" declares that the breasts "have a history of stories:/sighing children and oblivious lovers," while "The hips, we see,/are posing for Rubens." A long, hilarious rant ("Menopause Ain't No Tunnel of Love") makes vivid what women know but what men keep out of awareness. Lighter verses display imaginative lyrics, like "Bookmark" that becomes a "rooster crowing from the edge of the page,/prisoner condemned to the medieval press" yet "transformed from souvenir to consort/of the best words in their best order, what's it like to hold a place in time and space,/to separate yesterday from tomorrow?"

The last section offers superb odes to nature: "In a saddened land,/where birds fill us with obligation/waiting beside their clay bowl,/we take any fluff of sky,/however white and promiseless,/vow to love its finger shadow/passing over us, the only thing/between us and a dry god" ("Drought"). Its clever antidote, "Medley of a Mockingbird on a Rainy Dawn," reads "Finally, my color—gray!/Come, come and love me anyway, nearby mate./I am mockingbird; therefore I am."

Seale's poems in *Nape* (Ink Brush, 2011) provide a signature text in the title poem, precise poetry evolving line by line: "Here's praise to the nape of the neck,/a much neglected organ. Become a nape watcher/and you see strawberries stamped/at the turnstile of birth; an overhang of hair—/natural queue, leftover of the widow's peak,/or tail of a valentine. . ./the nape of the neck is a touch key of love:/feather-stroked, the whole board lights up./The hair at the nape stays young forever./Ancients go to their graves black-naped/which leads me to say: when I die,/I'd rather not be redeemed like a gymnast recovering/ on a trampoline, springing from grave/to feet blinded by an eastern sun. Rather/let God come like a thick dumb mother cat, pick up what's left by the nape of its neck,/and move it to safe quarters."

The Wonder Is truly is a wonder by the author of nine poetry titles, two short story collections, three nonfiction volumes, and several children's books, for which she has won seven PEN awards and an

NEA fellowship. Jan Seale stands taller than the valley of "regional-ism" to which her work has been wrongly consigned. While evoking the Texas border topography adeptly, she ventures deeply inward to the emotional and spiritual levels we will recognize in such diverse, exquisite poems.

Wendy Barker's *Way of Whiteness* (Wings, 2000) won the Violet Crown Award from the Texas Writers' League, containing master-ful poems that operated on several levels. As a scholar of Emily Dickinson and an astute reader of modern poetry, she has honed her craft in the medium-length lyric to a subtle sophistication.

Poems from Paradise (WordTech, 2005) breaks new ground by stripping away the allusions and references that animated *Way of Whiteness*, risking a longer form that explores an integration of the self set free from academia. But what has *not* been erased are the various realms of meaning, for this sequence of 47 brief cantos (and a final poem) can be read also as an Eve's soliloquy of love and loss and as a verbal stream of consciousness through wordless nature.

Considering the book's title and references to a God, a snake, a lush garden, and fallen apples, Barker clearly establishes this connec-tion to Edenic myth. Yet the poetry turns on the primacy of the senses not intellect; and the mind does *not* separate itself from the body, as the lovers of the sequence "did not think in halves."

The opening poems celebrate a glorious oneness: "Oh, You Said, Your/fingers and half-open/mouth pressing bits of me/I had thought were ordinary,/separate pieces of my body,/till they began to swim/together in your hands." "At First You Insisted" flows late into "there was no/space anywhere/between us, light and/air my breasts, your hands,/our breath, our breath, our/unbroken breath."

But too soon comes an inexplicable, wrenching separation, then the "Unsteady footing./Whichever way I set out/to find you I will sink." Yet "I Think/you never existed" but "Sometimes/when I am whispering/to myself about you/as I go, leaves begin/to sound like your voice." Everywhere she discovers memories of him and, even peering into a mirrored self-awareness, he emerges as her desire.

"So This/is what you saw. By/leaning down over/smooth stones around/the calm of the pond/I have seen my face./And to think I was/

worrying about/the flowers I would/wear when you found me. In the final poems of Part I, the narrator believes that her lover "will come when I least/expect it."

Part II acts as a two-page *coda*, when for the first time we meet a nameless God, suggesting a spiritual level of attention in surrendering to the divine. "If a God/comes to you/a small/fish in the night,/ simply become water." But the final stanza creates a counterpoint that preserves the mystery of identity.

> When a god comes
> to you as a man,
> you will have no need
> for questions, blossoms,
> or bracelets.
> Even a name.

Cyra S. Dumitru adopts several voices of dehumanized witnesses early in *Remains* (Pecan Grove, 2008), her third book after *What the Body Knows* (1999) and *Listening to Light* (2003). Her images in "A Western Woman Puts on a Burka" are startling: "—entertain/your own thoughts within this striding/curtain, this private theater. Here/ you can become the secret—the offstage woman carrying the pearl/ handled dagger, the leather book of potions/the key to the attic library,/the missing slipper,/the answer to the question:/who do you say I am?"

This display of empathy soars beyond mere identification, as her inner voice continues to be meditative, and lovely lyrics celebrate water immersion as a swimmer and an astute observer of nature. The most radiant of these begins "How the river fills. Carries/upon greater current/even as it compels you/to swim for your life, gives just enough resistance. . ." Later lines integrate a graceful poetic process. "As I shake my hair, syllables drop upon my shoulders/and the pebbled grass,//where they gleam/suggestively/of broken words.//Phrases drip from fingertips, and near rhymes run/down my arms.//Stanzas that glistened/among the river reeds/leave shadows on my skin.//Line breaks evaporate/from the middle of my back,/some splash to the grass.//At my feet, poetry/is silence breaking open/into song."

"A Swimmer Speaks of Keeping Company with Rivers" sets a convincing example of a text as body. No matter how modern or ancient, poetry never forgets the human body-in-nature, even while lyric imagination leaps beyond earthly limits. Cyra Dumitru has inscribed poems on her body of poetry with sensual and aesthetic élan in these meticulously crafted texts of pastoral contexts.

Marian Aitches' first collection, *Fishing for Light*, won the chapbook contest from Wings in 2009. It opens with these startling lines from "In the Stories": "I am the tough sister, the one/who saved the others,/the one who stayed awake,/stood in the door, trying/to keep the monster at bay." Many portraits of fascinating females and powerful elegies about family grief find balance in joy. "It is loud, like God laughing./Thunder, when a drought/has gone on too long." And it is like that "cry of the baby you were told/you'd never have, born/healthy in your middle age . . ."

Other poems range from an experience at age ten to speculating about a future millennium. "Spelling" prepared her for "ambitious, loquacious, even extraneous—/and then out of nowhere—get/a one-syllable test,/a word close to death—" That word was "dearth" and she misspelled it. "Bones" declares that "Having been young once,/I think it is too much/to embrace maturity with one dumb face," predicting "A thousand years away/I will be the bones/some anthropologist holds up to the light, amazed//by the music they make."

In Aitches' first full-length book, *Ours Is A Flower* (Pecan Grove, 2010), succinct lines—jagged and stony—expose dark politics, as her spirit illuminates "rough justice" in the context of ethics. "We have a moment, they have an hour/theirs is a stone, and ours a flower," reads Langston Hughes' epigraph, paralleling her edgy critiques of savage behavior by the powerful against the *Other* throughout history. Part Choctaw and a professor of Indian Studies, she writes pointedly about the treatment of Native Americans, plus several heartfelt poems on the plight of ordinary Palestinians, Iraqis, African Americans, and Mexicans on both sides of the border, as well as the ongoing mistreatment of women.

In a brief prose poem ("For Jon"), Aitches writes devastatingly.

A young man returns from Iraq to American History class. Wears shorts that expose his left leg from the knee down—metal structure ending in a size twelve shoe. The shock is not this limb but the other—his loss laid bare by smooth brown skin; how the full calf traces a beautiful arc to a muscled ankle that anchors his power to the ground.

One of her strongest poems ("Hunger") ends with these stanzas: "Last helping of spaghetti in the pan/when you're the oldest—the two siblings/wanting more. Scared at night,/when Mama's at work, that approaching/footsteps aren't your father's/or that they are.// Anger that flares when you're asked/to sign the petition—to keep/the percentage of poor people/down—in the urban-renewed projects/that kept your family from sleeping/on streets.//Never growing beyond your past./Not being able to sit at the table—/even when you realize—/there is more/than one way—/to starve."

Carol Coffee Reposa's fourth collection of poems, *Underground Musicians* (Lamar University Press, 2013), contains all the attributes of great poetry. The imagery is original, the structure of each poem and the book's formal cohesion reach the epitome of poetic craft, while every line carries the rhythmic flow of underground music. A rare bonus—the poems are clearly understandable, but without ever sacrificing significance or witty allusions. This may look like a travel book, since sections carry geographical titles—Gold Hibiscus: Mexico, Peru, and Ecuador; Light Bent Blue: Western Europe; Otherworldly Red: Russia; and A Web of Green: principally San Antonio—but the precise language penetrates other cultures as tourist guides cannot.

"Machu Picchu" ventures beyond the guidebook: "I think about Pizarro's men/Toiling up that steep incline/Their fine Castilian horses/Lathered in the mountain air/Saddle leather molding,/Orchids dangling from strange trees//While water flowed above them/Over stones and terraces/Down green slopes draped in clouds/Like shawls around the shoulders/Of a woman/Lost in thought."

Following impressive sonnets on British royalty, we gaze at Michelangelo's ceiling in "The Expulsion of Lucifer, Sistine Chapel": "As God hurls him from heaven/In elongated rage/. . . His luminous finger/Pointing the way to ruin.//Lucifer does not yet know/What awaits him,/How he'll darken/. . . Until his thoughts are opaque/As the space around him/And he has no memory/Of light . . . //Above him/Saints are saved/Prophets speak/The sky stays blue/And God remembers."

In Russia, Reposa hears "Underground Musicians": "Somehow solitary/In the noise/Separate from everything//Except the melodies/Of Schubert/Bach and Mozart/. . . Folksongs from the steppes/Remote as ice floes/In the heat of passing flesh.//We stride along,/Throw rubles, dollars/Into hats or open cases/Colors of the currency/Lost in the wider spectrum/Of a baritone's crescendo/Or the flutist's final trill."

Under the ground of Reposa's lyrics, sumptuous music can be heard. Even the cover art features the animals of Lascaux cave in France, with a young violinist smuggled into the scene. From the lovely painting to this title poem, music is either directly composed or indirectly alluded to in her lyrics.

In the final section, we learn from "How to Stop War": "Put Yo Yo Ma in every doorway/Pavarotti at each checkpoint/Perlman on the road to Kosova/Or in Rwanda's thick green hills.//Let the hands of Artur Rubinstein/Float slowly over Belfast/Have Marsalis/Shoot cadenzas into Gaza.//When we fill the bores/Of AK 47s/With scores of Brandenburg concertos,/When we arm the Stealths with Mozart//No one will hear the voices/Calling them to blood. Remastered/They will find their families/Building ballads in the streets/See them tuning old guitars/Inside their tents/Chords shimmering/In Kabul's radiant dust//Rising/Past minefields/Into melodies."

"One Night in a Cheap Motel" is a witty take-off on T.S. Eliot's "The Love Song of J. Alfred Prufrock" as "A tomcat sits by my door, courting me/In plaintive yowls. Doors lock and unlock/All night long, and through the walls/I hear disembodied laughter, sultry tones/Set to raucous country-western songs./In the room above, people come and go/Probably not talking of Michelangelo."

Lee Robinson's *Creed* (Plain View, 2009) celebrates the vital-yet-aging body, but with sophisticated wit. The title poem reveals that "it is the body of a ninety year old/straining to stand upright/each vertebra/a testament, each muscle a miracle." It ends with "Fold your flesh into her bones//until you do not have to ask me anymore/what to believe in: It is the body//the body,//Amen." Her voice moderates sassy ruminations at windows between home and nature. The time frame becomes set during a comfortable second marriage, but laments attempts to "parent" grown children from a distance, while other poems map her own youth and young motherhood.

Robinson's best poems gauge the disappearance of nature's creatures and our ecological stupidity. "Verge of Extinction" tallies this loss, ending with "We argue over global warming and complain/about the price of gas; revise, re-think;/waiting for more evidence of ruin/than twelve thousand species or more on the brink./Busy sawing off the limb we stand on, we miss the news of our own oblivion."

Her critique has deep roots in ethics. She has a fine musical ear in "The Goldberg Variations," a take on the late Glen Gould, featuring his 1955 and 1982 recordings of J.S. Bach's masterpiece. Wending through Gould's interpretations as "the playfulness amid the utmost/ seriousness, the childhood notes/that play and skip, then slow//to somber canon, things lost/and things that are not/what they seem." Her reason for Gould's gift is that "You gave me these variations/as if to say *Listen to me*,/listen to all the years of recitals,/the competitions, listen to the girl/who wanted to be famous,/the woman who earns a living//selling Steinways, giving lessons,/who gets up early every morning/to practice in the dark."

Sybil Pittman Estess' *Labyrinth* (Pecan Grove, 2007) faces primal themes about dying loved ones. She tends to be direct but vulnerable in personal narratives. "I Have No Story/I Have No Tale" concerns her mother's denial (in pitch-perfect dialogue) of having been a Mississippi migrant worker in California during the Depression. The second section strikes a fanciful tone in outlandish variations on *Wuthering Heights*. The third enters those labyrinths, ending with "Labyrinth, Fourteen Ways" where we are walking but "there are other people on their own path." Every life has its metaphorical conundrums, convergences of experience, and memory. "When you walk in, you get to a still-point," but "you are not finished yet." The only way out is enlightenment, "you must exit as/Christ did: down the Mount/ of Transfiguration."

In Janet McCann's *Emily's Dress* (Pecan Grove, 2004), for Emily Dickinson, stands before the museum case and slips into this delightful title poem.

Does she put it on, the British guide,
the dress, when no one is looking,
she looks about the right size

and she is so stern! *Don't touch that*,
as I press my face to the glass of the case
just trying to see. Tonight she'll be leaping

through the dark and dusty house, Emily's dress
thrown over her British underwear.   But no,
it's me, I put it on, the way she did,

buttoning it as she did, carefully,
not slipping into it like my own brown shift
as daily as hers, but button after button

lovingly smoothing it out, its white panels
slightly yellowed, sliding its sleeves
over my arms grown suddenly slim

and of course I've got Emily's underwear,
the secret garments they never spoke about,
but I am thinking of a plain white shift

and loose white drawers with a string, that's why
they call them drawers, or else
no underwear, certainly nothing complex

and Victorian, or earlier, and I understand
in the 18th century many wore no drawers
making a simple fall a social disaster. No, Emily,

I am putting on your dress and only that,

the fabric against your skin, my skin.
No one is here but us girls.

In *Pascal Goes to the Races* (CustomWords, 2004), McCann displays witty sophistication about Pascal, Kafka, Proust, the mystic Julian of Norwich, and a brilliant pastiche of memoir, newsreel, and nightmare ("1936"). "Answering Machine" depicts a simple act. "I call my house, it's empty/my own voice responds,/painfully hesitant, saying I'm unavailable. I can hear/gaps in the apology, the whirring/tape, a stammer, a repetition,/an indrawn breath,/then finally/and blessedly, the beep." The final closure dials up lucid profundity. "If it was all that difficult/just to express absence,/than how can I begin/to tell you that I'm here?"

Jenny Browne's third book, *The Second Reason* (University of Tampa Press, 2007), reveals fresh depths beyond *At Once* (Tampa, 2003) and *Glass* (Pecan Grove, 2000), while keeping alive a witty sense of experimentation. She plays with words without being a "language" poet and her leaps of consciousness occur in domestic realms, which are neither domesticated nor self-consciously surreal.

"Multiple Choice" illustrates Browne's strategy. "So if house is to barefoot/as God is to laughter,/what's rocking chair to orange?" No answer, followed by a final stanza. "The second reason is this/suckling child/who will one day hold/up the fruit and say/*can you start this for me?*" Perhaps the fruit and the rocking chair hold the source of such ideas that arise while holding a child? Her wit resides in such questions and in playful disconnection, creating an exquisite nonsense.

Whereas in "Not an Aubade," which begins with a parental discourse on their child's lineage and ends in a subtle seduction scene, we have clear connections. Her sensual awareness emerges not in the bedroom, but through peering "into the glowing kitchen of our own life/for a glimpse of when the three we have become/resembles two again for a few moments/as the lengths of our bodies touch//at the hip, the shoulder, the occasional/fingertip and you reach deeper// into the soapy water then pass me/the warm dripping plates to rinse and dry//and stack front to back or back to front/each with its own particular fit, at last this//slight rub, the almost forgotten hum/of my body rising, spreading, leaving//the widows all lingered in steam."

The longest poem ("There's a Slow Green River I've Been Living By") reveals an impressive experiment in a fusion of lyric, narrative, and prose poetry. While it does not approach the near-perfection of some shorter poems, it flows through consciousness as a river "faithful/to the innate knowing what/is bank, what is flow." She means not only the river as a symbol and moving as a reality, but also Mother Nature with a healing blanket of green life for her new daughter. "I strap/my child to my back and walk/towards a river." There "water under the bridge is filled with tiny/black fish, a school of commas. They clarify//that once I waited, grew larger, multiplied/and became two. I divided, stood and walked//on a river of selves. No remainder." The final part reaches a compelling closure as a vast opening. "If a root swallows the corner of the path, if green, if nothing/lasts, not even a child's name written with a sharp rock//on the buckled sidewalk then we must hide/the rock beneath a low blooming rosemary bush." Rosemary of memory, nature's pungent scent. "It will be our secret. You can find it again, each/morning like a mind, a surprise. Or a sky."

Despite some darkly chaotic prose poems, the book feels *green*— vigorously fresh, yet not naïve. Browne's natural sensibility tends toward the lyric, balancing lucid observations with honest revelations, and the poems are replete with subtle surprises. She "can see//how I've become one of those/divided types/I loved as a child, books/where the astronaut's body fits/the mermaid's scaly tail . . . //I've become/one of those leaky souls,/hot and sweet//midnight milk beads/a blue translucent *we*.//Today on Mars, water./Today in a dimple, the universe.// The baby smiles/but doesn't mean it yet."

In *At Once*, she lives in the *only* moment we have, *this one* vibrating our being awake—especially when vultures appear near unfolding flowers, not as symbols of mortality but as "the hint/of a body taken higher." The cyclical poems are open-eyed skies gazing on infinite exchanges of death-in-life, intensely attentive to "the silence of everything/turning back to dirt." Her poetics are grounded in the slender intimacy of vulnerable perceptions, expressed in "Saying Yes"—"Somehow my voice sounds sure/as sugar concentrating her story/into all a wine grape knows, one drop/between perfection and ruin." The ending opens upon the next poem and the next, when a girl student asks for "some hard words/to look up in the dictionary," but the poet "can't think of one."

Instead "I tell her I like sentences/that end in then." *Then* resonates as memory and a story beginning with *And then*. "Rainsong" (another "drop" of inspiration in the metaphoric code she calls "a second language") insinuates a world of immediacy. "So easy to worship anything,/drizzle in a second language,/that reflected gratitude shining/back from one fat drop/considering her possibilities."

Both Browne's story of sugar and possibilities for a raindrop are strategic voices for the silent phenomena shimmering before our hidebound eyes, growing as we sleep. Poetry suggests what prose proclaims or reveals what amnesia hides. She creates "a second language" that transcends the literal one debased by the so-called rational public discourse. Her poems are immersed in direct realities *not* categories, and she does not talk in generalities or report the weather, but the effects are evoked in precise language.

"For the Morning" begins the complex unfolding. "Spiral of glory/poised on the vine/I never tire//of your white trumpet blazing,/flared edge/of color all/open to the oceanic/sort of end, thrashing red/snapper on the line,/an entire face falling/at the glacier's/distant crack." The aubade swiftly leaps from porch to ocean to glacier, connecting experience through arcing gerunds (blazing, thrashing, falling), and active verbs (spiral, flared, open, crack). Dynamics emerge in this "spiral of glory"—a palette of color transparencies, an interplay of the senses, and awe heard in a mute trumpet at the "flared edge" of the boundaries of sight and sound, perception, and metaphor. But the poem is not finished. Three subsequent stanzas turn a ruminating sensibility into direct speech. "Flower turning back/to the used-up/tissue, sticky//at the stillbirth?/Just as much work./You don't know how much//you can really give./You don't know how to live/but at once."

Flowers and fish live *at once*—and die. Even oceans and glaciers die, but in awe-inspiring proportion to our scale and duration. But are we alive *at once* or *only once*, if unaware that our own death will be future fuel for the planet. Browne's previous lines strike the true message: "You don't know how much/you can really give," suggesting that if we live only *at once* in the sensate reality, simultaneously we must learn to be in reflection. That is, we must live twice at once.

Jenny Browne flirts along the edges of meaning in *Dear Stranger* (Tampa, 2014), her fourth book that contains exhilarating tropes and strange, unmailed letters.

"The Multiple States of Matter," the first signature here develops like most of her sophisticated texts—facing brutal reality with a satirical attitude. She begins with an unanswerable question: "If four legs make a desk, a relationship, a donkey and its hee-haw switchbacking our slow descent, which way to turn first?"

Posed as a logical interrogation, the narrator pursues the absurdity of imagined dangers. "The back of the donkey I rode down into the canyon/quaked beneath me for miles. Every time we stopped,// she faced the rock. She didn't want to see where we going either. This desk faces a wall/of wooden masks, gods and monsters, some/with other bodies coming out of their foreheads." These are metaphors for writing. Browne is *not* really riding a fearful donkey in the mountains, and the gothic wall grotesques are artifacts or imaginings—not real gods and monsters.

Browne's work tends this unmapped path, keeping alive a witty experimentation. Playing with language, her leaps of consciousness go directly to the page, perhaps more self-consciously than in earlier books. Her narrators keep interrupting to remind that speculations can create sudden reversals. In "Studies for the Monster"—who turns out to be us, she writes: "Amazing/how many subdivisions named for the trees they destroyed." Then later, "Once upon a time a place survived our naming of it. It didn't really grow smaller in the distance. We did." The poems are not usually this explicit, but meaning creeps in between acerbic statements and clever, disjointed exclamations. Yet Jenny Browne remains in control of her voices and visions, but like everyone else she has no control over our commonsense reality.

Natalia Treviño's first book, *Lavando La Dirty Laundry* (Mongrel Empire Press, 2014) reveals a similar uncanny accomplishment in narrative poetry. Treviño grew up in San Antonio, but was born in Mexico City. The opening sections tell the stories of the consequences of poverty for female relatives, as well as her difficult first marriage. The narratives tend toward pain and drudgery, relieved by moments of humor in "The Mother Who Tried": "Before bed, my son told me,

You're not you anymore./You're like my shoes. When they're tied too tight!//I'd been reading discipline books,/experts' rules for four-year-olds, and he spoke his first poem."

The title poem is a fascinating tale retold, followed by a charming prose piece about learning how to make tortillas. Later "It Was the Chef Who Finally Explained" how to make a delicious sauce. "You can't throw everything in together, he said.//You wait. First you let the onions cook/for a while in their own oil.//And you listen for them to crackle./Only then, press the clove of garlic you will need.//Stir. They'll take each other in—the two layers./Create their own liquid."

Treviño admits in "Enriched Wife" that "I was not trained to cook by my mother," but while in Mexico she learned from her grandmother how to make Mexican rice "so fluffed, so golden and red"—not the American white rice of no nutritional value.

The last section focuses on a second marriage to an Australian, which "is converting my circuitry.//Reversing the current/in my angry blood." The book ends with "Forgive Me That My Empirical Self Still Rules": "We are both foreigners in this country./Yet my ex would have me ash again,/while I dine on our Phoenix.//They called you a gray fool when you came here,/yet our garden is too lush./We have double the time, the seasons,/so many lives—/too many to display/on our shelves.//When you plant a/garden in the heat,/the roots of the Passion Flower//must/stay/cool."

In *Bedrock* (Pecan Grove, 2011), Bonnie Lyons faces aging and the loss of loved ones with necessary adaptations and a seasoned wisdom. Here are touching narratives of early Jewish family life amid painful elegies about the passing of her parents. Yet she seems most deeply wounded by the death of younger sister. "On your fiftieth birthday/you've been gone sixteen years./Your children approach your age.//Little sister,/I wanted to take the bullet for you/to be a wall, a moat, around you./I never dreamed the enemy would grow inside you."

"At Kennedy Airport" reads of shared grief in this same inexplicable loss. "My father and I could/always be counted on/to weep at all occasions—//but meeting at the airport/after my sister died/we fell into each other's shaking arms/stretched open our mouths to howl/ and no sound came out. . ."

There are several other silent screams and clarifying yet tender observations of dying parents. "Sylvia and Irving Play" opens a charming lens on her parents as "Veteran actors playing/lifetime roles: his and her versions/of anxious duty and numbing routine…/but some mornings before the alarm//I'd find them offstage, in bed, entwined,/ her huge breasts released,/limbs flung over each other/every which way, exuding/the luxurious abandon/of hibernating bears/in pin-striped cotton and ivory silk." Obviously, we cannot control events but Lyons possesses the stratagem of memory in "Cypresses": "When my mother's vacant face peers out/earnest with the strain of remembering/nothing, I give up trying to forget."

Lyons recalls and accepts the inevitable (in "Revision"). "Just like you/I have always wanted to fly,/but now I know/I will never soar.// Even my body says tree/not bird, so here's my revised dream: to be like that lemon/leaf outside my window//Palmed up up up/floating and somersaulting/before the quiet descent/to earth." She learns unexpected lessons from "three sage Airedales." "Dog Training" lays down witty insights, like "First, yelp when you're in pain/but let it go when it's gone.//Second, travel the earth/with a quivering nose.// Third, answer the needs of your body/with shameless relish//but then go right on/to the real purpose of the day: play.//And finally, whenever possible/leap right//into the arms of someone/who loves you."

As a literary critic and professor of English, Lyons also sets literary references into ingenious contexts. After lamenting the horrors of war (in "We"), she points out that "one of us/not a dolphin—not a dolphin" created the masterpieces of art. It closes with "Nietzsche/ was right: I would die/without art. And Nietzsche too,/arms thrown around the cab horse,/was one of us."

"Oysters" presents a different turn. "Given the choice, I'd choose to be Chekhov./Sweetness waltzes with irony—/he loves his characters and laughs at them/as I suppose God must.//Instead I'm more like his black-clad Masha/announcing she is in mourning/for her life." From celebrating art over death, "Dulcinea Tries to Comfort Don Quixote" reads "Back then,/with my full breasts,/lean hips and flat belly,/you loved my body/because it was beautiful.//Now when the downward/pull of gravity and the grave/have taken a little here/added a lot more there,/you can love my body only//because it is my body./ Absurdly unexpected as all/these predictable losses,/we enter the real/ age of romantic love."

Marian Haddad's *Somewhere Between Mexico and A River Called Home* (Pecan Grove, 2004) embraces life and the death of loved ones in a voice both earthy and spiritual. This passionate cycle leaves no doubt about the narrator's identity or viewpoint. Water flows from the Syrian desert of her parents' origin to her El Paso birthplace, as the youngest child. "House of Children" begins with "I lived first/in the house of my mother,/not in-between walls/of stucco or brick,/but in the one house of children, there,/in the uterus/that held and cupped/ the fetus . . ." This series catalogues a painful yet deeply respectful relationship with her mother, followed by poems on her aging father. In "Coddling the Father" she has "become/a mother, here,/in a room/ where time/has turned. My father, my/child, now/burrowed/in this corner."

The long title poem flows through the pages of a childhood album, turning over a family saga of the parents' tale of courtship, emigration, and survival in a new place. This river meanders through the familiar immigrant experience, but with its own pulsing current that pauses at the shoreline. There her father "tends his backyard haven/ his fruit trees/tomatoes red with life/his little forest/where he finds that young man/strong as a rock/who dug the earth beneath him/and made it rise again."

The third section about sister Nawal ("the eldest and wisest one") includes ruminations on dying in simple, healing narratives. In "The Body" the youngest sister finds an elegiac antidote to death: "lying back and quiet, beautiful again./How you looked more than eighty/at the moment of your leaving./How death casts age upon us,/ the death of a flower in its ragged/and terse unflowering."

The final part transforms stifling hospitals into mythic gardens beyond place and time. Incarnated as Saturn ("Resurrection"), Haddad creates fresh turns. "She bids me to immerse myself in water,/past the patch of trees. She prays I will bear/children, that they will swim like truth/around my sphere." Then the evocative lyric of "Cypress,

Daughter of Fertility," who does *not* pray to a male god but speaks from the female godhead: "We are florid/and fecund./We are/the umbilical cord/to the underworld/and the higher world/and the world rotating/around us. We,/the nexus,/the bearers/and birthers./I have carried/you, sweet pit/of fruit/inside me./Go then/likewise,/and bear/the fruit/of your being . . ."

In Haddad's next book, *Wildflower. Stone.* (Pecan Grove, 2011), flowers bloom and stones endure as her lines travel flat highways, sweetly romanticizing a symphony of light, while her spirituality looks to the heavens. She opens with a lovely homage to Wallace Stevens' "The Man with the Blue Guitar," establishing the female body as her center of sensibility. "Through this blue guitar/the unconscious river sings.//Body of woman/entwined about helm and prow/of songs and strings, rivulets/of cadences between brows.//Body of wood and flesh/dressed in blues and violets/colors of sky and sound/colors of woman wound//about hips of harmonies/wide as water."

"Her Body Is a Guitar" has neither flowers nor stones, but water flows through it as the essential metaphor connecting all life. "In a San Diego Courtyard" brings us to "this fountain/water folding over itself/and back;//water has softened the edges it skirts./Persistence drives a stone mad.//Softening the edges.//The way the world would be/if only we let the water/roll over the edges//and back." Her title poem sequence constitutes the second section, traveling desert regions near El Paso and wetland areas of the Gulf coast, separated as elements yet encircled by sky and memory.

Poets Toni Heringer Falls and Janice Rebecca Campbell have joined voices in this charming collection of thematically related texts, which they call *Braided Stream: A Poetry Duet* (The Very Idea, 2014). "We began with an idea to do a collaborative poetry reading, a kind of call-and-response," even as they have "have different voices." Yet they "began to find correspondences, echoes," in their work, creating a "weaving, a braided stream." Their currents move in a hopeful direction, revealing observations with a simple clarity accessible to all. Both speak directly to an understanding reader, who will identify with these humane tropes.

Campbell declares in "Sacred": "You are a sacred site./I am a sacred site.//Face-to-face/at any place in this wide world/the sacred/ is in the presence of the sacred." Speaking directly, yet with a sense of wonder: "How we might shine,/each in to the other./What could we not accomplish?/What darkness could stand/against the light of such a sun."

Falls also speaks directly, as in "Tell Me," which flows out of its title: "is your heart rich,/could another take//taste the full/of you/and all/you have become?//Is your mind so clear/another could know/ it and come/away changed?"//Do you leap with/the arc of a fetus/in womb/whenever/another speaks//the truth?//If your answer is Yes/ take my hand,/we will walk/in the present/together."

In "The New Car Has No Clock," Campbell plays with time. "Now when we look for the time while driving,/there is only a restful blank space/where time is usually measured.//Without reminders/of time passing or appointments pending/we relax/cruise life's highway/ enjoy the scenery.//We bought the stripped-down model,/to save money./But we ended up/saving time."

In "Ice Storm in San Antonio," Falls dwells between vignette and poem. "I sit in a world that is mostly silent, except for the tired heater as it tries to warm this leaky house. My costume is comical— long johns peeked from under wool pajamas that flare from a fleece vest. I wear my husband's hunting gloves, the ones with the fingers cut off, a knit cap that was jaunty until mice nibbled the edges." Then she looks outside, asserting that "Deciduous trees hold up best. Eve's necklace, pecan, and walnut stand straight and tall, icy fingers pointing to the sky. Even the hackberry—Medusa's head of limbs—is unbowed. Hardy live oaks—laugh at the sun during our murderous summers. But the ice has them cowering. Heavy limbs sag under their own weight, each leaf encased in glass."

Neither is a "nature poet" or a "confessional poet" in the doc- trinaire sense, but they recreate natural and human environments in thoughtful ways. The collection generally alternates poems in a thematic balance that enhances the poets' connections, but also points out subtle differences in styles. Falls tends to write longer poems that utilize strategic spacing, while Campbell charges some shorter texts (and haiku) with irony and occasional lighthearted humor. Yet Campbell's succinct voice does not lack seriousness, as in "Enlightenment": "I've lived to see/Santa Claus debunked/and to know that childhood/was not the idyll my parents proposed/and I understand the purpose of education/is indoctrination and/deceit is politicians' stock-in-trade/while business exists to maximize profits/ no matter the cost/which brings me to religion/which fell along with the Twin Towers/vaporized/by men of perfect faith."

The book becomes a script for reading together in public, which was the original point of collaboration, but the poems also work on the page. There are no obscurities in *Braided Stream*, yet Toni Falls and Janice Campbell are courageous enough to write honest, vulnerable lines, evoking the mysteries of existence.

Lynn Hoggard's *Motherland* (Lamar University Press, 2014) combines poems and "stories" (memoir in vignettes) about growing up Protestant in Catholic South Louisiana as a blue-eyed blonde in a brown eyed-family. She would become an author and a translator (of French poets Michaud and Valéry), president of the American Literary Translators Association, and a university professor.

In her Introduction it is made clear that these vignettes (and many of the poems) are autobiographical, but since she writes "about places and people who didn't ask to become public, I've changed the names of both." As for "that time and place"—the 1950s and 60s in Cajun country—"have now both vanished." The vignettes of childhood are charming and bring immediate sympathy for "Cassie"— dreamer and outsider—whose sensitive tales often focus on others.

The portrayal of her mother is impressive, but particularly in a chapter about desegregating the elementary school where "Martha" was principal. "Everything in her mother's nature and in the historic circumstances during the start of the school year in 1969 had been slowly moving toward confrontation . . . One as a group of angry protesters ready to explode unless it could return the community, by force if necessary, to its segregated past. The other was an impromptu, nervous, shifting coalition of educators, churchgoers, and National Guardsmen, who—in different rhythms—all were moving in the same direction." During the 15 years after the Supreme Court declared segregation illegal, Louisiana's public schools remained in violation, thus desegregation was mandated. "Martha" walked 40 African-American children by the hand, two by two through the gauntlet, until all were in the school. Many difficulties followed and this riveting chapter explores every detail.

Laura Van Prooyen's 58 poems in *Our House Was on Fire* (Ashland Poetry Press, 2015) remind of a long, restless insomnia—interrupted by dreamscapes, memories, fantasies, and touching portraits of an unnamed husband and their young daughters—punctuated by startling images and fascinating observations. The house is not burning except in imagination; there are allusions to a child's serious illness and others about youthful vitality; saying no, perhaps meaning yes. These are not domestic texts, but rather a journal of mysterious variations. "Listen, then. Quiet as a dream," begins "Migration" and the book: "As the moment/she held her breath to see the man who touched her//all night was not the one next to her sleeping. If/that was a dream. The man she met in the woods . . .//even within a dream, she knew/to put her plume in his hand was never to go back."

"Happiness" reveals that "Once I wore/an impossible dress to a party and drank so much/I woke with a mysterious bruise. You should have known/that was what I called happiness. Not/the bruise, but the not knowing. Anything can happen./I like it like that." She can be prosaic, but also succinct. "Self in the Dark" reads entire: "If I'm honest,/I'm most myself//alone/and in silence./Clock and sunrise/quiet/your protests!//My heart, too,/resists,/screeching//like a note, blown/by a novice/on her new clarinet.//Solitude,/my black instrument,//how long can I stay/unschooled?"

"I know the world can be broken,/yet beautiful," reads the final poem about her daughter: "I want to believe loneliness//is not menacing, but can be a window/from which I watch her walk away." Laura Van Prooyen's second collection was nominated by Philip Levine as winner of the 10th McGovern Memorial Prize.

Dave Oliphant's poems in *The Pilgrimage: Selected Poems* (Lamar State University Press, 2013) are gathered from 50 years and 11 books, including conversational narratives, subtle rhyme schemes, and erudite connections. The best poems honor innovative authors (Joyce, Twain, Stevens, Neruda) and composers (Ives, Ellington, Ornette Coleman), featuring allusions to the arts throughout.

In 1965 Oliphant traveled with a University of Texas student group to the University of Chile, meeting Nicanor Parra and later translating the wry antipoet. The next year he met Maria, his Chilean muse (and wife of 46 years). *Maria's Poems* (Austin Book Award, Prickly Pear, 1987) includes his tenderest poems. Listen to "Maria's Mandolin"—"inside its orange-lined case/with its hollow form unembraced/its neck not held nor danced upon/its strings untuned & uncaressed/can lift no song nor lilt a phrase//but even now can feel it ring within/its tremolos recounting all the nights/she's held this head & kissed the frets/till her music's filled all emptiness."

In the title poem Oliphant journeys to Danbury, Connecticut, in search of places related to a favorite composer, Charles Ives, while delivering a witty pun about Ives' loving wife and artistic supporter (Harmony Twitchell): "to most/instead of Harmony he'd married dis-cord." "An Occasional Ode" is an homage for "teachers of the second tongue," those translating Spanish-language literature, which ends with a dash of humility: "if never fully to master/yet to know with love & respect/to impart with passion & pleasure/& in gratitude to Ortega y Gasset."

The cleverest design is "Fessing Up to David Yates" (a touching elegy for poet/editor of *Cedar Rock* magazine, who committed suicide at age 45 in 1985), consisting of lines that can be read down the left margin, a second set at the right margin, and a third poem when read straight through. Yates' tabloid "had opened to the priceless poems/ at times a photo/of your own face's inner glow/a pose in that final number/no mirror will ever return." Like many poets Yates published, Oliphant felt "unable to live with the way you left/after you'd written in public to stay in touch."

The book ends with a section from his unique verse epic in rhymed quatrains (*KD: A Jazz Biography*, Wings, 2012) about the Texas-born trumpeter Kenny Dorham (1924-1972). The 192-page biography based on discography, stands as an innovative and ironic (because rhymed) postmodern long poem. "I had no idea I would stick with the format when I started this," says Oliphant, who worked on the book for eight years. "KD was a musician's musician. You know how we talk about call-and-response in jazz? Dorham had the ability to do that within a solo. He would play a phrase like a question almost and then he would answer it. Back and forth, a call and response to himself. I don't know too many players who could do that."

Oliphant's wandering narratives in *The Cowtown Circle* (Alamo Bay, 2014) rummage through the underbrush of seemingly trivial memories until readers trip on a significant epiphany or witty turn hidden in the brief stanzas. His cleverly subdued style allows making almost anything into a poem. Those about music are fascinating, because he characterizes it evocatively, and his roving eye observes details that make every event a possible poem, displaying a confidence and a caring for what most poets miss. The same is true of the "Maria" poems (begun in 1976)—a mixture of love, charm, and soft comedy that long marriages reveal—yet elements that poet-husbands rarely register.

The poetry of David M. Parsons, 2011 Texas Poet Laureate, seems paradoxical on the surface. We do *not* think of ex-Marines and former athletic coaches composing poems, especially of high caliber. *Feathering Deep* (2011), his third book after his other two titles from Texas Review Press, *Color of Mourning* and *Editing Sky*, continues to reveal unexpected depths. In *Color of Mourning* (2007) he presents a series of homages for poets, elegies for loved ones, and reflections on communal history—all illuminated by honesty and humility. His narratives are conversational, comprehensible, and touching. The title poem, a moving meditation on the color yellow, observes a woman mourning on the morning of her niece's funeral, realizing that "yellow should not feel like this." That book ends on a light note with "Keys"—"There is a certain amount of amazement, when/you have been typing for a while/and glance up, finding/that you have been writing in some foreign untold language, coming/with the greatest ease, hands/flying through the wrong keys." This prompts a darker thought. "I have been living with great confidence/a life based on false premises." Despite a clever reversal, his premises have not been false, and throughout he embraces the correct keys.

While we may expect traditional verses on hunting and fishing, Parsons' poems (like "Blinds") turn suddenly inward to illuminate the unexpected.

I could discern
in my blind of artificial
trees, and yet, I
am, also, a witness

and citizen of the ancient
tribe, that coalition
that exists in the universal
chain of fear
and food—the aiming
eyes behind our many
individual stands—
those many faceted irises,
eyes we see through—
not with.

The unexpected is not merely wordplay on "blind" but an insight of connecting our "chain of fear/and food" to the chain-rattling anxiety of mortality.

In the title poem, the narrator's canoe, reflecting an inward, spiritual quality, is a metaphor without saying so. "I believe it to be/ unlike any other/conveyance//the manner in which/it carries us in/ upon its own silence//the way an idea drifts/into the great divide/ where we find ourselves//in that sacred state—easing/quietly into the dark *duende*/to unconscious understanding//a lone canoe at midnight—blades/paddling deep—smoothly/and deftly feathering//that largest of bodies."

This unpunctuated poem, afloat on immense waters of unknowing, drifts where meditative poetry always goes—from the "inscape" of Hopkins to Wordsworth's "spots of time" to Emerson's "moments" to Joyce's "epiphanies" to Denise Levertov's extensions of her exploratory "organic form" beyond the sensorium to include the intellect and emotion, which she calls "the inscape of an experience."

"Portents of Inscape" envisions "inscape" as "the distinctive and essential/inner quality of something, especially/a natural object or scene in nature/like the manner in which a poem resides," perceiving "enigmatic possibilities//for something new, fruitful,/an entity/

lit from within." The intrinsic light of poetry clarifies the experiences most readers share but cannot express.

Rarely lacking words, "Stepdaughter" stumbles adroitly across the time of this loving relationship, paralleling the social awkwardness of *that* word. "The term has always felt clumsy in my mouth," he begins, working through it, while metaphorically brushing her "stunning locks in complicated snares and rats,/demanding gentle/concentration, occasionally evoking a snagging yelp/and pain." This confession ends with "two smooth syllables combed together as two pig tails/woven carefully around /each other—naturally . . ."

Parsons also reveals social consciousness in texts that expose white racism. Not overtly political, they resonate with honesty and self-criticism. In "Midnight Montana: Little Big Horn" he hears "the true sound of the coming/of the Valkyries" and has an epiphany that ends "Integration 1964" with "in after hours' deep in East Austin,/when it was the 'bad part of town'/and we were like giddy young tourists . . ./through the sixties and we didn't have a clue/that we were like Ugly Americans." But Parsons' fine poetry is anything but ugly.

Larry D. Thomas, 2008 Texas Poet Laureate, mounts a figurative Harley in *Fraternity of Oblivion* (Timberline, 2008). It may assault pale aesthetic sensibilities, but its evocation of the land and roadways maps the ethics of a biker tribe, and contains a rough-hewn lyricism and thematic control. "The Initiate" suggests double imagining, "Through mirrored,/dark sunglasses/he sees the stars/clustered in the fraternity//of oblivion." This pack of "hogs" riding under a starry sky reflect each other's light in a crafty line which, even though bound by grammar to referencing stars, simultaneously mirrors in metaphor the exuberance of the bikers below.

Thomas' *Skin of Light* (Dalton, 2010) contains an imaginative sequence on art (by Renoir, Van Gogh, Chagall, Franz Marc, Hopper, Rothko, Picasso), which is about as far from bikers as one can travel. Yet all tribes will understand "Crow No. 4" (based on a drawing by Leonard Baskin). "His calves/are so massive/they ridicule the heft of Satan's.//The bulging muscles/of his humanlike torso/tremble with the weight/of his beak.//He squats a plumed/behemoth/blotched with the bile/of blasphemy.//To make him, Baskin/dipped his pen/in God's/worst nightmare,//and daubed his paper/with the fetid,/black mulch/of original sin."

Thomas' *Uncle Ernest* (Virtual Artists, 2013)), presents an epigraph by Roethke—"What's madness but nobility of soul/at odds with circumstance?"—that makes one wonder, following these acts through brutal and effective episodes. But the narrator visits the heart of darkness without flinching, suggesting we might all be capable of doing what Ernest has done, if we had been deprived of humanizing influences. Ernest ends in an asylum, where the graphic scenes startle. In "Windowsill," he sits in "the garish light/of purest science," observing "the row of jars/on the cousin's windowsill,/the jars of hearts,/the perfect,/pickled hearts/of little sparrows."

Only Thomas could create a book of contemporary poems about a goat herder, (*The Goatherd*, Mouthfeel Press, 2014)—in this case, an actual farmer in the Chihuahuan Desert during the early 1900s. His narrative internalizes the herd's survival instincts (and his own), adapting appendages into cloven hooves, taking sustenance from the herd, while protecting them from predators (but not from his own predation). He explores stark paradoxes of the food chain, as it once was in an earlier era. Nothing was wasted then, and Larry D. Thomas wastes nothing now—especially his poetic precision and prolific imagination.

No one is safe from the satiric wit of Reyes Cárdenas. In *Chicano Poet (1970-2010)* from Aztlan Libre Press (2013) we are treated to (and playfully mistreated by) the imaginative humor of his 40 years of work. This Chicano master of antipoetry exposes social truths in a cackling lexicon of critical insight, wry puns, and hatchet wordplay. His tone leaps from savage to the absurd, from ironic to dry, from bitter anger to tender concern. Neither victim nor clown, he must be among his "Survivors of the Chicano Titanic," who reveal "That swaggered/humility."

From the beginning Cárdenas had inner confidence, as the ending of his early manifesto attests. "If you come by you'll see me in the back writing about/Chicano territory./Out of my life have gone all the nagging doubts./And with them even my vieja./But I keep on writing as if nothing has happened./Sounds and colors drift into the poem/and go out of it./This is what peace is all about./And when this poem passes by/no one has to move out of the way." For a poem that blasts open with: "My long black and white hair attracts too much attention./Especially in a little redneck town like Seguin," "Chicano Territory" closes with humility and a bit of whimsy. His transparent poem knocks us awake with an invisible feather.

Cárdenas is a sly recluse who invents various personae in recent sequences. The longest is "Homage to Robinson" (2008), the adventures of an anti-hero told in the third person. Then the voice of Artemio Sánchez (2009), who "tries to explain/how he, as a poet, got to this point/in his creative career.//. . . groveled his way up/from nothing in the white man's eyes,/to nothing in his own brown community."

In "Meeting Mr. Incognito" (2010), the anonymous narrator describes a Russian poet's reading and time in Manhattan with his lady, realizing "There is nothing between us/except the dark matter science has been looking for." Several other texts are gossipy takes on famous Anglo poets—sarcastic, naughty fun.

The final section, "From Aztlan to the Moons of Mars" (subtitled "A Chicano Verse Novela," via Mexican soap operas), is a verbal cartoon of Mexicans exiled from Anglo Earth, who get revenge. Not great narrative poetry, but hilarious fantasy. And in "Poems From chicanopoet.blogspot.com" (2004-10), the imaginative masks slip intentionally. "Mirada" opens with a witty paradox: "I knew I was Mexican/by the way white people/looked at me," ending with "Today I know I'm Chicano/by the way the Mexicans/look at me."

"Flor y Canto" closes with "The years have passed./Now we're either stuck/with Hispanic or Latino writers.//They, of course, can never be Chicano,/that's why they fester/out in the open." Never a "militant Chicano," Cárdenas' bold political and social critiques draw blood with truthful thrusts. He remains a Chicano in the sense that one is always a human rights activist. "My barrio had gravel/streets,//only the/white side/of town was paved.//I went to Juan Seguin/ Elementary. . .//The only/white kids/I knew/when I was/growing up/ were Dick and Jane."

This seems to be his real voice, along with a masterwork from

1990 ("Epilogue to an Age" in the spirited "Elegy for John Lennon" section). Written "in the modern day language/in the Stonehenge of landfills," while openly admitting to being "In the anesthesia/of having been a rebel all my life." He riffs on "The poetry of Bogart's face/shimmering from a Sahara mirage," along with wild leaps and wry ripostes that paint the arid desert of civilization.

If Reyes Cárdenas is a "neglected" Chicano poet, this 370-page selection—six books from the 70s-80s, plus five new booklets of even stronger work—will bring this crafty, entertaining poet to our delighted attention.

Michael Gilmore's *Restless Astronomy* (Dalton, 2008) stirs a complex brew of erudition, cross-cultural allusion, and sophisticated shapeliness. His elliptic lines never lose control of their intensity. He opens the book with "Your smile is a ladder/I climb into your beauty," a fanciful encounter between cultural icons that signals the range of his imagination ("Achilles Proposes to Isadora Duncan Near Athens: 1903").

"Madame Pissarro Sewing" is a lovely poem about the wife of Camille Pissarro, that under-appreciated French painter who was a catalyst for the Impressionists. "There exists an ambiguous mystical life/Within the stitched parameters you sew//And parallel to what there is at hand/I am as rent as lace caught on a button."

"Vita Nuova" goes beyond Dante into "Merciless satire/Companionship distilled/Beyond conversation/No guesswork left/In the empire's realm." After a question— "Why is boredom/So fundamental a condition?"—Gilmore concludes: "We are equal now./Loneliness the most/Democratic form of exile.//Whatever we mean to do/is meant absolute.//When the fallen have landed/They rest."

The brief title poem casts a flash of awareness over the entire enterprise. "Unifying fields of force/Bind us heart and bone//Two half-lost souls/In the subaqueous lunar light//Waiting for the promise/Of a new school of thought." While *Restless Astronomy* does *not* invent a "new school of thought," it does chart an original path across our contemporary landscape.

Tony Zurlo's *The Mind Dancing* (Plain View Press, 2009), winner of the Peace Corps Writing Award, remains calm toward the still-point of meditation. These poems about China make it clear that he is neither Western-centric nor egocentric, and he has remained open to the ancient wisdom of the East. He opens with "Dao: The Elusive One" who "consumes scholars/in missions of the mind,/convinced they can analyze/and split it like an atom,//attracts philosophers/like gravity, confident/they will tame it with syllogisms and logic,/lures pilgrims to mountain tops,/guided by monks who promise/paradise to all who yield/to the scripture of bliss."

Not all the poems are brief Zen lyrics, as there are also longer discursive texts with witty turns and several about love for his Chinese wife, artist Vivian Lu, who provides a few verses and lovely artwork. In a send-up to Confucius ("Household Disharmony"), one of Zurlo's plays on Yin and Yang goes like this: "How to develop my undeveloped Self,/Sir, is why I come to you for help." His funny satire ends: "I go for some masculine advice, and you're out,/wandering the mountains dreaming up witty/one-liners. What kind of a man are you, Confucius?" A serious text on their love ("The Anarchy of Love") reveals that "To know her better,/is to know her less,/each day an invitation/into turmoil, each week/a temptation into chaos.//Exploring different threads/of her quilted character,/I uncover an uncharted world/and soar like a whirling dervish,/addicted to intrigue and suspense.//Enchanted by her mystery—/Lost in the bedlam of love—/I release, yielding and embracing/the endless universe of madness,/and together we explore anarchy."

Zurlo creates an alternation of cosmic and comic tones that keep minds dancing. His title poem hints that "To love China is to love not/the thing itself,/but the idea of loving, and never knowing.//Born in turmoil and nurtured/in mystery, China/leaves a vapor trail/of newborn stars.//China is the/mind dancing."

The title poem from Zurlo's next book, *Quantum Chaos* (Big Table, 2010), reaches its apex "By joining Chaos with Quantum Theory/we know that every nothing is something,/and something isn't that is./Even Time.//Time and Space are said to be but a creepy/parable of something unknown." Not exactly metaphysical, it is a satire on our ignorance. "We do know,/though,/that atoms and quarks and dark matter//Will explode into oblivion. You, me,/the fish and trees,/someday we'll all meet/our anti-matter, and we'll all be history—//Which itself is likely an illusion."

Zurlo spins this idea set by way of "New Age Philosophers" and fictional friends. In "The Picasso Corollary for the Many Worlds Theory" he imagines "Dali slipping from a parallel universe/ Michelangelo/from the rims of heaven, Rembrandt from the shadows." He declares we "shouldn't trust anything Picasso says." He also takes a turn with Matisse's cutouts and fragmented takes on mirrors. In "Through the Looking Glass" he inserts the phrase "The Mother of All Theories," only to be "sucked into a whirlpool of chaos,/brainwashed by fuzzy logic, then ejected/into a land where the truth, the whole truth,/and nothing but the truth is jabberwocky."

The collection carries the subtitle "Learning to Live with Cosmic Confusion," but one wonders if we have learned anything. "Quarks of Nature" asks intriguing questions. "Could the dance of/subatomic matter be/improvisational?" and "Can Reality/be determined by a/ probability curve?" When grappling with theories beyond what we can measure, what do we really know? "So I switched to creative writing, rumored to be a fuzzy branch/of the English Department," he says in "How I Became a Bona Fide Fuzzy Poet" and we discover "that all modern poetry/is based on the same fuzzy logic that runs artificial intelligence."

Charles Behlen's deft narratives of disappearing rural life, *Failing Heaven* (Lamar University Press, 2014), also reveal a vivid childhood. "Grandfather's farmhouse, vacant//now: windmill above the dried up/ horse trough charging the air still/with spent minutes, the blackberry/ tree where someone's sandals tracked its/bloodied fruit to the porch, past/the screen door drunkenly slung/on one hinge. Inside, there's a/ bent syringe on the sill, rusted//bathtub littered with beer caps,/a red sports coat in the stove: teens,/maybe, from sun-spanked suburbs/ that year by year, claim these fields one//house at a time, farm-to-markets/now packed with traffic you can/hear from windows that once brought only thunder, wind and chickens."

Yet "All that's gone. What's left persists/in a new kind of silence./Outside, newspapers blow in/from work sites, catch on the fence.//They tell how families vanish/overnight, one step ahead/of foreclosure . . ." Behlen's small town portraits (specifically west Texas and eastern New Mexico, but they could be anywhere in America) are filled with the wilted voices of country folk and textured sketches of soldiers scarred by wars. His precise evocations of handmade clocks, wicker chairs, or porch swings are not antiques, they are old and dying out, like the country people who inhabit the shacks and disappearing landscapes of the poet's past. "Depression era houses/throw their cats/ and little blue squares of TV light/out on the lawns."

B.V. Olguín's poems are never ridiculous in *At the Risk of Seeming Ridiculous* (Aztlan Libre Press, 2014), and his self-deprecating humor attests to the validity of his affection for and dedication to the process of becoming a peaceful revolutionary. Olguín made four trips to Cuba as a member of Venceremos Brigade, including men and women worldwide, who find ways to work with Cubans in the fields and everywhere else on the island blockaded by U.S. regimes since the 1960s.

This handsome paperback (with vintage photographs of Cuba) begins with texts that place the Brigade in historical/political context. The poems' plain speech and charming anecdotes provide insights into the conscience and humanity of the Brigade. Dedicated to poet Raúl R. Salinas (1934-2008), known internationally as raúlrsalinas, a mentor to writers, who were launched from Salinas' *Resistencia* bookshop in Austin (read Salinas' *Indio Trails*, Wings, 2007).

In an empathetic poem drawing on Salinas' words as its epigraph, Olguín writes: "We are all storytellers in the brigade/trying to figure out what it means/to pull weeds, cut cane, pick oranges,/scrape paint, haul concrete and stack fresh/yellow copies of "The History of America"/as the poor remember it./This is what a book is: sharp corners/of pulped wood cut into a weapon/by industrial blades, each page/sharp as a machete, and words,/words, words with letters curved/ and cut like miniature swords, daggers, rifles . . . A poem is most dangerous/when it doesn't tell the truth./Stories are most dangerous/ when writers become so certain/of a beautiful line they don't notice/ the children of wood cutters and/paper makers who will never learn to read./There is no time for metaphors/when an irrigation ditch needs to be dug./No one has patience for metaphysics/when the printing press needs repairs/to ensure students have books/when school starts after harvest."

One does not doubt the sincerity of this Chicano's concerns and commitment to a cultural revolution that "will take decades and lifetimes," according to Salinas' words to the author, yet always concluding, "we don't have a choice but to win." Time ran out for Olguín's mentor (an early volunteer in Cuba), but perhaps there is yet time for this UTSA poet and scholar of the 45-year-history of the Brigade's engaging support of the Cuban mission of valuing people over profit.

B.V. Olguín's *Red Leather Gloves* (Hansen Group, $12.95) emerges authentically from his experiential perspective as an undefeated amateur boxer, examining the seedy side of machismo. The gritty narratives express what it means to train for coaches in a gym, to be hungry since you had to run on fight day to make weight, and to overcome real fear and pain. Exploring boxing terminology as titles and themes—knockout, gladiator, killer instinct, the sweet science, pound for pound—Olguín counterpunches clichés into human reality. Most portraits are of losers, has-beens, or liars, but odes to Muhammad Ali, Ray Mancini, Ronnie Shields, Emile Griffith, as well as poems on the jab and double right cross, are enlightening.

Tad Cornell's resourceful Imagist poems are often satirical—laced with insights and playfulness—about theology, philosophy, literature, and pop culture. The aperture into his poetry is the delight in writing one's way through thinking. Five sequences are seamlessly fused into one grand book (*In Whom Is My Delight*, Juggling Teacups Press, 2015) by the variations of his witty voice. The first section is a narration of incarnation, reflecting Chesterton's views. The second section narrates a social worker's monologue of ethical crisis. "Today I am an 'on call' worker, and so/the phone may ring, and I be majestically shot/into my own denial before the cock's crow./'Welcome to the historical present,' I say/to St. Mark, or anyone who may know/his use of Greek in that gospel where he'll play/with language at life's core./ All this before my foot even touched the floor./Go figure. He also serves who doesn't care." Yet a reprieve, as the patient's "eyes searching mine and not mine into his soul/is what drives me through the rain to his side, to undo/my own hollow, loveless acts of control,/hoping for Sam's childlike verdict reading into/my soul the star of Bethlehem, the songs of hope . . ."

The third part peers into the brain of poetry, where Cornell has "staked my life/on an obsolete craft," discovering that "It's only when you can't find the last thread that clarity/and mystery can occupy the same space at the same time." A clever "Suite" sings as confessional poetics in the fourth section: "Compelling as/masterful origami, the point is fragile, elegant pointlessness." The last reminds of Shakespeare in sonnets to the body, where "The garden of the moon is utter gift/like heart to heart and spousal loin to loin/or sighting land when all you had was drift." As readers "drift" through the musing texts, Cornell's images will be unforgettable.

Mo Saidi's third collection, *Between A and Z* (Wings, 2014) spans the qualitative range from compelling narratives to a few unconvincing homilies, but is augmented by an impressive story telling tradition by describing scenes vividly. "The Mansion of My Childhood"—about life in Iran before Saidi immigrated to the U.S. in 1969 to become a physician—recalls a family expecting him to become a mullah, while he "always dreamed to be a writer," and "We made peace: they burned the chess board/and the pieces; I buried the Holy Book."

"Chaos" begins as youthful reverie: "On a clear summer night, I lie/on a thick mattress on the flat roof./I gaze at the myriads of stars/ the enormous universes and climb/the ladder of imagination/in search of an answer." It evolves into perceptive, mature observations: "We need miles of DNA strands/to decipher truth—nature is not/curious about your fate.//The sun rises and sets and warms up/our planet; we walk the green pasture/and look for a nest, a mate/watch the flight of hummingbirds."

"African Sojourn" is a precisely detailed sequence suggesting a documentary, yet finds subtle ways to embed critical insights. "On dry land, gangs follow the herds./Packs compete for meat; nature remains/ neutral among leopards, hyenas, and vultures.//The elephants walk as a team to defend/their young, yet they are powerless against/the men who kill the largest for ivory and sport.//Beware of armed holy men, the false saints/who usurp paradise and dig into the sacred/earth. Look at the hills of dirt,/dispossessed of their diamonds and gold."

Floyd Collins' *What Harvest: Poems on the Siege & Battle of the Alamo* (Somondoco Press, 2011) accomplishes in poetry what Stephen Harrigan's novel, *The Gates of the Alamo*, delivered in prose. Both are insightful narratives of the saga that do *not* negate the humanity of all its participants.

Collins does not plot a chronology but approaches the siege through fascinating character portraits and texts on the actual "things" of that era. "Kentucky Gunsmith: Long Rifle, 1833" begins "in the forge, wrapping a pressed bar/Of wrought iron braced on a swage block," and continues to detail the fascinating process of fashioning a rifle. In the third stanza, the gunsmith "starts to carve in earnest. Virtuosity/In the pursuit of form lies in slickest/Evasion. Everything flows, sinuous/Lines holding plane and mass forever/In the present tense. The stock tapers/And flares all the barrel's length. He raises/In low relief a baroque C-scroll..." Later "he chases/Rime-encrusted floral. . ." What harvest do we have here? The construction of a rifle as sculptural art masterfully expressed in poetry. Near the end we discover this "Blacksmith, mechanic, wood-sculptor, jeweler" to be the relatively-unknown Daniel William Cloud, who was "Bound for rebellion in the Texas province."

There are stunning portraits of the famous (Crockett, Bowie, Bonham, Travis, General Santa Anna), but what stands out are the detailed backgrounds each poem sketches. Three on David Crockett dispel the Disney legend that "Davy" died on the ramparts. Rather, he and a few others surrendered, thinking they would be treated as prisoners of war but "Santa Anna's/Gleaming entourage cut him down as tailors/Would a legend grown too large." (This debated fact of Crockett's fate was clarified in Walter Lord's history, *A Time To Stand*, which drew upon the field diary of Lt. Colonel José Enrique de la Pena, an unbiased eyewitness.)

Three poems concern James Bowie, including two that reenact his duels with Major Norris Wright. The first ends with Norris' shot "Lodged in the dial plate of Bowie's watch," but the second "Interval was Bowie's. His whetted Damascus/Cut the major free of both liver and lights." In "James Bowie: Bexar, 1836" we stand inside the Alamo sanctuary: "What harvest is forthcoming/As he watches from the delirium,/Hoping to lure into his gleaming arc" where "Sabbath sun streaks the bayonets,/And the brackish light begins to go."

"Gregorio Esparza"—a 60-line narrative on the courageous Tejano who manned a cannon at the Alamo—stands among the most engaging poems. "Esparza casts his lot/With the insurgents in the old mission/Hoisting by rope and pulley onto a scaffold/In the apse of the church a terrible/Deus ex machina, the iron tube/Of a Spanish twelve-pounder adorned/With twin dolphins. Thirteen days he abides/Aloft his makeshift ramp./His *niño* Enrique/Shrinks from flames, the crumping roar/Of the three-piece battery." We sense the absurdity of war and feel the fear of trapped families. Esparza "knows how futile his attempt/To break the generalissimo's hold./The siege tightens; a mineral sweat/Lurks in the limestone walls by day,/Making the chapel dank as a sepulcher./Catcalls drift across the river each twilight,/Words so serenely murderous they/Raise the hackles at Gregorio's nape./He sees men crouch around watchfires/In the Alamo compound, silence/And shadow the only realities/During a lull."

"Aftermath: Dawn at the Alamo" begins: "In the breast pocket of a slain defender/Impaled against the wall by a bayonet thrust,/A slim gold watch chimes the hour./Blood percolating through chill limestone./A young sapper's hand, brown and hardened by the toil of hefting retrenchment tools,/Seizes the precious heirloom." But the Mexican soldier "resists the impulse to remove/The broad brimmed hat, level his *escopeta*/At the blond head, and replaster with brains/The barrack wall." The chilling poem ends on a note of compassion: "Such stains, indelible, run deep enough."

The abiding value of Collins' viewpoint rests on the lucidity of precise details and intense feelings humanely rendered. War poems are generally impossible to write without spinning legends of glorious victory, and most writings that "Remember the Alamo!" are rarely unbiased. These fine narrative poems are the exception.

Geoff Rips and Noel Crook have seen their impressive first books published. Most initial volumes are weak, or perhaps promising; but these are fully-realized, mature works. Both know how to tell a story and, significantly, often as witnesses rather than as narrators. Rips, who has been political journalist (*Un-American Activities*, City Lights), award-winning novelist (*The Truth*, Western Michigan University Press), and editor of *The Texas Observer*, was always writing poems.

The focus of the first section of *The Calculus of Falling Bodies* (Wings, 2015) is on two young daughters. "Snow still on the mountains above Taos. My daughters/are growing older," begins "I Lift Her Up," a three part narrative with long, prosy lines, reminiscent of William Carlos Williams' "ordinary" language, while embedding subtle imagery and expressing great tenderness for his daughters.

In the title poem, Rips writes, "Looking the wrong way, I was told/what you fear will kill you. But there's too much/to choose from. One of them will get me, sure./Mortality has all the options, compared/to my one." Two elegies for his father are heartbreaking, yet there are hopeful poems. "At 51," he is "glad my losses are gradual./We outlive all our joys. But/just now I've been dancing on the front porch/ with my beautiful daughters as they gyrate/down the uncut trails of their green lives./Even the setting sun seems to pause/before it drops."

Noel Crook's *Salt Moon* (Southern Illinois University, 2015) won the first book award in the Crab Orchard Series and Red Dragonfly Press published her chapbook *Canyon* in 2011. Crook is a Texan, but lives in rural North Carolina, the setting for most of these powerful narratives that are precise, sharp, and bloody ("The Twins" and "The Secret Lives of Animals"). Deep concern for her children's safety comes forth in "Skull"—beginning with a skull hanging from a van's rearview mirror. That night she watches the hallway leading to the children's rooms—"all night I consider my options, my own/ black capacities: the baseball bat/nestled in the toy chest, its satisfying/weight and heft; a claw hammer gleaming/in the toolbox; in the kitchen, the cool handle/of the butcher knife that fits my palm like an answer."

Crook writes well about places outside North Carolina—a Manhattan art exhibit, a stay in Istanbul, a canyon in Texas, which suggests "a great scar, beautiful/in the way of a scar, in the story it tells," a place "with the scuttling of a million blind crustaceans./I was their sister, the warm sun whitening/my bones, the curve of my spine/ another decoration on the limestone floor."

In "Reading Ovid at Buzzard Rocks," Crook reveals that "I've come back to this blunt horizon/butting up against a bell jar of blue/ and a sun that can bake the meat off anything,//even loss. Where if you hold out our arms/at the bluffs edge and breathe deeply enough,/the sky will agree//to swallow you whole. But it's turkey mating season/again, the lovelorn, dusty hens congregating/over on Horse Hill, scooting willy-nilly in//and out of sage and prickly pear, addled/by their need"//yet, "waiting for kettle-drum calls of the gobblers/roosting solitary and oily in the cottonwoods,/their bristled beards swinging/like scalp belts. After this long coyote winter,/all of us still waiting to be stitched/into the old cloth of the world's desire. . ."

Octavio Quintanilla's *If I Go Missing* (Slough Press, 2014) does *not* read as an initial effort, but like a wise book that grapples with dark visions. The poems are not written for mere effect, but from depths reminiscent of the painful poetry of Peruvian César Vallejo, one of the poets quoted in the book's epigraphs.

The collection is divided into three sections that mirror the title. The first ("IF") suggests erasure in nightmares of losing a left hand and being lost in a labyrinth. Later he laments: "I carry my destiny like a corpse/of someone I've known/all my life./A faithful pet./A true enemy./Heavy like a bad deed/I have not yet committed." He has "no words,/no silence, no images to release/like frightened birds/ out of their cages."/Thinking of "the word 'forgiveness,'" Quintanilla "can't force it to forgive./Can't say, 'Forgiveness is like. . .'/No simile./ No metaphor./Just talk.//If you find beauty in this,/then you know the human heart/is made of words."

But the poet has heart and choice words. In the second section ("I GO"), he recalls Mexico: "My parents can't recognize the country of their birth," yet his "father wants to go back and harvest the fields he worked as a boy," the property that "belonged to my father and to his father," where "under a sky so wild, and so blue,/that it was impossible to imagine/any other existence." But exiles "have no land/ and the land of others remains quiet and pale/like a face adrift in a casket." There are strong poems about immigrants and *la frontera*, the "black heart/of the festering fruit./White grin of flies./Body hanging from a bridge," and where "In this light, things appear to be/made more of anger/than of flesh/like the history of all exiles/and of hands poisoned/by pesticide./Small heartbeats/that empty their grief/all over America."

In the last part ("MISSING"), Quintanilla observes his "father licking the salt/out of my mother's grief./My mother putting a band-aid/on my father's empty hands.//Some nights they talk about us,/their children, who live in distant cities,/who without knowing/also practice being alone." In "Café Triste" loneliness becomes absurd: "The man with the hat leaves/his ulcer sitting at the table./The wait-ress, not sad enough/to speak to me, pours herself/out the window.//I pretend I have what matters./A job. A plan. Hands that come off/with the gloves."

The title poem ends his collection. "What if we're taken in the middle/of our daughter's ball game, or from our beds,/minutes after making love,/never to be seen again?/But who takes us?/Where do we go when someone in the news/says, *He's been missing for days*." After speculation, the poet turns to his possible disappearance. "If you wake to find my toothbrush on the sink,/unused,/and my boots just right underneath the bed/as I tend to leave them,/slip back under the cov-ers and sleep/and dream new details—/a lit candle, a coffin, someone walking away/in the shallow of my eyes./Encounter once again so many/new images and words and trifles/that might or might not have been mine/so new your life by then,/like newly discovered scenes/in a movie you hadn't seen in years."

While he writes in "Fugitive" that "a greater mind couldn't fin-ish/the abandoned project/you became," Quintanilla ably finishes his project for those who can identify in human terms.

Jessica Helen Lopez, known for exciting slam poetry perfor-mances, has an intriguing first book, *Always Messing With Them Boys* (West End Press, 2011). While we may expect line-breaks to echo voice pauses, we also discover deft narratives composed for the page. Hearing these fetching performances will entertain, but her lines offer more than meets the ear. The title poem opens with a provocative image. "The night permeates like a blood orchid/bursting with the smell of wet caliche/through my open bedroom window.// One lamp is lit, the color of dusk./Curled like a fist around my cigarette,/I am stuck in the knuckle of my thoughts." Yet it concerns her pre-pubescent body that will *not* flow like ink. "I still do not/pick up my pen" but "I pinch/out the memory of one afternoon/I kicked ball with the boys, before the blood came." The poem bleeds into the story of an abusive father, a caring mother, while "still clinging/ to the inside of my head,/like clean white linen,/Mama's laundry/ and the idea of love."

"Dangerous Woman" questions societal stereotypes. "Where do I fit/between dainty decent/and vulgar truth?//saintly and slutty?/ maternal and murderous?" "This Sunday Morning" celebrates without guilt ("I like the honesty/in the swelling of this skin"), making the carnal spiritual. "In the hollowed church/of our bed, our shared/Sundays are holy//Together we make/our own religion."

Several concern marriage, separation, divorce, and the birth of a daughter, inscribing the body as text. In "Custody" "Our daughter is a dividend/carved from my hip/and a piece of your rib." "Beauty" revisits "your birth/colored the sky a certain shade of rose/I will never see again," and "your father shed his ego/on the day you were born and I never/saw him so naked and pure."

Jessica Helen Lopez was a member of the National Champion Poetry Slam team from the University of New Mexico in 2008. Dynamic, seductive and witty, *Always Messing with Them Boys* provides us with another younger poet who deserves national attention beyond her stunning performances.

José Antonio Rodríguez's *The Shallow End of Sleep* (Tia Cucha Press, 2011) explores childhood in south Texas where his family picked crops to support their bare existence. In "Resident Alien Card," a five-year-old boy is "being walked/through the immigration process." He meets a photographer who "has no face,/only a voice steady like the low light/from the corner of his studio,/the light that sometimes falls/on still bodies." Instructed to look at a teddy bear on a wall, he notices that "It is faded, small and gray with dust/and dulled eyes, nailed to the wall,/a stab of rust through the belly." And as the man "barks" directions, the boy's "tall mother stands/outside the lens trying to make herself small."

These unsentimental narratives tell a heart-felt story of parents exhausted from "stoop labor" and of hunger shared with older siblings. Without politicizing poverty (yet evident in the haunting details), it becomes clear through the "dust that coats everything" this resilient Mexican immigrant family does *not* "deserve" to be poor because of laziness. Their harsh conditions are neither romanticized nor over-stated. "The blades of the window fan/hypnotize my dirt brown stare,/dry away the sweat and urine/of wind-laced days without baths/in a bucket of well water." The ramshackle houses they inhabit have "one room with two beds and a stove,/a flimsy curtain dangling between/and no doors to slam shut."

Pablo Miguel Martínez's first collection, *Brazos Carry Me* (Kórima Press, 2013), begins with "Ecclesiology"—"Splayed on our bed, your arms are cruciate splendor, blazing;/my kisses, the fourteen stations." In this secular church of intimacy, "I worship here. Your offering, a slender spire reaching past/dreams of paradise." Not only do the lovers re-consecrate religious imagery in sexual passion—"Your rose window seduces the heavenly light. Your back arcs,/moves heav-enward"—but they have committed the culture's "sin" of gay love.

A later, brief counterpoint ("Crime Scene") brings this to street level. "With righteous chalk/They've marked the place/Where it ended suddenly./There on the scarred sidewalk./A few stop to ponder and gawk/At the outline of two men/Locked in a fast embrace." It would be insufficient to limit *Brazos, Carry Me* to the annals of gay or Latino (or even human rights) literature, even though Martínez writes eloquently from these personal viewpoints. Yet, since these realities have been ignored or derided, and his lyric voice represents *otherness* authentically, the strongest poems reflect this consciousness.

"A Map of Aztlan"—the longest and most complex—bleeds mythology into reality from Albuquerque to El Paso to Los Angeles to home town San Antonio, and finally to Mexico, where "The innocence of a thousand/Juárez girls float/at the water's edge,/where duck bills scythe unceasingly,/and a brace of egrets waits, patient/for startled schools to reconvene."

Trey Moore's poems in *Some Will Play the Cello* (Pecan Grove, 2011) strike a fresh variation on the theme of contemporary spiritual enlightenment. His lines echo both Robert Frost's sage dialogues and the wild open yowls of the Beats. But his street-level savvy never leaves a pedestrian imprint, and he is always an observant witness of landscapes and cityscapes. Following a public route in "Started at Luna's and Finished On Martin Luther King's National Holiday," Moore uncovers his inward path. "It is this way./One day we awake!/ Each star shining in dawn's headdress." During the march, "The children play the Dream/making do with scraps of paper/holding handmade signs./Can't resist the kick of a can/singing *we shall overcome*!// Unite in a tide/with one face dreaming," which also emits an epiphany, "Oh it's a new world/this one changing."

The poet listens intently to his late grandmother, Felice Moore, to whom this book is dedicated. "Love Never Fails" is a monologue in her voice, as he sets the scene of their tender visits, sitting in the chair in which she rocked him as an infant. This charming eulogy looks like an open spreadsheet in this large handsome format. Other spreads, bordering on prose, project the simmering oppression of summer streets and city dwellers. In "The Last Time I Used Sign Language," he is nearly run down by an angry truck driver, who speeds up as he attempts to cross. When the narrator proffers a single finger, the driver curses, stops the truck and steps out with a pistol. Even while recognizing "the *other*" as himself, Moore knows the difference, and runs into a store to call the police (as the driver leaves the scene).

Interspersed with the rambling poems are tight lovely lyrics, like "After School Practice" that holds the book's title.

A listening boy carries a cello
bigger than two of him. He daydreams
from Garner Middle School.
Furious flashing light and steel.
A thin black vinyl protects the cello, the bow
of purposeful pernambuco and horsehair.
Nothing protects the boy.

The tender helper's unsocietal
feeling of matchstick puzzles.
My heart scoops him up with wings.
It will take all of us. We'll each
have our part. Some will play the cello.

"Pursuit of Happiness" projects a humane perspective. "Underneath the concrete bridge./Caretaker of our streets/homeless, beaten-up/push broom wizened face/grocery basket filled with garden hoses.//Stolen land?/We are called here./Not asked." His empathy reaches out, knowing the difference is in circumstances. Moore admits the same, remarking that it "is a long way from crushing/beer cans until you have eighty pounds." It ends with a stunning couplet. "Some build prisons for their person./Others are the world without a roof." Trey Moore's *we forget we are water* won the 2008 Wings Chapbook Award, but he takes his music beyond that in *Some Play the Cello*.

Witness for Justice

Even as millions have viewed the photographs of Alan Pogue since the 1960s (in *The New York Times Magazine*, *The Washington Post*, *International Herald Tribune*, *Texas Monthly*, *The Texas Observer*), his profound documentary vision in *Witness For Justice* (UT Press, 2007) can be contemplated in a book for the first time.

Pogue's stunning images not only attract the eye to clarity and form, stirring primal emotions of anger and compassion, but most become transformative encounters. We are taken by these 100 masterful black & white documentary photographs to some of the world's most oppressed places—from the Middle East to Central America, Cuba, Haiti, Mexico, and to the punitive Texas prison system—a searing panorama that challenges our inculcated prejudices and exotic fantasies. Then there is Austin—his "beat" since the beginning—featuring street scenes of protest against injustice juxtaposed with portraits from the state capitol's glittering halls of power.

Pogue's camera eye reveals humanity's essences in its faces—from memorable portraits of the late César Chávez and Dolores Huerta (co-founders of the United Farm Workers of California, in a two-page spread) to various unheralded social reformers, to unnamed children in war zones. The images strike an immediacy that commands full attention. The most haunting faces are of children, including the Iraqi girl, Asraa' Mizyad, who survived with a severed arm and multiple injuries from fragments of a U.S. cruise missile and César Gardado, who lost a leg at age eight when he stopped on a landmine in El Salvador. Other lovely children are here, those who are not so obviously damaged, like the unnamed girl on a farming co-op in Nicaragua (fittingly entitled "Wise Eyes"), and six children of Florida farm workers, bursting with innocent delight and charm.

Everywhere in these pages, we meet compelling faces peering back—Palestinians and Israelis in dialogue, Mexican peasants and teachers at work, oppressed minorities, political students marching, and esteemed portraits of conscience: Barbara Jordan, Sissy

Farentold, Molly Ivins, Ed Krueger, poet Raúl Salinas, and Cindy Sheehan (in a witty juxtaposition with George W. Bush in full fluster).

Every page evokes the unmistakable viewpoint of a progressive activist. "Perception is judgmental and consciousness is communal," Pogue writes. "One need only avoid prejudice to experience the truth. I merely relearn the original lesson on a larger scale. The political activity and the photography were the same activity. If you are really trying to produce understanding in the act of photographing people, you must join with them and leave them alone simultaneously." His *Introduction* reveals the source of his truth telling. He volunteered for Vietnam in 1967, becoming a chaplain's assistant. From the "well-fortified base camp," he saw the war as "distant thunder," taking pictures with an ordinary camera.

When the chaplain had a breakdown, Pogue volunteered as a combat medic. "Now there were scenes to be kept from my mother's view: napalm-burned mothers, children hurt by bomb fragments, rice farmers shot in the back, fields destroyed. I felt an urgency to record what shocked me as well as what was beautiful." On leave in Japan, he bought a 35mm Nikon, three lenses, feeling that "it was important to record what I was seeing because the reality didn't match my preconceptions."

Returning home, Pogue worked at his craft, becoming a student of the legendary Russell Lee, one of our premiere photographers, when Pogue's energies were put in the service of the farm workers' struggles and crimes of the penal system.

Roy Flukinger's *Foreword* provides a clear survey of documentary photography, establishing a useful context. "For, even more than representing any one particular subject or story, they represent a threnody for this age and a strong call for us all to be continually alert to and aware of all the good and the evil that mankind is capable of engendering." Flukinger quotes Marita Holdaway, director of a Pogue exhibition in Seattle, pointing out his unique vision: "Many people document severe conditions, but not many bring out the warmth and humanity, the love and hope that are the qualities we all share that make it possible to believe in peace."

Alan Pogue's chosen images, their sequence and juxtapositions, and his direct and often pithy captions, all harmonize into an unmistakably empathetic viewpoint, a clear aperture of suffering and beauty. *Witness For Justice* is not merely a random collection of well-framed pictures, but a self-contained work of art.

Face to Face

While it will be impossible to overlook the art of portraiture evident in 50 large black & white photographs by Michael Nye, the photographer is otherwise erased from the naturalness of these powerful images. *About Hunger and Resilience* is inhabited by the faces we gaze into while their voices relate their own stories (via headphones). Originally at the Witte Museum in San Antonio, this and other Nye exhibits have been touring the country, and like his last exhibition *Fine Line: Mental Health/Mental Illness*, this one also depends on the viewer's openness and empathy.

As we enter a dimly lit spiritual sanctuary each station presents a unique encounter. The effect of peering into exquisitely detailed portraits and hearing authentic voices, compel us to forget our preconceptions. The participants do *not* speak in the cliché of the victim, but document in human terms the daunting circumstances beyond their control.

Nye points out that "These stories are not intended to summarize or explain anyone's life," since "explanations and solutions are profoundly complex." We can see why he was moved by "the human presence" in these lives.

Nye traveled around America four years, spending three days with each person, listening with an open mind before making photographs. The astonishing exhibit reveals faces in unselfconscious reflection rather than subjects captured in a dramatic moment. In search of a "longer moment," as Nye puts it, we can witness instants of unfolding illumination into a reality about which we know only slogans. This is not a strategy to win a political argument, but an artistic process that does not judge. "Everyone in this exhibit knows something important and valuable, a wisdom about their experience that only they know," for when it comes to understanding personal disclosures, Nye believes they are the teachers and we are the students.

The reasons for hunger are legion, and anxiety has spiked since formerly middleclass workers have lost jobs and homes. A catastrophic illness or serious accident can bring down a family without sufficient health insurance. Natural disasters have created exiled communities of the homeless and hungry, whose situations are exacerbated by mental illness, alcohol, and substance addictions, by incarceration, and the loss of dignity. Hunger is *not only* a present reality that carries past baggage, but also a tangible fear of future hunger.

For those who have been malnourished for years—one participant describes hunger as "your belly rubbing against your backbone"—they experience desperation, loss of vitality, and deep depression daily. Many have been supported by food banks, soup kitchens, charities, and churches that include the generosity of volunteers. But these are stopgap measures, which do not affect the roots of the larger crisis that has expanded with the recession and the phenomenal growth of agribusiness that has moved small farms off the American map.

There are heart-breaking comments made by the participants in this exhibit, including one recording that is an anthology of voices responding to the question of what do they hunger for beyond food? The responses are varied, telling, and basic—for acceptance and understanding, for meaning in life, for being heard, for knowledge, for optimism to keep on living, and for wisdom.

"I have felt with even a greater conviction that we all need to speak of the essential needs of our human family," writes the photographer. "These stories are about all of us as we live with our uncertainties and the realization that we too could experience hunger."

Being confronted face to face with the universality of suffering due to hunger, we cannot dismiss them as *others* who deserve their fate. "Hunger is an issue of human rights," declares Nye, and we would be human *and* right to agree.

While we hear a humane "documentary" in these recorded voices, Michael Nye's magnificent portraits are true works of empathy and art.

On Extended Wings

Wings Press was founded in Houston in 1975 by poet Joanie Whitebird and Joseph F. Lomax (from the famous family of folklorists and blues discographers). It began as "an informal association of artists and cultural mythologists dedicated to the preservation of literature in the nation of Texas," publishing a Townes Van Zandt songbook, and the poetry of Vassar Miller and Naomi Shihab Nye, whose voices soared above the quaint notion of Texas as a nation. As significantly, the imprint's survivalist instincts for literary works paralleled Alan Lomax's preservation of American music, which struck one as visionary rather than naïve.

When Bryce Milligan assumed the Wings perch in 1995, the literary community recognized him as a serious poet, as the publisher of the literary magazine *Pax: A Journal for Peace Through Culture*, and as the experienced editor of the groundbreaking anthologies of Latina writing he assembled for Penguin.

Wings continues to defend artistic freedom, to represent cultural diversity, and to battle the insidious domination of the publishing cartels (most recently against Amazon). Milligan has accomplished this by making handsome books of challenging content instead of manufacturing products that mask a wordy void with flashy covers and huge budgets. This may sound extreme since Wings is an independent imprint based in San Antonio and not a massive corporate mill, but alternative publishers provide a vital antidote for the bottom line mentality of bestsellerdom.

What Wings lacks in quantity, it delivers in literary daring and aesthetic quality, remaining open to the new, in stark contrast to those houses of Gotham, whose gated stables locked out authors long before the small press revolution of the 1950s-1970s created a wider world. Instead of selling what marketing managers claim customers want, independents continue to offer readers what they need—the contemporary fresh voices in a multi-cultural dialogue. The following books and authors tell part of the Wings Press story of this independent press that has existed for 40 years.

The late E.A. Mares became a leading Chicano poet when *The Unicorn Poem*, one of America's signature long poems, was published by San Marcos Press in 1980. The narrative about "Old Town, Albuquerque" was expanded as *The Unicorn Poem & Flowers and Songs of Sorrow* (West End Press, 1992).

Mares' recent 55-page poem, *Astonishing Light* (New Mexico University Press, 2010) is based on "Conversations I Never Had With Patrociño Barela." This imaginary dialogue between the great wood-carving artist and Mares' persona harmonizes a witty, rhythmic text in English, in Spanish, and in the international language of metaphor.

The woodcarver speaks the "truth of knife, chisel, wood and dreams. . ./I can't speak a lie there." The narrator declares: "I don't lie, but I say the truth/with a little salsa." Mares creates a masterful homage to Barela's primal and humane art. *Astonishing Light* illuminates these pages with lucid insight, charming humor, and lovely lyricism.

Between these two memorable long poems resides *With the Eyes of a Raptor* (Wings, 2004), a stunning collection of poetry. There are heart-breaking poems about the life and death of his daughter, in Spanish and English, beginning with "There are Four Wounds, Miguel" (based on lines by the Spanish poet Miguel Hernández). "One by one the days slip into history,/and where there was a voice/ there are only documents, evidence/that my daughter once walked this land./Now she leaves footprints only in memory.//There are four wounds, Miguel,/the wound of life,/the wound of love,/the wound of death,/the wound of silence."

Mama Yetta and Other Poems (1999) by Hermine Pinson closes with the title piece, an exuberant prose poem in praise of her paternal grandmother. This earthy and wise African-American matriarch taught her the lessons of Yoruban lore and family stories from the bayou regions of the South. "This is your daughter talkin'," Pinson begins, with self-deprecating wit and naked honesty, "the one who peed in the bed and didn't walk till twelve and a half months, the one who was left-handed and stuttered with strangers, the one who rolled her eyes until they crossed one day, the one who loves you still." Pinson's lyrics (like "Left-Handed Poem") read like jazz riffs with an attitude, a set of sassy, signifying variations.

Left hand turns inward
then rises like an ominous
hump from the limp neck
of the wrist
when I am making a point
or begging
    to differ
fingers and thumb poised
to pick up some subtle thing
        beyond themselves
came out of the womb that way
left hand turned inward
hard against the heart
transparent knuckles
but worker's hands
    like Papa Johnny's
came out that way and
    almost broke my arm
the doctor pushed me back in again
so I could come out
right

Pinson plays the instrument of her becoming, mindful of the orchestra that shaped her, and the doctor who had to rearrange her first solo, so she would emerge right. She continues from the distaff side of the bandstand.

I used to play saxophone
now I press fingers to soundless keys
the task:
    reach through the space on the pages
for some subtle thing
half-turning motion of pincers
    in the ocean of heartways—
at rest the left hand lies:
    a failed balletic exercise
an invalid's carelessness

a pulse
a time signature
  a womb's knowledge
of life's ceaseless motion.

This stands as a personal creation myth, a musical take on the poetic process and a left-hander leaping through metaphors of identity. Even if some notes slide past, her tunes are not bent toward obscurity. She swings in original ways, inhabits the beat, slips behind it. What begins as a tribute to Nina Simone evolves into a moving portrait of her parents ("Nina or somethin' like happy"). "Mama would turn on Nina's/scratched record and sit down/after she and daddy had been/drinking and screaming/exercising blues/two prairie chickens/ on unholy dancing ground."

Later their hot dancing becomes a *danse macabre*. "Mama and Daddy/reached for each other/with murderous hands/two blind minds." Pinson's blues lyrics are sung in startling rhythmic turns, emotional shifts, and edgy thoughts. These signatures are never ornamental, but essential to recomposing the risks of memory.

Margaret Randall, poet, writer, photographer, and human rights activist has authored more than 100 books. *As If the Empty Chair* (2011). This exquisite hand-made book includes photographs by Annabella Balduvino and Randall, with translations by Leandro Katz and Diego Guerra. The handsome limited, signed edition presents heartbreaking poems on the "disappeared" throughout Latin America during the 1970s and 1980s.

Randall writes of "a new form of state terrorism" that "took root and spread," becoming "known as disappearance: paramilitary forces aligned with national dictatorships, themselves supported and funded by a succession of U.S. administrations . . . kidnapped people from their homes or plucked them off the streets. They were never seen again. They became the *desaparecidos* of popular discourse, mourned in homes and communities, immortalized in song and poem. Disappearance. Disappeared. Strangely passive words to describe such brutality. From the rich Latin American lexicon, we might have invented a word that better fit the crime. What happened instead was that this word shed passivity and took on new meaning, one instantly and painfully recognizable to anyone living on the continent. . . ." She focuses on families of lost loved ones rather than on the horrific violence that "disappeared" more than 150 thousand victims.

In "At Exactly the Right Time," Randall writes, "Disappeared is a word/like some sleight of hand:/the rabbit that won't come out of the hat,/the macabre magic trick gone bad.//All those frantic days and nights/making the rounds of prisons,/hospitals, morgues,/then making the rounds again,//a routine that kept them alive/until hope tripped on its own feet/and memory turned inside out,/blurring the contours of his face.//She remembers a time before hope/had to claw its way to the surface:/her baby brother/still laughing...//Then she remembers to forget./No body. No tombstone/she can cover with flowers,/no goodbye."

"Disappeared"—that haunting word offering no closure, "unable to describe/its burden of loss" for "sons and daughters,/lovers and workers/who still walk the scarred streets/of a city peopled by ghosts,/whispered conversation,/truncated songs/whose fading words/can only be read on old walls/or echo inside the heads of those who remain://still searching, still in love."

"Another Dimension" begins with "Macabre vectors twist memory/their dance mutes a history/where some humans//live swollen with power/that erases others." In light of the horror "As If the Empty Chair" expresses the viewpoint of denial: "Can't we just put it behind us, those untouched ask//Can't we just move on. . ." The response to heartless questions, "as if the empty chair/isn't tucked beneath table rim,/that side of the bed isn't barren and cold/or the mirror reflecting a single face,/doesn't taunt these lives/we inhabit//without those plucked/from the air we breathe." For "Without them/we cannot move on,/for where will they find us/when they stumble home?"

The International Court proclaimed "forced disappearance" as a systematic attack on civilian populations, qualifying it as a crime against humanity in 2002. The United Nations adopted the International Convention for the Protection of All Persons from Enforced Disappearance in 2006.

Too little *and* too late, since such laws have had minimal effect in finding victims or bringing the guilty to justice. "The vast majority of victims of the crime of forced disappearance were kidnapped, illegally detained, tortured, murdered, and their corpses hidden" or "their bodies often dropped into the ocean from helicopters," writes Randall. "But there is a vast emotional distance between knowing this intellectually and having a body to bury and mourn." The crimes "not only punished the man or woman fighting for social justice, it also punished their families, communities, and nations. Hope is that most tenuous but tenacious of human emotions. Without a body, hope refuses to die." These painful poems give hope in the midst of despair. "Do I get out of bed this morning/yet again? Do I wash my face?/Do I speak?" For Randall, and all those who have lost loved ones in the fight for justice, the answer must be an unimpeachable yes.

Margaret Randall's latest collections of poetry are, as usual, boldly political and deeply personal. If one agrees with her truth telling against the lies perpetrated by those in power, then this poetry is for you. If not, you will get "news" from TV or the establishment newspapers, but not from poetry (as William Carlos Williams hoped). Randall's viewpoint is clear in texts of protests and in nuanced poems.

Her collection, *About Little Charlie Lindbergh and Other Poems* (2014), mentions the famous kidnapping in the opening stanza of the title poem, but it is merely part of the public background about growing up. Her poems are usually more direct, as in "Everyone Lied": "We lied to protect our own and then/to justify not protecting our own./We lied on a need to know basis,/parroted our leaders/even when they pretended genocide away."

A subtler, witty poem (in its entirety) reads: "Irony and unassuming wit/paint my everyday mask./A question mark/where the mouth should be/adorns another./A mask of kindness/always works /when promise comes up ominous.//I have fashioned these masks/ through a lifetime of fear/and certainty, a step back/for every two steps forward.//I cannot remember/when the last mask dissolved/in a moment of blinding silence./Touching raw skin still surprises."

The final two poems break through their narrative frames. "Your Poems Are So Political" responds: "What moves me is the delicate membrane/where love's pulse/beats against submission,/subjugation erases will,/Big Guy versus everyone else," continues about an intimate partnership with artist Barbara Byers. "Your gentle fingers braid mine/as we transit streets/where it's a crime/to love/outside the rules.// Yes, I respond, *my poems/are political like a razor/against your throat,/the word no when you expected yes,/spit in the eye of the powerful.*"

In "This Poem's Got a Problem," she cleverly injects her political poetics. "This poem wants to serve,/provoke chuckles/even outright laughter,/transmit the magic/of a charmed life.//But it slips from my grasp,/wanders under the railway bridge/where a family of seven/takes scant cover from the cold." Stanzas declare poetry's solidarity with the pain of others, expressing itself as the voice of conscience, closing with "I am an optimist, light-hearted/and believe it or not/have a sense of humor,/but my poetry insists/on recording what it sees."

In *Beneath a Trespass of Sorrow*, a hand-made chapbook from Wings (2014), with Barbara Byers' maps (lovely cartographic paintings), Randall commits a long poem that covers the internal map of global grief. "Their National Security litany urges us/to be afraid of difference,/kill anyone unlike ourselves/before they get us first.// We are taught our nurture of hope/wears the wrong clothes/settles accounts too easily./Laws mock our every ritual.//We are too young, too woman/wrong shape or color;/our bodies un-white, unclean/ meant to serve in shame." In a later section she writes of what poor people know experientially—"Poverty draws its own boundaries, toxic/waste confines, evicts./Foreclosure pushes spatial limits/while the big boys redistrict solutions."

Like most of Randall's poetry, these collections reflect the outsider's view of the injustices undermining our sense of humanity. She knows about injustice, since in 1985 the US government ordered her deported because of views expressed in books. But she won her case in 1989, despite living and working in revolutionary Cuba in the 70's and in Sandinista Nicaragua during the 80's. She was awarded the Lillian Hellman and Dashiell Hammett grant (1990), and is the subject of an hour-long documentary ("The Unapologetic Life of Margaret Randall").

Sheryl St. Germaine's *Preface* to Darrell Bourque's third book suggests an elegant parallel between his *Burnt Water Suite* (1999) and Johann Sebastian Bach's *Suites for Cello Unaccompanied*, in that each voice is "*both* cosmopolitan and confidential, and speaks to us about what really matters, the single instrument's voice explored so deeply and fully that one cannot imagine ever needing another one."

He begins a 90-line discourse ("Inhabiting Separate Bodies").

> We have always been told that wanting rises,
> but there is something like longing asking
> for another reading. This is not desire
> if by desire we find ourselves driven toward
> the edges where exacting begins to clarify itself,
> where urge itself begins to set out trotlines
> for its own translations, where necessity begins
> to see its own measurability.

Borque's meditation reflects a complex sense of the cultural psyche and a primal awareness. Subtle comments follow on poetics. "This travels without sense/of strictness. It travels slowly and mostly down/with all these other bodies through paths skewed/for collision." Matter ascends until it begins its slow descent through stages, bringing pain to the poorly designed lower back, to the constricting chest, and finally to the limbs that "sing *desire* and *parting* and how."

> early on these two lie easily in the same bed
> and how it all is as happy an arrangement as
> marriages ever get until we find ourselves somehow
>   all the way up here;
> here, moving like moons circling the planet
> of whatever your matter and my matter make,
> never able to move any closer to whatever
>   has this pull on us and will not let us go,
> never able to read the something we know is written
> there if only we could bring the right light to it,
> before we begin to sense recession, the sweet descent
> we have come to recognize the way we recognize our hands,
> our feet, the face that falls into the field
> where we look for ourselves. We sail past,
> are comforted by this configuration memory tells us
> we once took for ourselves, called by our very name.

Desire animates matter, flowing like blood through the body of poetry. The "burnt water" of the title refers "to the opposition that engenders all creation and to the created thing itself," Bourque observes. "It is at once both the phenomenal and the pervasive Urge that creates all being. It is then flower, sex, poem, person as well as the necessitating force or desire that resides in all matter." He discovered the phrase in Octavio Paz, who interpreted it as "The opposition of water and fire is a metaphor for cosmic war. It is an image of cosmos and man as a vast contradictory unity. The cosmos is movement, and the axis of blood of that movement is man."

Burnt Water Suite is in seven sections, each technically varied but thematically integrated into one cohesive text. Poems can be read separately as self-contained entities, but fresh depths are illuminated by reading from beginning to end, because passages are composed to reveal wisdom patiently (as in "Holy Water").

Your mother is water.
You are water.
She runs Tigris
and Euphrates
through your veins.

Her Nile flows
into the waters
of your longest river.

Rivers she gives
are not gifts.
They never separate
themselves enough
from the two of you for that.

She will give you a drum river.
It will beat over you
sleeping in the high branches
in a sling she made
just for you.

One day you will fall
suddenly.
The fall will force you open.

You will hit the skin
of the drumhead yourself
for the first time
and it will change
everything.

You will be music
from that moment.
Everything else you do
will be accompaniment.
You are a sacramental
thrumming. You are
making all of time
a vigil.

Darrell Bourque's poetry balances the tension of contrary opposites within his harmonium of solitude. Desire and parting are a marriage of *yin* and *yang*. Mothers and children swim rivers of memory, as water and fire flow into burnt water. Spiritual life is sacred energy and sacrament. The complex ferment and contemplative vision of *Burnt Water Suite* are reminiscent of the expansive poems of Paz, returning us to the intimacy and sophistication of Bach's solo cello suites.

Hook & Bloodline (1999), Chip Dameron's third collection, evokes the palpable resonances of a changing world from the vantage of mid-life. Since his perspective evolves through precise diction that uncovers deeper levels of experience, the lines never fossilize into object lessons. Mature perceptions reveal a lively and thoughtful dialogue with middle age, neither indulging in cheap nostalgia nor courting this culture's denial of death. He often contrasts past and present, without wallowing in vanity. Even when the "creative process" becomes a sub-text it feels natural rather than manipulative.

"The Journey" begins "When his heart/was hollow/the ringing phone/could fill it wither her redolent gifts,/but someone else's voice/ would empty out his ear,/and he would one again wonder/where to find his second skin,"

the one that stretched around
the landscape of his life, tattooed
with the glyphs of another's
headlong living.

And yet
to find the voice he had to first
absorb the morning birds
and talk at work, he had to find
a satisfaction with the tone
of his voice, feel in
its timbre a fullness that he
could live on. He had to turn
his inner landscape out
and outer in, and hike across
them both, leaving the plain
tracks of being.

While the self-portrait is introspective, there are portraits of fellow inhabitants along his South Texas coast. Further south we encounter Tahiti in a lush sequence of paradisiacal poems, including one about artist Paul Gauguin.

the dark lushness of the jungles
that are rooted in the humus
of his mind, finding those totems
that bring back a red and orange world
that has no factual existence, but comes
as quickly as shadows do, as shadows
turn the night into the thing
the day yearns for, intensely without form,
without color, humid with emotion.

Two of his most entertaining texts (one a fantasy on Hemingway and Picasso, the other a portrait of Faulkner) are Modernist without sounding dated. "Rendezvous" cuts against the grain of legend with satirical wit, picturing the Spanish painter and American writer in a French café, drinking wine and talking about women. "When live bullets nip their exaggerations/Hemingway, puffed with grenades/and pistols, nods goodbye and strides/into action." Then "Picasso turns the sounds/into the thin lines of a drawing/of a dream." After "the noise subsides,/Hemingway binds his wounds with words/and reinvents his shadow."

In the "Portrait of a Mississippi Novelist," Dameron depicts the Faulkner we know from the photographs but the mask is not quite right. Then he reveals the man, "seen best through the stitchery/of the sentence, the place/where the clarity of word/reveals the muddling of heart/and mind, impossibly complex/and unmeasurable. No one can know enough. All he can do/is puff on his pipe, habitually,/and follow his words through/their strange and resourceful/inclinations, driving them/along the muddy river bottom/as if they were wild beasts, amazed into submission."

Dameron's fifth book, *Tropical Green* (2005), navigates along the borders of acute awareness, evoking the varieties of *flora* and *fauna* natural to the Texas coastal regions, while also meditating upon a primal sense of place. The title poem explores depths "in the market, where snatches of meaning/are lost in a cascade of syllables/that leave you wet but still thirsty." But "So deep this green that it can choke/you in the night, its tendrils swelling/into ropes that wrap around your dreams."

At the shore of another poem "the grinding sea climbs through me as it rolls its tale inland,/a living salt stew that never stops for breath," and in a forest he challenges us to "Just try to rub the trees from your eyes,/this haze of particulate holding off the sun." The poems are never far from the great silence of the universe, reminding us how small we are, yet always from a view of awe. "South Texas Direction" instructs us to "Follow the aroma/of sound deeper than you'd/think you'd ever dare,/and there you may find/a pool to gargle in,/to go hip deep and sink/until you bubble like a fish,/a fat fish at rest at last,/eyes adjusting to each side/of the world, fins holding/

everything equilibrious, gills/beginning to filter truth from fact."

Dameron's resonances of a changing world deepen as his wise perspective crystallizes. "Where I've Come To" expresses it in the naked terms of being-in-nature, while also inscribing a linguistic subtext. "This is where I've come to,/this mountain pass, this marker,/this sky with rain clouds/building in the west,/the wind capable of cutting/the past into ribbons of regret,/the trees as thin and cold/as thoughts, the hawk along/the ridge focused on fur." Mountain passes mark his passage, wind breathes past regrets, trees become symbolic thought, before a real hawk soars beyond projections. He makes a simple turn, becomes grounded in elementals. "I stop and stake the tent,/swap boots for moccasins,/lie back against my pack,/and say the first words/of this day: *welcome home*." These introspective nature poems, always lucid and truthful, strike most deeply. Chip Dameron's accomplished style is not limited to quiet meditations. *Tropical Green* also contains tender family narratives, witty portraits of rural characters, social satires, and protest pieces of ethical conscience.

JoAnn Balingit, Delaware's 2008 laureate, winner of the 2010 Global Filipino Award and the 2011 Whitebird Series for *Forage*, writes remembrances of painful family narratives and lovely nature lyrics. "The Great Tree" (after cover etching by Leonard Baskin) weds both in one intense rush. "The great tree stands in the corner of your youth unhurriedly/gathering rings and massively sidles up close to your birth/while you are not looking. It peers down through your life as if/over a cliff…" Shedding leaves, "it lets you see how provisional things were…./great tree of/longings, of fledglings always about to fall/from that nest of feathers you dream."

David Lee—Utah's first Poet Laureate from 1997 until 2002, a professor at Southern Utah University for decades, and author of 16 collections—writes about imaginary misfits in Pipe Springs who speak in rural dialects that torture language. These may be the funniest characters ever overheard in print, despite their desperate lives shaped by extreme losses.

"Wheelis House: A Texas Tragedy" is an absurd romp that opens with an epigraph by Sophocles and a perfect imitation of the hilarious ignorance. Since Lee was raised in West Texas, he knows these voices, turning them into woe begotten fictions like Odus Millard, who was "apparently unaware of his universal appraisal/of being neither useful nor ornamental/in their familial pecking order. . ."

David Lee shares the stage in *Moments of Delicate Balance* (2011) with narrative poet William Kloefkorn (1932-2011), author of 20 volumes, who was professor emeritus at Nebraska Wesleyan University, and the state's poet since 1982. His intimate poems reveal absolute attention during his last years. Every precise detail recalls incidents from childhood and epiphanies of aging.

In "Sunday Morning on the Patio," he hears everything. "No bells or whistles, no/hosannas in the highest,//just the first robin of the season/posing dark-eyed and orange-breasted/on the rim of the empty birdbath,//beneath it a familiar resurrection/of green, and because suddenly/I have this odd urge//to use love, in a sentence,//I tell my wife, who's sunning/nearby in a recliner, that//I love her, and when she looks up/I confuse her eyes with the/robin's, my confusion doubled//when she takes wing and glides/into the kitchen from where/very shortly she returns,//pot of coffee in one hand, cookies/in the other, her feathers molted/to reveal the skin I touched//last night before I went to sleep. . ."

The first stanza of "Sitting Next to a Young Woman Who Plays Classical Violin" begins with "Because in my childhood I learned the art of pilfering/I continue to nurture it, this time/to take from the young woman beside me/something to help me live my life/more musically, something that/by way of a quaint osmosis/will enable me to fall from the high notes/without shattering the delicate counterpoint/of flesh and bone." How joyful his music, ending with "the spirit of wood and of string/so precisely on-key joining in, eye and teeth,/brown and skin and so on, restoration/in the presence of what, each time we recover,/can never be fully explained."

As Kloefkorn turns over roots of consciousness, he discovers the ineffable in the everyday. In "Waiting" (for a poem in to emerge), he realizes that "I have more than enough light/to write by.//I write that with its front paws a squirrel/reaches into the grass and brings forth/an acorn." But when he applauds, "the squirrel/cocks its head, drops the acorn,/and disappears in the branches of the oak." Not intending this result, he waits for the sun to set, and "When it does, I will write about/whatever it is the fallen sun reveals.//I meanwhile wait. I write that meanwhile/I wait." While relating the process of waiting for a poem, one appears.

Frances Hatfield's first book, *Rudiments of Flight* (2012), alludes to decades of immersion in mythology, Sufi mysticism, and Jungian archetypes, creating a sweet lyricism that rewards careful rereadings.

In "Three Names for a Spider" the narrator watches a "tiny blond spider" on a goddess statue. "She adorns the stone body with silken/hair extensions, a filmy veil." Each morning the poet discovers "subtle new connections/she has illuminated between objects/of this world. . .// Thus she begins/the day's work for me." In the next stanza "my spider likes to pose. . .//as a starry necklace, wily eyebrow, shoulder tattoo." In the third incantation, the spider becomes a Hindu Avatar: "Worried she might starve/from her austerities and devotions,/I search for dot-sized bugs. . ."

Spider as Muse, Savior, Avatar? "I can't prove/it is her voice I hear, /or tell you how she answers/when I ask what she sees/from her perch/on the unfathomable/brow." The "tiny blond spider" may not be female, may not even exist. But the poetry of Frances Hatfield flourishes in such lyrical inspirations.

Wang Ping's *Ten Thousand Waves* (2014), her twelfth book, explores desperate realities of the voiceless. The title poem encounters the tragedy of 21 undocumented Chinese laborers who drowned at Morecambe Bay, England. They were collecting clams, and had been misinformed about the timing of tidal waves. This sequence is not as penetrating as the personae she inhabits in the vignette portraits of Chinese peasants, which are powerful and heart breaking.

In "Time to Go Down the Mountain," a young niece pleads with her aunt, "there must be something for me down there—washing dishes, doing laundry, cleaning, cooking, scrubbing toilets, babysitting, walking dogs, or shining shoes. Look at my hands. They're strong, nimble. No, I haven't learned Mandarin yet. You know I don't read or write. You tried to teach me when I was little, tried to send me to school on the other side of the mountain. But I was homesick, and the teacher beat me with a stick because I couldn't recite Chairman Mao's poems."

"The Price of a Finger" is a sequence of voices on both sides of the assembly line. "With your right hand, you slip strips of metal under a hammer back by four-thousand pounds of pressure; with your left, you sweep molded parts into a pile," writes a worker with crushed fingers. "You do this once a second for a ten-hour shift . . . . You must concentrate. You must not lose a beat, or it's all over." A lawyer for the factory bosses retorts: "We have always met the government's standards for safety. Otherwise, they would not let us operate."

Wang Ping includes an actual chart in the notes, revealing that "compensation" for such gruesome injuries—10 months salary for losing two fingers or 18 months salary for the loss of four fingers or both thumbs. Minimum wage salaries are less than 40 cents per hour in China, so the loss of a limb is no bargain.

Pamela Uschuk's *Blood Flower* (2015) is her sixth collection from Wings and her *Crazy Love* won the American Book Award for 2010. Vividly conscious of war, which she knows from loved ones—since brother, first husband, and father were in different ways victims of endless tragedies. In a poem for brother John: "You wrote me that you stood/on top of an ambulance while mortars/tore wounds in the green earth,/and you couldn't stop anyone's screams." Concerning her late husband, she remembers: "He'd point to the mean hieroglyphs of red scars/a pinched cummerbund of bullet/and stab wounds cinching his waist,/then ask me, new bride, too young/to be a Sphinx, the riddle I couldn't reason out./*What was this for? What for?*/as he headed to the kitchen for anesthetic beer,/the amber mattress of whiskey straight./ In three years he joined his company underground."

Uschuk's father was a tail gunner in WW II, who escaped death in a dogfight. "When his plane skidded in on its belly, mechanics counted a hundred holes in the tail alone," exclaiming, "*No way you could have been in this/and not been hamburger.*"//Fingering campaign medals,/my dad looked through me with eyes/liquid as the blue air above peaks./*That's why they send boys to war. No/grown man would go.*"

The opening section of growing up as a Russian in middle America rings true with other stories of prejudice against immigrants. Uschuk includes two pitch perfect takes on classical music. "Shostakovich: Five Pieces for Violin and Cello" evokes the parts with imagined scenes. "It's the Russian in me that charges out/in my dark velvet skirts, heart/as blood-gorged as Anna's watching/the train gain speed for her leap, when I hear/what your violin remembers . . ."

"Iron and Lace" hears a Bach violin piece again played by Kasia Sokol, a dear friend. "When a woman makes music, the course/of the river shimmies/free of ice as passionate stones/unbury their long grief. This lovely poetic motif mirrors the music in words. "When a woman plays music, glass/windchimes of fortune ring ecstatic in wind,/toss black roses on bedcovers with each deep tone."

Chapbooks

Contemporary chapbooks—known as "cheap books" in earlier centuries— continue to find their niche in this new world of electronic devices. "The debate between handcraft and more modern means of production in the book world," writes Bryce Milligan in *Publishing Perspectives*, "has been going on since medieval scribes threw up their hands in horror at Gutenberg's press."

> Over the past half millennium, the debate has resurfaced every single time there has been an improvement in the means of getting text before the eyes of a reader. The future is writ upon the wall for all to see, and it spells doom for lovers of the physical book. It's okay. We're human. We'll adapt. That much, at least, is in the DNA. But I do not think that the average reader—no matter how happy he or she is with their voluminous digital libraries on their diminutive screens—will be satisfied to never have access to a true literary artifact, something tangible that connects them to a favorite author. It makes perfect sense that larger printed works violate both our economic and our evolving green sensibilities, but small artifacts of the author may remain a necessity, if only a psychological one.

Milligan also points out last century's literary highlights in chapbook form—from T.S. Eliot's *The Love Song of J. Alfred*

Prufrock (1920) to Alan Ginsberg's *Howl* (1965)— before these works became reining titles in the universal poetry canon. Since 1975 Wings has issued nationally significant titles in this format, like those by Vassar Miller (*Approaching Nada* and *Small Change*), as well as superb poetry by Naomi Shihab Nye, Michael Ventura, Hermine Pinson, Michael Sofranko, and Eleanor Crockett—all as handsome saddle-stitched chapbooks in limited editions. The chapbook was a predominant format for books of poetry during the "small press revolution" of the 1960s and 1970s, and Wings continues that tradition.

When Milligan brought his own talents to the art of the chapbook—not only his editorial eye for the work of younger poets, but also his imaginative eye for design—he began with the *Poesía Tejana* series, publishing Latina writers (under the age of 30), which yet remains one of the most under-represented groups in the country. Among the poets are Frances Treviño, Carolina Monsiváis, Greta de Leon, Nicole Pollentier, Victoria García-Zapata, Mary Grace Rodriguez, and Celeste Guzmán.

In 1999, Wings brought out one of its loveliest chapbooks, *Winter Poems from Eagle Pond* by Donald Hall, with woodblocks by Barry Moser—and in the adventurousness of hand-made production. The Colophon, a page which usually means little in book publishing, herein gives due credit to the contributors and some insight into the complicated process.

> Seven hundred copies have been printed on 70 pound Nekoosa Linen natural paper, containing fifty percent recycled fiber, by Williams Printing and Graphics of San Antonio. The text was set in Bernhard Modern type, titles in Caslon Openface type. The cover was printed by Paul Christensen of College Station, using a 12x18 Chandler & Price sheet-fed letterpress.
>
> *Winter Poems from Eagle Pond* was entirely designed and produced by Bryce Milligan. The sugar maple leaf used as a printer's device throughout came from Robert Frost's farm in Derry, New Hampshire. The first three hundred copies off the press were numbered, signed, and dated by the author. These were hand-sewn by the publisher into

cover stock made by Austin papermaker Kristin Kavanagh. This handmade paper incorporated maple leaves from Eagle Pond, gathered by the poet's grandchildren on an autumn day in 1997.

The most distinguished U.S. poet published by Wings—Donald Hall—has won nearly every significant literary award: the 2010 National Medal of Arts, U.S. Poet Laureate (2006-2007), Ruth Lilly Poetry Prize for lifetime achievement, Robert Frost Medal, National Book Critics Circle Award, Poet Laureate of New Hampshire (1984-1989), and a Caldecott Medal for *Ox-Cart Man*, a picture book for children. He edited the groundbreaking anthology, *New Poets of England and America* (1958), and has written memoirs, biographies, novels, and textbooks.

Like Hall's sheaf of Christmas verses (including one by poet Jane Kenyon, his late wife) from the Eagle Pond house where he grew up, Wings produced an equally lovely chapbook by novelist Robert Flynn, *Burying the Farm* (2008) a memoir of early life in Chillicothe, Texas. While chapbooks are usually collections of poems, Flynn's 30-page personal essay is the perfect text for gentle hands-on treatment, surrounded by a magnificent decal-edged cover by Amy Gerhauser, incorporating north Texas mesquite leaves. Both spines are hand-sewn by Milligan, who does much of the intense handiwork while watching movies with wife Mary, a librarian and writer who has been an essential contributor to the press. The Flynn chapbook includes charming family photographs and tender verbal portraits.

Ana Castíllo's flash fictions, *Bocaditos* (2009), is another example of a perfect fit for the chapbook concept. The stunning cover includes a cutout, allowing Castillo's painting to show through from the title page. Another significant aspect of chapbooks is that internationally known writers, like Ana Castíllo, poets Rosemary Catacalos and Margaret Randall, the late Spanish master Ángel González, and the heralded Chicana Lorna Dee Cervantes, have seen their brief manuscripts transformed into beautiful chapbooks. In the case of these five authors, the press has also produced trade edition collections of their other works.

Chapbooks are also a way to feature newer poets like Joseph Trombatore, who reflects on the arts in sophisticated allusions.

Screaming At Adam (Whitebird Chapbook Contest winner in 2007) opens with a lovely homage to Debussy's "*Clare de lune*" beginning, "you loved the sea/like an Impressionist claiming all the light/for yourself,/devouring colors like clouds/pink blush of sand dollars, pale tint of an afternoon kiss." Others allude to Caruso, Fellini, Matisse, Toulouse-Lautrec, and Hart Crane in serious or comic modes. But Trombatore can also be introspective. "This morning will be measured in quantity, quality/value of conversation from a minimalist's point of view/graded, categorized/filed away for next year's assessments/quantum leaps for those last minute needs will be calculated/as a Passover meal." "Anticipation" ends with "diligent spies/waiting like lions, for the tamer's wrist to tire."

In Joseph Trombaore's title poem we read a more cosmic overview. "I inherited what you did not want/thunderstorms upon mountaintops/you could not descend." The poem closes wonderfully: "the woman trembling beside you/like a Monarch clutching onto bark/ blood rushing to its singed wings."

A recent Wings chapbook, *The Log from the Sea of Cortez* (2012), a series by David Taylor, is based on the published log of Ed Ricketts and John Steinbeck's trip through the Sea of Cortez in 1940. Taylor's poems, in Milligan's assessment, "articulate the ways in which the trip became an exploration of themes and concerns which resonate today—a growing concern for the overuse of the natural world, the legacy of colonialism, the intersection of the arts and sciences, and the uneasy place of spirituality in a modern worldview."

Milligan ends his essay about the chapbook thoughtfully:

> Inevitably, in the very near future, publishing a paper edition of a book, even of moderate size, will no longer be a viable economic option. At that point, the sole surviving physical publication of this press and many others may in fact be the chapbook, consciously (and shamelessly, I might add) created to be a literary artifact, designed in consultation with the author, sometimes using materials associated with the author. . . You just can't appreciate (or own) an illegible signature on screen the way you can one on paper. And besides, what are all those writers going to sell and sign at their readings, downloads?

Epilogue:
Angela De Hoyos

Poet Angela De Hoyos (1924-2009) is celebrated by a Wings chapbook, issued in conjunction with the tribute, *Poeta del Pueblo* (Poet of the People), at The Guadalupe Cultural Arts Center in San Antonio, on January 9, 2010. The booklet includes a long personal portrait of De Hoyos by Bryce Milligan:

> If anyone has ever been truly "larger than life," it as Angela De Hoyos. A bit shy of four-eight, she was, as Rudolfo Anaya put it, "one of our giants." She was a walking contradiction in many senses. Born in 1924, she was older than even the oldest of the activists who created the Chicano movement in the 1960s—and older by over a decade than writers like Anaya and Tomás Rivera. Yet Angela always seemed part of a younger generation. Such was her passion.
>
> Partly that impression came from the fact that she surrounded herself with younger writers, especially when her press, M&A Editions, was turning out ground-breaking books by young Chicanas like Carmon Tafolla, Evangelina Vigil, and Inés Hernández. Angela had enormous respect for other people's talent, yet she was so self-effacing that it could be disorienting. If you were a writer in the same room with Angela, she made a point of making you feel like *you* were the best writer in the room.
>
> Among other projects, Angela, myself and Mary, my wife, edited two large anthologies (*Daughters of the Fifth Sun* and *¡Floricanto Sí!*) and a few issues of her magazine *Huehuetitlan* together. I also interviewed her several times. When the question of her age came up, she'd just chuckle and hand us some authoritative reference book that indicated she was 16 to 20 years younger than she actually was. "*They* say I'm . . ." she'd begin—and then never finish the sentence. She liked being in reference books and text

books. "It's the only immortality I'm likely to qualify for," she told me. . . .

The Chicano political movement did not begin in one place or another, or on any specific date. Political awareness threw throughout the country from the 1920 on, with a few highlighted events like the pecan shellers' strike led by young Emma Tenayuca in 1938 and the 1954 Supreme Court case, *Hernandez v. Texas*, all of which led to the activism of the 1960s. The Chicano literary movement, on the other hand, was essentially proclaimed at the 1969 Chicano Youth Conference in Denver. Two poems defined it: Corky Gonzalez's "Yo soy Joaquin" and Alurista's "El Plan Espiritual de Aztlán." Both movements were very male dominated.

Then along came Angela De Hoyos. In introducing her own poems at readings, Angela often chided "the guys"—meaning Corky and Alurista, Lalo Delgado and Ricardo Sánchez, among others—for being blind to half of the workers for the revolution. Within a very short time, Angela's first two books, *Arise, Chicano!* and *Chicano Poems: For the Barrio*, were being used interchangeably as literary works and as political documents. But very importantly, they were among the very first Chicana feminist statements. . . .

The late poet Raúl Salinas once famously called Angela the "den mother of the Chicano movement." He was *not* referring to cub scouts, but to wolves. It was, in many ways, a perfect description. Angela was fierce in her advocacy, yet the gentlest of guiding spirits. . .

Angela, along with husband Moisés Sandoval, were not only central to the culture of San Antonio, but powerful forces in the Chicano/Chicana movement. Moisés, Mary and Bryce Milligan, poet Carmen Tafolla, and many other artists are yet with us, working toward a humane reality outside the margins of definitive mediocrity.

Angela De Hoyos provides the last word in a defiant poem ("The Final Laugh"), which graces the back cover of this charming chapbook celebrating her life.

On an empty stomach,
with the pang of mendicant yesterdays,
I greet my reflection
in the dark mirror of dusk.

What do the entrails know
about the necessity of being white
—the advisability of mail-order parents?

Or this wearing in mock defense
the thin rage of ethnic pride,
saying to shivering flesh and grumbling belly:
Patience, O companions of my dignity?

Perhaps someday I shall accustom myself
to this: my hand held out
in eternal supplication, being content
with the left-overs of a greedy establishment.

Or—who knows?—perhaps tomorrow
I shall burst these shackles
and rising to my full natural height
fling the final parting laugh
O gluttonous omnipotent alien white world.

Acknowledgments

Earlier versions were published in *World Literature Today*, *National Catholic Reporter*, *Library Journal*, *San Francisco Book Review*, *Southwest Review*, *New Orleans Review*, *Vortex*, *Texas Observer*, *Balcones Review*, *Cedar Rock*, *Small Press Review*, *Voices de la Luna*, *December*, *Houston Chronicle*, *Fort Worth Star-Telegram*, and *San Antonio Express-News*.

Others are revised introductions to *El Paso Days* by Elroy Bode, *Tender Spot: Selected Poems of Naomi Shihab Nye*, Marjorie Agosín's *Among the Angels of Memory*, and *Tropical Green* by Chip Dameron. The essay on Vassar Miller was in *Heart's Invention*. The Rumi essay is from *Reading Rumi in an Uncertain World*, a DVD featuring readings by Robert Bly and Naomi Shihab Nye. Thanks to the journals and book publishers in which earlier versions of these pieces appeared.

The translations of César Vallejo's poems are my efforts. All other translators have been credited in the collection.

I have been fortunate to work with generous and loyal editors over the decades, currently with Steve Bennett, at *San Antonio Express-News*. Margaret L. Hartley, former editor of *Southwest Review*—who published the work of mentor John Howard Griffin—was interested in essays on literature. And three editors at *The Texas Observer*—founder Ronnie Dugger, Greg Olds, and Michael King—were supportive of essays about Latin American and Texas writers.

Appreciation to friends for exquisite, thoughtful prose works: Paul Christensen, Russell Hardin, Julio Ortega, H.C. Nash, and Daniel L. Robertson.

Thanks to Maggi Miller for her collage as witty cover art, and to Kamala Platt for her excellent indexing skills.

About the Author

Critic Robert Peters praised Robert Bonazzi's first book of poetry, *Living the Borrowed Life* (New Rivers, 1974), for the poet's "consummate style" and poems "sophisticated in their patterns and designs." The book was recommended by *Library Journal, Poetry Now* and praised by poets Mark Van Doren and Thomas Merton. *Fictive Music* (Wings, 1979) was cited in *The Prose Poem: An International Anthology,* and praised by *Publishers Weekly, Choice* and *Library Journal.* Critic Paul Christensen wrote in *The Pawn Review:* "Bonazzi's books advance our culture. He is a Prospero of this heat and sunlight, a visionary, an enchanter, an amuser." *Perpetual Texts* (1986) received praise in the *Austin American-Statesman* and *Dallas Morning News.* "Like all good art," wrote *Way Magazine,* "Bonazzi's lucid poems become a weapon against whatever profaning spirit says that truth is only a matter of opinion."

Of his post-1990 poetry, Guy Davenport wrote: "Bonazzi's style can do all sorts of things and the poems have a balance and grace all their own." Paul Christensen, writing of Bonazzi's *Maestro of Solitude: New Poems & Poetics* (Wings, 2007), said "Bonazzi has taken poetry to its limits of subtlety, where sense nearly but not quite gives out into silence and awe." His latest collection of poetry is *The Scribbling Cure: Poems & Prose Poems* (Pecan Grove, 2012).

Bonazzi is the author of the critically-acclaimed *Man in the Mirror: John Howard Griffin and the Story of Black Like Me* (New York: Orbis Books, 1997, 2003). He only recently completed a decade-long project, the authorized biography of John Howard Griffin, to be entitled *Reluctant Activist.* Bonazzi has written introductions or afterwards to Griffin's *Black Like Me; Scattered Shadows: A Memoir of Blindness and Vision; Street of the Seven Angels; Follow the Ecstasy: The Hermitage Years of Thomas Merton; Encounters with the Other; Available Light: Exile in Mexico* and other titles. His work on Griffin has appeared in *The New York Times, Bloomsbury Review, Motive, New Orleans Review, Southwest Review, The Texas Observer* and *The Historical Dictionary of Civil Rights.*

His essays, reviews, short stories and poems have appeared in hundreds of publications—in France, Germany, the U.K., Japan, Canada, Mexico, Peru and the U.S.

Born in New York City in 1942, Bonazzi has also lived in San Francisco, Mexico City, Florida and several Texas cities. From 1966 until 2000, he edited and published over one hundred titles under his Latitudes Press imprint. He lives in San Antonio and writes a column on poetry, "Poetic Diversity," for the *San Antonio Express-News*.

About the Cover Artist

Maggi Miller's "Falling Chairs" (2010) is the cover art for this volume. She creates collages from her own hand-made paper. Her inspiration comes from dreams, literature, photographs, and snatches of overheard conversation. Miller's pieces have been exhibited in group shows in Austin and beyond. She is the author of *The Baby Who Wouldn't Say, "Mama"*—a charming children's book with her illustrations. Miller's artistic website can be accessed at http://maggimiller.com

Index of Authors

Catacalos, Rosemary, 118-20, 274
Celan, Paul, xi,
Cervantes, 24
Cervantes, Lorna Dee, 119, 274
Chagall, 233
Charara, Hayan, 78
Chávez Castañeda, Ricardo, 51
Cheever, John, 131-33
Chekov, 100, 224
Christensen, Paul, xi, 98, 137, 176-86
Chumacero, Ali, 52
Ciardi, John, 139
Clemens, Samuel, 124, 130, See also
    Mark Twain
Cohen, Marvin, xi
Coleman, Ornette, 230
Collins, Floyd, 242
Coltrane, John, 151
Cornell, Tad, 240-41
Cortez, Luis A., 171
Cox, Mark, 102
Crane, Hart, 275
Craven, Jerry, 206-07
Creeley, Robert, 134
Crockett, Eleanor, 273
Crook, Noel, 244-45
Cross, Elsa, 53
Cú, Juan, 53
Dahlberg, Edward, 186
Dali Lama, 87
Dario, Rubén, 3
Darwish, Mahmoud, 63, 67-71
Davis, Glover, 109-11
Davis, Miles, 34, 150-51
Debussy, 274
Degas, 31
De Hoyos, Angela, xi, 276-78
Delacroix, 143
de la Garza, Beatriz, 158
de Leon, Greta, 273
De Palchi, Alfredo, 56
de Rokha, Pablo, 24
de Unamuno, Miguel, 3
DeVoto, Bernard, 125
Dickinson, Emily, 61, 96, 100, 123, 218
Dinesen, Isak, 131
Di Piero, W.S., 56
Dobie, J. Frank, 153, 157

Dogen, 114
Donatello, 61
Doreski, William, 138-39
Dorham, Kenny, 230-31
Dostoevsky, 100
Douglass, Frederick, 84
Drummond de Andrade, Carlos, xi,
Du Bois, W.E.B., 84
Dugger, Ronnie, xi, 141-42
Dumitru, Cyra S., 213-14
Duncan, Robert, 134
Dylan, Bob, 136
Eatherly, Claude, 140-42
Eberhart, Richard, 139
Eco, Umberto, 131-32
Ekelöf, Gunner, 80
Eldridge, Roy, 150
Eliot, T. S., 14, 18, 134, 190, 216, 272
Ellington, Duke, 34, 230
Ellison, Ralph, 151
Elizondo, Salvador, ix, xi,
Elmusa, Sharif S., 78
Emamuel di Pasquale, 58
Emecheta, Buchi, 132
Emerson, Ralph Waldo, 131, 133, 232
Enheduanna, 189
Erofeev, Benedict, 132
Esquinca, Jorge, 53
Estess, Sybil Pittman, 217-18
Falcón, Leticia M., 153-58
Falls, Toni Heringer, 226-28
Farber, Norma, 106-08
Farber, Sidney, 107
Faulkner, 267
Feldman, Ruth, 56
Fellini, 275
Fernández, Macedonio, xi,
Fick, 52
Fisher, Rudolph, 151
Flaubert, 131
Flynn, Robert, 147-48, 274
Ford-Brown, Stephen, 98, 138, 139, 140
Franklin, Benjamin, 131, 133
Franzen, Cola, 37
Foner, Philip S., 125
Frost, Robert, 100, 139, 273
Freud, 125-28
Fuentes, xi, 50, 52

Snyder, Gary, xi, 133-34, 136
Sofranko, Michael, 273
Sokol, Kasia, 272
Sophocles, 268
Soto, Lilvia, 143
Soutine, Chaim, 111
Starnes, Sofia M., 60-61
Stevens, Wallace, 208, 226, 230
St. Germaine, Sheryl, 262
St. John, David, 110-11
St. John of the Cross, 34
St. Martin, Hardie, xi, 14
Stowe, Harriet Beecher, 140
Swann, Brian, xi, 56
Tafolla, Carmen, 208-09, 276-77
Tanizaki, Junichiro, 132
Tate, Alan, 134
Taylor, David, 275
Temple, Thea, 01
Terkel, Studs, 140
Thomas, Larry D., 233-34
Thomas, Lorenzo, 103-05
Thompson, Clifford, 150-52
Thompson, Robert Farris, 84
Thoreau, 100, 203
Tolstoy, 131
Toulouse-Lautrec, 275
Trakl, George, 80
Treviño, Frances, 273
Treviño, Natalia, 222-23
Trilling, Lionel, 127
Trombatore, Joseph, 274-75
Truesdale, C.W., xi
Twain, Mark, 124-30, 230, See also
    Samuel Clemens
Turner, J.M.W., 31
Twichell, Chase, 111-14
Twitchell, Harmony, 230
Ullmann, Liv, 40
Underwood, Evelyn, 97
Updike, John, 131
Urroz, Eloy, 51
Uschuk, Pamela, 271-72
Valad, Bahauddin, 62
Vallejo, César, ix, 14-20, 51, 80, 100, 138
Van Den Broeck, Lillian, 53
Van Doren, Carl, 125
Van Doren, Mark, xi,

Van Prooyen, Laura, 229
Vargas-Llosa, Mario, 131-32
Ventsel, Yelena Sergeyevna, 132
Ventura, Michael, 272
Vigil, Evangelina, 276
Villoro, Juan, 51
Viramontes, María, 158
Volkow, Vernóica, 53
Volpi, Jorge, 51
Waldman, Anne, 135-36
Webb, Walter Prescott, 153-55,
Whalen, Philip, 133
Whetstone, David, 62, 66
Whitbread, Thomas, 98
White, E.G., 131
Whitebird, Joanie, 96, 256
Whitehead, Colson, 151
Whitman, Walt, 134, 138
Williams, David, 78
Williams, William Carlos, 52, 134, 140,
179, 244, 261
Wilson, Edmund, 131
Wilkinson, Robert, 139
Wison, Eliot Khalil, 78
Wordsworth, 232
Wright, Bruce, 148
Wright, James, 14, 100
Yates, David, 230
Yeats, W.B., 100
Yo Yo Ma, 216
Zurlo, Tony, 237-38

Index of Titles

Wings Press was founded in 1975 by Joanie Whitebird and Joseph F. Lomax, both deceased, as "an informal association of artists and cultural mythologists dedicated to the preservation of the literature of the nation of Texas." Publisher, editor and designer since 1995, Bryce Milligan is honored to carry on and expand that mission to include the finest in American writing—meaning *all* of the Americas, without commercial considerations clouding the decision to publish or not to publish.

Wings Press intends to produce multi-cultural books, chapbooks, ebooks, recordings and broadsides that enlighten the human spirit and enliven the mind. Everyone ever associated with Wings has been or is a writer, and we know well that writing is a transformational art form capable of changing the world, primarily by allowing us to glimpse something of each other's souls. We believe that good writing is innovative, insightful, and interesting. But most of all it is honest. As Bob Dylan put it, "To live outside the law, you must be honest."

Likewise, Wings Press is committed to treating the planet itself as a partner. Thus the press uses as much recycled material as possible, from the paper on which the books are printed to the boxes in which they are shipped.

As Robert Dana wrote in *Against the Grain*, "Small press publishing is personal publishing. In essence, it's a matter of personal vision, personal taste and courage, and personal friendships." Welcome to our world.

Colophon

This first edition of *Outside the Margins* by
Robert Bonazzi, has been printed on 60 pound
Accent Opaque paper containing a percent-
age of recycled fiber. Titles have been set in
Colonna type, the text in Adobe Caslon type.
This book was designed by Bryce Milligan.

On-line catalogue and ordering:
www.wingspress.com
Wings Press titles are distributed to the
trade by the Independent Publishers
Group
www.ipgbook.com
and in Europe by Gazelle
www.gazellebookservices.co.uk

Also available as an ebook.